Aeschylus' *Prometheus Bound*

A LITERARY COMMENTARY

D.J. CONACHER is Professor of Classics at Trinity College, University of Toronto.

This book provides a thorough analysis of the literary and non-literary aspects of Aeschylus' *Prometheus Bound* essential for an understanding of the play. Although it is designed primarily for students, with or without a knowledge of Greek, it will suit a wide range of interests and expertise. As an introductory study it includes discussions of the poet's adaptation of the mythological tradition of Prometheus and the fragmentary evidence for a 'Prometheus trilogy.'

In the central chapters Professor Conacher presents an overview of the main structure and theme of the play, followed by detailed commentary on its various parts and their relation to the whole. Here he offers answers, based closely on the text, to the main problems of the play: the nature of the struggle between Prometheus and Zeus over the fate of man, and the question of the degree of dramatic development to be discerned throughout the action of the play.

This analysis leads to discussion of various theoretical reconstructions of the fragmentary tradition of the 'Prometheus trilogy' and an assessment of the main scholarly positions taken regarding the nature of Zeus as represented in *Prometheus Bound*. In appendixes Professor Conacher provides a summary of the much-debated question of the authenticity of the play and a discussion of some aspects of its original theatrical presentation.

UNIVERSITY OF TORONTO PRESS

Toronto Buffalo London

D.J. CONACHER

Aeschylus' *Prometheus Bound*

A LITERARY COMMENTARY

© University of Toronto Press 1980
Toronto Buffalo London
Printed in Canada

ISBN
0-8020-2391-6 cloth
0-8020-6416-7 paper

Canadian Cataloguing in Publication Data

Conacher, D.J., 1918–
Aeschylus' *Prometheus Bound*

Bibliography: p.
ISBN 0-8020-2391-6 bd. ISBN 0-8020-6416-7 pa.
1. Aeschylus. Prometheus vinctus. I. Title.
PA3825.P8C66   882'.01   C80-094411-9

To my students

Contents

Preface

This book is designed primarily, though not exclusively, for students of *Prometheus Bound*, of various kinds and levels, some 'Greeked' some Greekless, such as I have taught over the years. The wide range of interests and expertise in such a group of potential readers has dictated certain features in the content and format of the book which require, perhaps, a few words of explanation. For readers new to the play and its problems, I have supplemented my detailed analysis with some discussion of the mythological background of the play and a summary of what evidence we have concerning the possible trilogic development of its theme. I make little claim for originality in the presentation of this ancillary material, much of which will already be familiar to classical scholars from various editions and other studies of the play. However, since classicists (both more advanced students and instructors lecturing outside their own areas of specialization) may also wish to review this material, I have included with it a fair sampling of scholarly opinion, along with my own, on the various questions raised. My hope is that these chapters will help various different kinds of readers in their study of *Prometheus Bound* and of my own discussion of the play in chapters 2 and 3.

In both the detailed commentary of chapter 3 and in other chapters concerned with specific problems, I have included rather a larger amount of material than is usual in the notes. The reason for this is twofold. First, and most important, I have not wanted to interrupt the main lines of discussion (particularly when dealing with the dramatic structure and dramatic effects of the play) with arguments over details of interpretation involving the consideration of various scholarly views. Secondly, while I believe that all of these arguments are important for a thorough understanding of the play and its problems, the notes will, in some cases, be aimed at students with more specialized interests and competence. Perhaps I may say in defence of this some-what discrete treatment of different levels of discussion (both of which I regard as important) that it is a device which I have found rewarding in seminars on Greek tragedy. On the one hand, even fairly 'advanced' students tend to appreciate an overall analysis of a scene, or the general presentation of a problem, before returning for a closer look at points of detail (and divergent views on them) of particular interest to them. On the other hand, good students unfamiliar with Greek tragedy (including those reading it in translation) often raise surprisingly searching questions about some specific issue or passage in a play, once they have seen, in overview, what some of its problems are. The latter point is, I believe, particularly worth making at this time (and, indeed, it is germane to much of the purpose of this book) when classicists have, perhaps more than ever before, the opportunity, with its contingent difficulties, of discussing Greek and Latin literature with students well versed in critical and scholarly techniques acquired in disciplines other than classics.

Certain intentional omissions from my study of *Prometheus Bound* (in addition, no doubt, to numerous unconscious oversights) should also be noted here. In my discussion of the mythological background of the play, I have purposely limited myself to the more obvious literary material. Discussions of the iconography of the Prometheus myth or of its ramifications in relation to the cult of Prometheus and of other divinities associated with fire have been deemed outside the scope of this introductory study of the play. Readers interested in these wider aspects of the Prometheus myth and cult should consult, among several excellent studies: L. Séchan *Le Mythe de Prométhée* (Paris 1951); J. Duchemin *Prométhée, Histoire du Mythe, de ses Origines orientales à ses Incarnations modernes* (Paris 1974); and (for a comprehensive account of the iconography on Prometheus) L. Eckhart's article in Pauly-Wissowa *Real Encyclopaedia* 23[1] (1957) 704–30; for certain specific iconographical references and treatments, see also Séchan *Etudes sur la Tragédie grecque dans ses Rapports avec la Céramique* (Paris 1926) and A.D. Trendall and T.B.L. Webster *Illustrations of Greek Drama* (London 1971).

One further omission might be noted, this time in the 'Detailed Commentary' (chapter 3) which forms the central and longest part of this study. I have attempted, in this and the preceding chapter, an analysis of the structure of various parts of the play in relation to the theme and structure of the whole. Since the commentary is addressed to students reading the play in translation as well as to those reading it in Greek (all Greek quotations are translated or, less often, paraphrased), I have not attempted to include in it, except, occasionally, in the most general terms, any adequate discussion of the poet's style. While matters such as theme, structure, use of Chorus, and various kinds of dramatic effects can, to some degree, be discussed in the same terms with Greek-reading and Greekless readers, it is difficult to do so successfully in the matter of style, especially of poetic style. To do this properly obviously involves discussion of the words, and their particular effects, in the original version: an attempt to discuss the poet's style in a book of this kind would lead either to a sense of frustration in Greekless readers or to irritation among classics students ... and quite possibly to both. One partial exception here is the discussion of imagery; thus I have made reference, both in the bibliography and at specific points in the discussion of the play, to relevant studies of style and imagery in *Prometheus Bound* and in Aeschylean tragedy in general.

The recurrent questions concerning the authenticity of *Prometheus Bound*, that is, concerning its Aeschylean authorship, I have postponed, for reasons indicated in chapter 2, to an appendix at the end of the book. Moreover, both sides of this disputed question have been thoroughly presented in recent times in the studies of Professor C.J. Herington (*The Author of the 'Prometheus Bound'* (Austin and London 1970)) and of Mr Mark Griffith (*The Authenticity of Prometheus Bound* (Cambridge 1977)), whose book appeared only as I was completing the present work. In the shadow of these two detailed investigations (as well as those of Wilhelm Schmid and his earlier opponents and followers) I have contented myself, in the aforementioned appendix, with a summary of the main arguments there provided and a tentative indication of my own less expert opinion on the matter.

Chapter 4 of this book, together with pp 48–52 of chapter 3, is based, with minor adaptations, on my article 'Prometheus as Founder of the Arts,' *GRBS* 18 (1977) 189–206. I here make grateful acknowledgment to the publishers and editors of *Greek Roman and Byzantine Studies* for their permission to republish this material. Similar grateful acknowledgment is due to The University of Chicago Press for permission to quote, in the appendix to chapter 3, translations by David Grene of the passages from *Prometheus Bound* there noted; reprinted from *The Complete Greek Tragedies* edited by David Grene and Richmond Lattimore, volume I, *Aeschylus* (published 1959), by permission of The University of Chicago Press, *Prometheus Bound* © 1942 by The University of Chicago; and to Oxford University Press for permission to quote, in the same appendix, the corresponding passages in Greek from *Prometheus Bound* in *Aeschyli: Septem quae supersunt tragoediae* recensuit Gilbertus Murray (Oxonii: E typographo Clarendoniano 1938); by permission of Oxford University Press.

Debts of a different kind are owed to scholarly readers, anonymous and otherwise, of this work in manuscript form. Mr T.C.W. Stinton of Wadham College, Oxford, read two earlier drafts of the work. It would take an additional lengthy appendix properly to describe my debt to his patience, scholarship, and judgment; here I can only express my gratitude for the truly exceptional generosity with which he shared his much greater knowledge of the numerous matters on which he has advised me and to add that any errors and oversights which remain in my work are entirely my own. I have also profited from various helpful suggestions and criticisms from anonymous readers for the University of Toronto Press and for the Social Sciences and Humanities Research Council.

I should also like to express my thanks to Ms Cynthia Grainger-Burton and to Mrs K. McCallum for their patience and efficiency in typing this work and to the editors of the University of Toronto Press for their unfailing helpfulness and courtesy at various stages in its publication.

This book has been published with the help of a grant from the Canadian Federation for the Humanities, using funds provided by the Social Sciences and Humanities Research Council of Canada. I also express my grateful acknowledgment of a Research Grant from the Canada Council in 1976 which I made use of for research at Oxford University and which consequently assisted greatly in the preparation of this book.

Aeschylus' *Prometheus Bound*

A LITERARY COMMENTARY

CHAPTER ONE

The mythological tradition and its adaptation in *Prometheus Bound*

1 Preliminary comment

In his opening chapter on Aeschylean tragedy, a celebrated scholar of the last generation used the *Prometheus Bound* to illustrate Aristotle's statement about tragedy's transformation of the 'small myths and ridiculous diction' belonging to an earlier stage of its development.[1] There is, of course, an important sense in which the illustration is true and one must not, in any case, press the rhetorical use of a 'text' too closely. There can be little doubt that the re-creation of Prometheus from his relatively humble origins in the Hesiodic tradition into the great founder of the practical arts was almost entirely the work of Aeschylus. Nevertheless, there are several ways in which this emphasis may be misleading, particularly to the casual reader of Aeschylus. For one thing, Aeschylus' transformation of the mythical figure of Prometheus has so appealed to the imagination of readers and poets of later ages that they, in turn, have carried that transformation a great deal further than Aeschylus did – a process justified in new re-creations of the myth but not in the interpretation of the *Prometheus Bound*. Here one thinks particularly of two related kinds of exaggeration: that which attributes to Prometheus rather more of the civilizing arts than he himself claims in his specific statements on the matter; and that which regards Prometheus and his quarrel with Zeus in terms too

---

1 See Murray *Aeschylus* p 13 and n2, p 14, pp 19–32, esp p 32 for the conclusion summarized above. Cf also Aristotle *Poetics* 1449A 20 ff. It seems unlikely from the context (apart from other considerations) that Aristotle was thinking of Aeschylus' development of Hesiodic myth, but we need not, perhaps, take Murray's illustration too literally.

allegorical, even romantic, for the text of the play or its cultural and mythological background to justify.[2]

One should not, of course, attribute such exaggerations and distortions to all critics rightly observing the great development which Aeschylus did give to the Prometheus myth. However, because such (humanistic) exaggerations have occurred and because the central (divine) struggle of the trilogy involves a mythological background with which the original audience was thoroughly familiar, it is important that the modern reader should have that background clearly in mind. Most important, this entails an awareness of Hesiod's treatment not only of the Prometheus myth but also of myths concerning the struggles for the divine governance of the universe and the evolving conceptions of the gods.[3] And an examination of this material should, incidentially, allay any misconception that, whatever the 'small myths' of Aristotle's statement did involve, they could not have been the great cosmogonic myths in Hesiod, with which (as well as the Prometheus myth) the present trilogy is intimately concerned.

Before embarking on this comparison of Hesiod and Aeschylus on the mythological matter relevant to our study, some warning of the restricted scope of our treatment of Hesiod should be given. Much work has been done in attempts to distinguish the thought of Hesiod himself from the traditional material with which he was dealing. Moreover, the text of Hesiod has been the subject of dispute at numerous points, particularly on matters of sequence and possible interpolation. (Recent scholarly opinion tends to deprecate too radical a tampering with the text of Hesiod as we have received it: classical standards of coherence and consistency cannot be applied to a poet of the eighth or

2 Cf, for example, Havelock *Prometheus* part I, chapters 5 and 6, passim (eg, 'Prometheus represents the intellectual humanism of the Greek mind in competition with all the inherited terrors of traditional Mediterranean cult' (p 56). There are some fine, imaginative illuminations of the Prometheus myth and of *Prometheus Bound* in these essays, but the strain of humanistic allegory which prevails seems (at least to this reader) to distort the central *divine* figure of Aeschylus' play.

For a brief but excellent account of the influence of the Prometheus myth and of *Prometheus Bound* on the imagination of poets and thinkers especially from the seventeenth century onwards, see Smyth *Aeschylean Tragedy* chap 4, pp 92–7. For a much more detailed study of this topic, see Duchemin *Prométhée* esp chapters 8–14.

3 There has been much difference of opinion among scholars as to whether the Greeks would ever have accepted the idea of an individual god, such as Zeus, 'evolving' in any way, but few, I think, would question that some kind of evolution in the concept of the godhead was involved or implied in the myths of the divine successions (Ouranos-Kronos-Zeus) or, more specifically, in the myth of the overthrow of the Titanic order of gods by Zeus and the Olympians.

seventh century BC dealing, perhaps at the very beginning of written composition, with traditional material going back to the Mycenaean Age.) These problems will, for the most part, have little relevance to our study: for one thing, as Wilamowitz has reminded us, Aeschylus would not have exercised textual criticism on the *Theogony* as he received it.[4] Our discussion of Hesiod, then, will be limited to a selection of passages relevant, in one way or another, to the mythical material which Aeschylus develops in *Prometheus Bound* and its trilogy (as far as we can know it).[5]

2 The 'divine overthrows' and the battle of the Titans

The first 'divine overthrow' of which we read in Hesiod's *Theogony* is that of Ouranos ('the Heavens') by Kronos, the youngest of the first and dynastically the most important brood (later called the Titans, *Theog.* 207ff) of Ouranos and Gaia ('Earth'). When Ouranos kept pushing their children back into Gaia, she produced iron, fashioned a sickle and persuaded Kronos to castrate Ouranos (*Theog.* 132–8; 154–82). No formal succession is described but it is Kronos who is next spoken of as having 'kingly power among the immortals' (*Theog.* 462; cf 476).

Kronos and his sister Rhea produced offspring (later called 'the Olympians') ending with Zeus, the youngest. Kronos kept devouring his children (up to the birth of Zeus), 'for he had heard from Gaia and starry Ouranos that it was fated for him to fall by his son through the

4 Wilamowitz *Interpretationen* p 130.
5 Readers wishing to pursue further the various Hesiodic problems mentioned should consult: West ed *Hesiod, Theogony* and bibliography, pp 101 ff; West ed *Hesiod, Works and Days*; Sinclair ed *Hesiod, Works and Days*, Solmsen *Hesiod and Aeschylus*. Solmsen's study, despite certain idiosyncrasies, will be of interest particularly for the author's attempt to discern Hesiod's own contribution to the mythical material and for the author's views on the relation between Hesiodic and Aeschylean thought. Of the many other works dealing with the mythological background of *Prometheus Bound*, cf also (for points relevant to the present discussion) Wilamowitz *Interpretationen* pp 130 ff; Reinhardt *Aischylos* pp 29–39; Séchan *Le Mythe de Prométhée* esp pp 9–10, pp 26 ff; Mazon *Eschyle* I² pp 151–9; Duchemin *Prométhée* chapters 1–5. For a somewhat subjective but interesting view of Aeschylus' adaptation of the 'divine overthrows' motif in the *Prometheus* trilogy, cf also J.A.K. Thomson 'The Religious Background of the *Prometheus Vinctus*.' Finally, Jean-Pierre Vernant in his recent article, 'Mètis et les mythes de souveraineté,' provides several interesting observations relevant to the present study. (Cf also Detienne et Vernant *Les Ruses de l'Intelligence: La Mètis des Grecs* chapter 2, 'La Conquête du Pouvoir,' which contains an expansion of the above-mentioned article; this book has been translated by Janet Lloyd as *Cunning Intelligence in Greek Culture and Society*).

plans of Zeus – for all his great strength' (*Theog.* 453–65). Rhea, with the help of Gaia and Ouranos (*Theog.* 469–71) outwitted Kronos; she gave birth secretly to Zeus in Crete, then gave Kronos a stone, wrapped in baby clothes, for him to swallow, while Gaia hid the infant Zeus. Later (*Theog.* 468–500), when Zeus had grown to strength, Kronos vomited up both the stone and his progeny, 'tricked by the cunning counsels of Gaia ... overcome by the strength and devices of his son' (494–6). Kronos like Ouranos before him now disappears from the power struggle; once again, there is no immediate statement of Zeus' succession, beyond the prophetic lines that the son, who had escaped by the stone trick, 'would soon overthrow him by force, drive him from office, and then himself reign among the immortals.' (*Theog.* 488–91).

The divine successions end with the battle of Zeus and the Olympians against the Titans. Here again (as in the case of the 'succession myths') Hesiod does not provide a clear consecutive account of the struggle, but we may set down its most significant features (for our purposes) from a number of different passages and contexts. First of all, Zeus sets about securing powerful allies, particularly from among disgruntled members of the older generation of the gods. To any god who fights on his side, he promises the same honours as he had under Kronos, and he offers 'promotion to office and privilege' to any god who had lacked such distinction before (*Theog.* 390–6: the passage is interesting both as the most political one in Hesiod's account of the Titanomachy and as the only one referring directly to the rule of Kronos in connection with it). Of his own accord, Zeus releases the Cyclopes, the one-eyed giants who had been imprisoned by their father Ouranos and who in gratitude now give Zeus thunder and lightning which Gaia had hitherto kept hidden (*Theog.* 501–6; cf 139 ff). By the cunning advice of Gaia, Zeus also releases the other monstrous, 'post-Titanic' brood of Ouranos and Gaia, 'the hundred-armed ones,' Obriareos, Kottos, and Gyes, and thus gains fresh and powerful allies when the battle with the Titans had already been going on for many years (*Theog.* 617 ff; cf 147 ff). Gaia prophesies that with these three the victory will be won (628); Kottos, in turn, congratulates Zeus for his intelligence ($\pi\rho\alpha\pi\acute{\iota}\delta\epsilon\varsigma$, 656), perception ($\nu\acute{o}\eta\mu\alpha$, 656), and prudence ($\dot{\epsilon}\pi\iota\varphi\rho\sigma\acute{\upsilon}\nu\alpha\iota$, 658) in this manoeuvre. (Again both passages will be of interest in our comparison with Aeschylus' treatment of the Titanomachy.)

In the long and splendid description of the actual battle (*Theog.* 629–726), it is 'the Hundred-Armers' who are finally given the credit for driving the Titans to Tartaros (713–25). Nevertheless, some ambiguity remains as to whether it is this fresh alliance or the Cyclopes' earlier gift of the thunderbolts which is most responsible for the victory: the sudden description of Zeus' terrifying deployment of these weapons (687–712) neatly divides into two parts the longer account of 'the Hundred-Armers'' exploits and seems, moreover, to provide the crucial turning-point in the battle (711; cf also 506).

What are the more striking features of Aeschylus' adaptation in *Prometheus Bound* of this traditional material concerning the divine successions and the Titanomachy? First of all, the personal overthrows and take-overs involved in the divine succession (Ouranos-Kronos-Zeus) are stated more sharply and succinctly in *Prometheus Bound*. In Prometheus' account of the beginning of the Titanomachy, there is a direct reference to the intention of one faction of the gods to overthrow Kronos (*PV* 201); Prometheus also refers later to the curse of Kronos on Zeus (910–12) and to the fall of the preceding 'tyrants' of the heavens (956–7). The less clear indication of these personal overthrows and take-overs in Hesiod is, no doubt, due mainly to the peculiarities of the *Theogony*'s composition. Nevertheless, by presenting the sequence more starkly, Prometheus is able to exploit the previous overthrows in a manner which is quite foreign to the spirit of the *Theogony*. In Hesiod's account, there is an air of finality about Zeus' victory over the Titans and this is reinforced, as we shall see, by Zeus' unhindered and majestic punishments of individual (non-Titanic) rebels such as the cunning Prometheus (*Theog.* 521–34; cf 535–616) and the monstrously powerful Typhoeus (*Theog.* 836 ff). There is no such sense of finality and security attaching to Zeus' rule in *Prometheus Bound*. Indeed, in the two passages referred to, the divine successions are themselves emphasized by Prometheus to suggest the vulnerability of the current ruler of the gods who is subject to Kronos' curse (*PV* 910–12) and may ('will,' in Prometheus' more arrogant moments!) himself suffer the fall that his predecessors have suffered (*PV* 955–9). And even in the mouths of Zeus' minions, emphasis on the newness of Zeus' rule as an explanation of its harshness (*PV* 35, 310) further conveys the suggestion of its vulnerability.[6]

Of specific adaptations of this tradition, the major one (from which

---

6 In *Agamemnon*, the divine succession, involving the two overthrows, is also described (by the Chorus at *Ag.* 167–72) in rapid sequence, but the implication is very different from that in Prometheus' account. In *Agamemnon* the emphasis is on the complete demolition of Ouranos and Kronos in turn and on the finality of the triumph of Zeus, the 'winner of the third throw' (*Ag.* 171–2).

several others follow) is, of course, Prometheus' own role in the over-throw of Kronos and the Titans. In the *Theogony*, Prometheus is only the son of the Titan Iapetos and Klymene (*Theog.* 508–10) and plays no part in the Titanomachy; in *Prometheus Bound*, he is the son of Gaia (and so himself, a Titan) and as such can be closely involved in the power struggle in which Gaia gives the essential advice. In the *Theogony*, Gaia herself is the purveyor of the cunning plans and she works consistently against Kronos and in favour of the coming generation of the gods: in the stone-feeding and the 'sickening' of Kronos (469–71; 494–5); in the Cretan fostering of the infant Zeus (479 ff); in the prophetic advice to Zeus about the necessary alliance with 'the Hundred-Armers' (626–8). In *Prometheus Bound*, it is, of course, Prometheus who offers Gaia's (here rather vague) prophetic advice as to how the Titanomachy will be won; significantly, he offers it first to the Titans and only when they spurn the advice does he turn to Zeus, taking Gaia with him in this new alliance (*PV* 204–18). The change and, in a sense, impoverishment of Gaia's prophecy is also, of course, an essential part of the adaptation: in contrast to Gaia's direct advice to Zeus in Hesiod about 'the Hundred-Armers,' we now have Gaia's prophecy, through Prometheus, that guile not strength will win the victory (*PV* 211–13). Thus Prometheus, both the purveyor of Gaia's message and the epitome, as it were, of guile (δόλος), becomes the new ally of Zeus by which he defeats the Titans, and so replaces 'the Hundred-Armers' of the original prophecy. (No mention is made, either, of the Cyclopean thunderbolts so that, at least at this point in Prometheus' account, Zeus' victory *appears* as entirely due to guile.[7] Throughout the evolving action of *Prometheus Bound* this Promethean element is to be localized in the special knowledge (again from Gaia) which Prometheus, now Zeus' adversary, holds over Zeus. Zeus, on the other hand, at least in his relations with Prometheus, now appears to revert to sheer force and the present play

7 Cf Vernant 'Mètis et les mythes de souveraineté' pp 62–5, who compares the sufferings and release of Prometheus in the ensuing action of the trilogy with the sufferings and release of the sons of Ouranos, namely the Cyclopes and 'the Hundred-Armers' in the *Theogony*. The latter two groups were released to aid Zeus in his victory over Kronos and the Titans; Prometheus will be released by Zeus because '... il lui faut intégrer à son pouvoir de sourverain l'astuce, les feintes, la préscience secrète du Titan.'

The Aeschylean Prometheus does not *deny* the role of the Cyclopes and 'the Hundred-Armers' in the overthrow of Kronos and the Titans; rather, it suits his version to suppress mention of these 'power-allies.' Later, in connection with the reduction of Typho and of Prometheus himself, Zeus' use of the thunderbolt *is* mentioned (*PV* 361–2, 372, 1044 ff), though the Cyclopes are still not mentioned as its inventors.

is to end with the cataclysmic use against Prometheus of the thunder-bolt of which Prometheus has omitted mention in his account of Zeus' victory in the Titanomachy.

It will be clear from the foregoing account of this part of Aeschylus' treatment of the tradition that no simple contrast can be made between the brute force of Zeus' victory in the *Theogony* and the victory by guile related by Prometheus in *Prometheus Bound*.[8] Even in the *Theogony*, the prudence of Zeus in securing 'the Hundred-Armers' as essential allies has been stressed by those strong ones themselves (*Theog.* 656, 658). Nevertheless, the actual victory in the *Theogony* comes about by force ('the Hundred-Armers' and the thunderbolts) while in Prometheus' account the emphasis is all on guile. Paradoxically, the Zeus of the *Theogony* later appears to acquire, after the victory over the Titans, the various intellectual and cultural qualities necessary for civilized exist-ence. This would seen to be the significance (at least in part) of Zeus' swallowing of the pregnant Metis, 'wisest of mortals and immortals,' and producing Athena, 'the equal of Zeus himself in might and good counsel' (886–900; 924–6);[9] of Zeus' propagation of the Seasons, Law and Justice and even the Fates (Μοῖραι) from his mating with Themis (901 ff); and of the propagation of the Graces and the Muses from his matings with Eurynome and with Mnemosyne (Memory), respectively (907 ff; 915 ff). There is no doubt that in this emerging conception of Zeus towards the end of the *Theogony*, Hesiod shows us a great ad-vance over the more primitive gods, Ouranos, Kronos, and the Titans, and their activities in earlier times.[10] It would, perhaps, be going too far to say that the nature of Zeus himself actually 'changes' in the

8 It is possible, of course, that Aeschylus' treatment of the Titanomachy was influenced by other, post-Hesiodic accounts. That some of these accounts *were* post-Hesiodic seems probable: see the arguments in Dorig and Gigon *Der Kampf der Götter und Titanen* vi–xxiv. There is, however, nothing in the sparse extant tradition on the Titanomachy, the 'cyclic epic' of Arctinus or Eumelus (see Dorig-Gigon, pp 10–11, for the fragments), which relates to Aeschylus' treatment.

9 On the other hand, the formulation of this myth is still too primitive and literally meant for us to regard it simply as allegory. We must not forget that the reason given for Zeus' swallowing of Metis is still the old fear which plagued his predecessors: the fear, here based on the warning from Gaia and Ouranos (890–8), that Metis would produce a son who would overthrow him. I cannot agree with the arguments of Bergk, Wilamowitz, and Jacoby (cited with approval by Solmsen *Hesiod and Aeschylus* pp 67–8 and notes ad loc.), adduced against the authenticity of this passage on the swallowing of Metis and the birth of Athena. See also West's long note on *Theog.* 886–900, which he accepts as Hesiodic.

10 Cf also Solmsen's discussion of the *Theogony* passages just mentioned, in his section, 'The Synthesis of Old and New Figures, Earlier and Later Generations' *Hesiod and Aeschylus* pp 66 ff.

Theogony; Hesiod himself would, no doubt, have denied that Zeus was not 'wise' from the start and indeed the recurrent epithet μητίετα first occurs quite early in the poem's account of Zeus (see v 520). Nevertheless, it is after the struggles of the Titanomachy and after the repression of individual rebels that Zeus by a series of suitable matings produces the various qualities necessary for a gradually more and more civilized cosmos; and the actual swallowing of Metis seems to suggest a fresh acquisition of wisdom on the part of Zeus, or at least a renewed emphasis on its importance in the divine governance of a changing universe. These passages may be instructive for our later consideration of the nature of Zeus, in so far as we can guess about it from the sparse indications of the trilogy's denouement, at the time of the reconciliation with Prometheus and later.

3 The offence of Prometheus and its punishment

A brief summary of this part of the Hesiodic background to the mythical material of *Prometheus Bound* will indicate that here Aeschylus has indeed transformed the career of a relatively minor rebel against Zeus' authority. Here the Hesiodic account given in the *Theogony* is supplemented with an account of a somewhat different nature and context in the *Works and Days*. We may begin with the earlier poem.

The context is Hesiod's telling of the reduction of the rebellious sons of the Titan Iapetos, for as we have noted above the Hesiodic Prometheus is one generation further removed from primordial Gaia. That the main emphasis of the tale (*Theog.* 521 ff) is on the supremacy of Zeus may be seen not only from the moralistic conclusion ('For it is not possible to hide from nor outstrip the mind of Zeus' 613 ff) but also from the fact that the punishment is described before the offence itself. The description is brief: Prometheus was bound to a stake (we are not told where); by day an eagle gnawed his liver which by night grew in again; eventually (we are not told when) Herakles slew the eagle and freed Prometheus at least from this anguish 'not without the will of Zeus,' so that Herakles might have greater glory ...

> And Zeus, though angry, laid aside the wrath which he had before because Prometheus set about matching wits with the powerful son of Kronos.
> (533–4)

Only now (535 ff) do we hear the actual offences of Prometheus. First, he sought to outwit Zeus in the matter of food-offerings which men were to make to Zeus: he gave Zeus the choice of two 'packages,' hiding the (delectable) meaty parts in an ox's stomach and decking out the mere bones in an attractive covering of fat. According to Hesiod, Zeus saw through the trick but chose the inferior offering (as Prometheus had intended) so that he might punish men. (Hesiod here seems to twist the tale in order to favour Zeus' insight: there seems to be a touch of inconsistency in saying that Zeus 'divined the trick' beforehand (551) and then that 'anger came on his heart when he saw the white bones of the ox in their cunning arrangement' (554–5) after he had made his choice). [11] As a punishment, Zeus deprived men of fire (562–4; no mention is made here of any punishment of Prometheus). Prometheus deceived Zeus again and stole back fire for men, [12] 'after hiding it in a hollow reed.' Zeus then punished men again by having Hephaistos fashion the first woman (570 ff). There follows a long description of the adornments of this 'replacement of good by beautiful evil' and of the train of evils which this 'utter deception' ($\delta \acute{o} \lambda o \nu \ a \acute{i} \pi \acute{u} \nu$, 589) brings upon men. No further mention is made of Prometheus or *his* punishment until the moral (to which we have already referred) is pointed out at the end:

… Not even Prometheus was able to escape the deep anger of Zeus but strong bondage oppresses him for all his great wit. (614–16)

The main point of the Prometheus myth as told in the *Theogony* seems, then, to be the glorification of Zeus by an illustration of the impossibility of getting the better of him – and a warning of the danger of trying. The context of the supplement to this account in Hesiod's *Works and Days* is rather different. Here the briefer reference to the Prometheus myth occurs in explanation of the life of toil and dismal sorrows which Zeus has inflicted on men.

11 Cf West's notes on vv 551 and 558–61 and Solmsen *Hesiod and Aeschylus* pp 48–9; both comment on the slight awkwardness of Hesiod's adaptation of a legend which in its original form clearly presented Zeus as really deceived by Prometheus' trick.
12 There might appear to be some doubt in the account above as to whether men had possessed fire before Zeus 'refrained from giving' ($o \mathring{v} \kappa \ \mathring{\epsilon} \delta \acute{\iota} \delta o v$ *Theog.* 563) it to them. However, this would hardly have been a very striking punishment if man did not have fire already, and besides the previous deception of Zeus, and its sequel, would seem to imply cooking and burnt offerings (cf esp *Theog.* 556–7). The point about man's previous possession of fire (which is repeated at *Erga* 50–2) is of some importance in our contrast of the Hesiodic with the Aeschylean version. For a different view, see West *Theogony* pp 305–6, and also his note on v 563; he infers from the *Theogony* account that in this version of the myth men did not have fire before Prometheus stole it for them. However, West does not consider in this connection the point just made about burnt offerings.

We are told first that the gods hid and kept hidden man's 'liveli-hood' (βίον); otherwise, man would be able to earn in one day's work enough to keep him for a whole year. The reason for this deprival and for the 'dismal sorrows' which Zeus inflicted on man is that Prome-theus cheated him (42–9). Only after this general account do we come to the statement of the specific deprival of fire.[13] This Prometheus stole back again for men (τὸ μὲν αὖθις ... ἔκλεψε: the phraseology makes it clear that men had had fire before) in a hollow reed (50–2). It was in punishment for this further offence of Prometheus' on men's behalf that Zeus in his anger caused Pandora, the first woman, to be fashioned and she with her jar of evils (the 'gifts' to men from all the gods) let loose all the woes which have since afflicted men (53–105).

This tale, then, with its description of Pandora and the list of woes which she let loose, is concerned with the explanation of men's hard lot rather than with the nature of Prometheus' initial offence (which is not described) or with his own punishment (which is not even mentioned). Indeed the myth seems but loosely tied to Prometheus' activities at all; one or two details are, however, of interest when we come to consider the Aeschylean version of Prometheus' role in men's affairs. One is that Prometheus sought to warn his brother Epimetheus (the arche-typal blunderer or 'second-guesser,' who first receives Pandora) against accepting any gift from Zeus 'lest it should bring evil to man, in some way' (86–8). Here for a moment, despite the fact that the tenor of the tale as a whole is to blame Prometheus for the origin of men's ills, Prometheus appears as the would-be guardian of men's safety, Zeus as the constant threat to their prosperity. Secondly, of the woes in Pan-dora's jar, 'only hope [ἐλπίς] ... remained under the lid of the jar and did not fly forth; for she (Pandora?) put the lid on before that could happen, by the design of aegis-bearing, cloud-gathering Zeus' (96–

13 Some may take the reference at *Erga* 42 to the deprival of man's livelihood (βίος) as an anticipation of the deprival of fire. But the result, a sudden plunging into the workaday world (43–4), seems not quite to fit the deprival of fire; even *with* fire, man has to work more than one day a year. The conflation of two explanations of man's deprived lot seems likely. See Sinclair's note to v 47; he argues, against Schoemann's view (and apparently against Paley's, though the latter's note is a shade ambiguous) that 'the hiding of βίος and the hiding of πῦρ are two different actions both performed by Zeus in order to punish Prometheus as well as mankind; βίος remains hidden to this day ...' Cf also West's subtler account (*Works and Days* p 155) of Hesiod's rather clumsy conflation of the two myths: 'There is no equation of βίος ['livelihood'] and πῦρ ['fire'], just a likeness which entices Hesiod into the myth [which he had told about Prometheus in the *Theogony*] which lands him on a familiar but not immediately pertinent track.'

9).[14] Here hope is regarded as one of many banes (μυρία λυγρά, 100), the only one which men escaped. In *Prometheus Bound*, as we shall see, with its more optimistic view of human initiative, under Promethean guidance, hope is one of Prometheus' gifts to men (*PV* 250–1).

It is, of course, by his radical adaptation of this triangle – Prometheus, Zeus, and man – that Aeschylus has transformed the Prometheus myth. To put the difference in the broadest possible terms, the Hesiodic Prometheus, by his deceptions and frustrations of Zeus in his relations with man, is presented (however 'artificially') as the indirect cause of all man's woes;[15] the Aeschylean Prometheus, on the other hand, by his interventions on behalf of man, is presented as the saviour of mankind, without whom man would have ceased to exist and with whose help he progresses from mere subsistence to a state of civilization.[16]

To this end Aeschylus first of all suppresses Prometheus' food-offering trick and changes Prometheus' retrieval of confiscated fire to the first bestowal, by daring theft, of what had previously been the gods' prerogative (see *PV* 7–11; 29–30; 82–3; 107–11; 252–4; 612). The two changes are, of course, connected, but their effects are several. Without the deception over food-offerings, Zeus has no occasion for just indignation with men and for depriving them of fire in punishment. Fire can thus be left as a hitherto celestial treasure far beyond man's lowly estate (as it is in the account of the 'Platonic'

14 Cf Wilamowitz *Interpretationen* p 131, who regards the Aeschylean passage as modelled on the Hesiodic one with the revaluation of 'hope' to a good by Prometheus on the grounds given in v 248, that (through blind hope) men no longer foresee their deaths. Note, in general, that the Greeks tended to stress the dangerously delusive quality of hope at least as much as its more gratifying aspect. Cf, for example, Sophocles *Antigone* 615 ff. (Others, however, regard the 'hope' of this passage as a good, and they may be right: this would, at any rate, explain why Pandora did not let it out; see England's note *ad loc*. West also regards the 'hope' which remains in Pandora's jar as a good but claims, by a complex and not entirely convincing argument, that (unlike the evils *escaping* from the jar) it was preserved for men by remaining in it. (See West *Theogony* p 307, n 1 and now, at greater length, West *Works and Days* pp 169–70.)

15 Cf Mazon *Hésiode* p 72.

16 Wilamowitz (*Interpretationen* p 130 ff) would make the cleavage between the Hesiodic and the post-Hesiodic (he does not say 'Aeschylean') Prometheus considerably sharper: he does not believe that the Hesiodic Prometheus, a part of the old generation of the gods removed by Zeus, could ever have been credited with the gift of fire. This fire-theft Wilamowitz sees as a post-Hesiodic development symbolizing the origins of civilized life but notes that in the account of the origin of the arts in *Prometheus Bound* it is kept in the background since the Aeschylean Prometheus is the founder of *all* human civilization (p 132). (Cf below n35.)

Prometheus),[17] which is, of course, just the situation needed for the new role of Prometheus and the new future of man. Secondly, the Hesiodic Prometheus' deception of Zeus over the food-offerings, though it showed Prometheus' cunning on man's behalf, was a relatively petty, even sordid trick and would have distracted attention from the theft of fire, which is now presented (at least in the earlier passages of the play) as Prometheus' great contribution to human civilization. Thus fire, with Prometheus as its bestower, can now be given its full symbolic force in the creation of the practical arts (see especially *PV* 7–11; 107–11;[18] 252–4).

Prometheus' championship of mankind appears in a somewhat different form, again original (as far as we know) with Aeschylus, at *PV* 231–6, for here he claims actually to have saved the human race when Zeus had determined to destroy it and beget another one. No details are given, but from this passage and from one other it is clear that the Aeschylean Prometheus, in his days of alliance with Zeus, was a figure of high authority and power. At vv 439–40, Prometheus informs us that he actually determined the prerogatives of the new gods, after the victory over Kronos and the Titans. These two passages, brief as they are, put the role of Prometheus in relation to Zeus' new order in a different light from that in which it is usually considered. Prometheus' alliance with Zeus, and the qualities of guile and foresight which he brought with him, were clearly, until his fall, essential elements in the new government of the universe. Only with regard to the destiny of the current race of men did Zeus and Prometheus differ, and even here Prometheus appears to have won the first round in preserving their existence with impunity when Zeus was bent on destroying them. And only when Prometheus attempted, by stealing a divine prerogative, to raise that existence to a higher level did he finally suffer Zeus' punishment. These points are worth remembering when we come to consider the denouement of the trilogy.[19] The previous elevation and fall of Prometheus, like the fall and subsequent resurrection of the Titans, illustrate the vicissitudes, the changing circumstances, of cosmic politics rather than any essential change in the natures of the gods con-

17 Plato *Protagoras* 321 c ff
18 Prometheus' first reference to his theft of fire also preserves a literal element of the tradition along with the innovation: 'I hunted down and stored in fennel-stalk the stolen source of fire ...': Smyth's subtle translation (Loeb edition) of ναρθηκοπλήρωτον δὲ θηρῶμαι πυρὸς / πηγὴν κλοπαίαν well expresses the verbal reminiscence to the theft of fire at Hesiod *Theog.* 566–7 (κλέψας ... ἐν κοίλῳ νάρθηκι).
19 See below, chapter 3, pp 64–5, and especially chap 5, pp 110–14.

cerned. It may be that the eventual reconciliation of Prometheus and Zeus can be viewed in this light also.

As far as one can tell from this preliminary glance at *Prometheus Bound* in relation to its Hesiodic background of traditional myth, there is no indication of a more advanced conception of the gods in the Aeschylean play.[20] Rather there is an interest in relating (and perhaps, at first, opposing) a new kind of civilization myth to the previous account of all-powerful Olympian gods. Indeed, there is even a suggestion of a kind of humanism, of a new independence on the part of man (for why else does Zeus so resent their possession of 'all-devising fire'?) through the development of the arts, under Prometheus. But, as we shall see, the great issue of *Prometheus Bound* – and of the trilogy – is the struggle between Prometheus, as the god responsible for this new development, and Zeus. Consideration of the possible outcome of that struggle must await discussion of the play and the fragments of the trilogy.

4 The secret of Prometheus and the Io theme

Two other important constituents of *Prometheus Bound* bear no relation to the Prometheus myth in Hesiod, though one of these, as we shall see, is present in a different form and context in Hesiod. The secret prophetic knowledge which Prometheus holds over Zeus – that if Zeus consummates a certain marriage (cf γαμεῖ γάμον τοιοῦτον, *PV* 764) he will beget his overthrower – is the chief plot device of this inevitably static play. The myth of Zeus' pursuit, in competition with his brother Poseidon, of the sea-nymph Thetis was, of course, traditional, but its connection with the Prometheus myth appears to have been an Aeschylean adaptation. At any rate the earlier account of the myth (in Pindar, *Isthmian* viii, 27 ff), has Themis herself warn Zeus and Poseidon of the danger and directs Thetis to marry Peleus instead.[21]

20 I cannot however agree with the implications of Solmsen's statement (*Hesiod and Aeschylus* p 148) that 'The Zeus of the *Prometheus Bound* is not Aeschylus' Zeus at all but the Zeus whose manifestations he found in the *Theogony*' – particularly, thinks Solmsen, the more unpleasant ones appearing in the Titanomachy and in the suppressions of Typhoeus and the sons of Iapetos. Solmsen makes this suggestion largely to contrast the Zeus of *Prometheus Bound* with the more truly 'Aeschylean Zeus' which he believes will emerge later; however, this aspect of his argument must be postponed until we consider the possible development of the trilogy.

21 The date of Pindar *Isthmian* viii (478 BC) precedes by some years the earliest dating of *Prometheus Vinctus*. An earlier source of this myth is probably to be found in the cycle of legends of Achilles, as Mazon indicates in his introduction to the *PV* (*Notice* p 155). Wilamowitz (*Interpretationen* p 133), in his comment on Aeschylus' joining of the

This skilful adaptation on the part of Aeschylus provides an essential element (not needed in the unequal contest in Hesiod) in the long deadlock between Olympian power and Promethean knowledge. On the other hand, the motif of the dangerous marriage and its avoidance by use of Promethean knowledge corresponds, in a sense, to the threat imposed on the Hesiodic Zeus by his marriage to Metis and Zeus' own frustration of that threat by his guileful swallowing of Metis.[22]

Aeschylus' exploitation of the Io myth for his particular dramatic and thematic purposes is unquestionably one of the most imaginative and innovative devices of the play. However, it is in the new significance which he gives to Io's career and its consequences by interweaving it with the Prometheus myth, rather than in any drastic changes in the myth itself, that this fruitful innovation chiefly resides. The main outlines of Io's own career and that of her descendants seem, for the most part, to be amply, though not always consistently, attested in one source or another independent of Aeschylus' treatment.[23] Io was an Argive princess who, because of the love of Zeus and the jealousy of Hera, was transformed into a heifer and sent in headlong flight over vast stretches of Europe and Asia, until eventually, on reaching Egypt, she was impregnated by Zeus and restored to human form by a single divine touch. Epaphos, the 'touch-engendered' offspring of this union, ruled over the Nile-lands. Five generations later we hear of fifty female descendants of Epaphos fleeing from fifty cousin-suitors. They take refuge in their ancestral land of Argos, but when, despite Argive protection, force prevails, they murder their cousin bridegrooms on their wedding night. Only Hypermnestra spares her husband (Lynceus) and from their union springs a new line

'dangerous union' myth with the freeing of Prometheus, observes that the reference to the trident of Poseidon in the prophecy of Prometheus (*PV* 925) shows that Aeschylus and Pindar are using the same poetic model. Cf also Lesky's good arguments for identifying the author of this 'original' (so differently adapted) as the poet of the Hesiodic Catalogue. See Lesky *RE* 191 (1937) p 296. Cf also Hesiod fr 80 (R)-210(M-W).

22 See Vernant 'Mètis' pp 30–3: 'Point de souveraineté ... sans Mètis': in Aeschylus it is Prometheus who incarnates the *Metis* element which, in Hesiod, Zeus incorporates by his own stratagem without foregoing the 'dangerous marriage.' In this article and in *Les Ruses de l'Intelligence* II. 3, pp 61 ff, Vernant expounds well both the difference and the essential point of similarity (the necessity of intelligence as well as power for the *lasting* rule of Zeus) between the Hesiodic and Aeschylean versions.

23 For a full discussion of the ancient sources of the Io myth, see Roscher *Lexicon* I.1. cols 263–9. (References to particular sources will be given for specific details and variants discussed below.) Cf also Garvie *Aeschylus' Supplices* esp pp 174, 177 f.

of Argive Kings. (The Argive protection of the maiden-fugitives, and its bloody but ultimately prosperous sequel, is the subject of Aeschylus' 'Danaid trilogy,' of which only the first play, *The Suppliants*, is extant.) Near the end of a genealogical list[24] of Hypermnestra's and Lynceus' descendants, we read the name of Herakles.

In Aeschylus' treatments of the pursuit, or the persecution of Io, there are certain minor variations which are worth noting. *The Suppliants* departs from the tradition in making Hera, not Zeus, responsible for the actual transformation of Io into a heifer; in *Promethus Bound*, the responsibility remains ambiguous throughout. The explanation, in the case of both plays, of Aeschylus' refusal to have *Zeus* transform Io may be that it would have suited neither play's depiction of Zeus to cast such emphasis on his fear of Hera's jealousy (and his attempt to hide Io from it) – which is the traditional motive given for the deed of transformation.[25] So, too, in *Prometheus Bound*, the narrative details about 'earth-born Argos' sent by Hera to keep track of Io, about his death at the hands of Hermes (sent by Zeus), and about the subsequent pursuit of Io by Hera's gadfly are all consistent with the other accounts, though they are slightly confused in Io's distraught utterances.[26] One other difference, both from *The Suppliants'* and other versions, in the treatment of Zeus' relations with Io in *Prometheus Bound* is that at no time (either before or after the transformation of Io) is Zeus said actually to have assaulted Io sexually,[27] despite the references to his sexual desire for her (*PV* 590–1, 649, 737 ff). Again, the point may be a minor one, but we may find it significant in our later discussion of the play.

However, as I have indicated, the most radical and dramatically significant feature of the adaptation of the Io myth in *Prometheus Bound* is the close connection effected, on various levels, between the suffer-

24 See schol Eur. *Hec.* 886, ad fin.
25 Contrast Aesch. *Suppl.* 299 and *PV* 591–2, 600–1, 673 ff, with schol. *PV* 561; Apollod. II.1.3 (Frazer); Hyginus *Fab.* 145.3; and Pausanias I.xxx.1 (where the transformation of Io by Zeus is implied by the close comparison of Callisto's experience). That the myth of Zeus' transformation of Io into a heifer in order to disguise her from the jealous Hera goes back at least to the time of Hesiod seems likely from Apollodorus' citation of Hesiod at II. 1.3, 1; see Hesiod *Aegimius* fr 187 (Rzach) = Merkelbach-West *Fragm. Hes.* 124 *Eoiai* (M-W reject the ascription to *Aegimius*); Sophocles *Inachus* (Nauck *TGF* pp 188 ff).
26 See *PV* 567–73; cf 590–2. Compare the more explicit account at *Suppl.* 295 ff.
27 Contrast the omission or suppression of this point in *Prometheus Bound* with the explicit statements about it at Aesch. *Suppl.* 295–302 and in the other sources cited in the preceding two notes.

ings and destiny of Io and those of Prometheus. It was probably Aeschylus who chose a Scythian mountain crag for Prometheus' punishment (the locale remains unnamed in Hesiod). The wanderings of Io (one of the oldest and most traditional features of the Io myth) provide a natural though no doubt original opportunity for the meeting of Io and Prometheus – a meeting where the vast range of Io's sufferings readily provides a theatrical contrast with the static figure of the martyred Titan. Io appears both as a fellow victim with Prometheus of Zeus' violence *and* as one whose ultimate liberation by Zeus affords us hope for Prometheus' future: again, this potential ambiguity in Io's role is present from the start in that, from one point of view, Zeus is the cause of Io's sufferings, while from another, Zeus is her defender against Hera as well as her ultimate liberator.[28]

The actual course of the wanderings of Io in *Prometheus Bound* and her encounters with many mythological peoples and legendary phenomena are no doubt largely the poet's own invention: they are chosen, at least to some degree, to suit the theme of the play and are by no means consistent in all details with the fragmentary references in the early epic *Aegimius* (of Hesiod?) or with the later account in Apollodorus.[29] Also, it seems likely that in the earlier versions of the Io-Danaid myth, the 'Egyptian connection' did not come through Io and the Egyptian birthplace of Epaphos. According to a scholium to Euripides' *Hecuba* 886, Io's descendant Danaos, father of fifty daughters, drove his brother Aigyptos, father of fifty sons, out of Argos. The

28 Cf Aesch. *Suppl.* 556–82. Granted that the emphasis on Zeus the liberator from *Hera*-induced sufferings is, for obvious reasons, much more emphatic in *The Suppliants*, there is, nevertheless, a hint of this at the climax of the prophecy of Io's future at *PV* 848–9 and in the more subdued references to Hera's role in her sufferings at *PV* 591–2, 600–1 (if the scholiast and Hermann's nearly certain emendation are right), and 704.

29 That the wanderings were an essential aspect of the Io myth from the beginning appears likely even in the brief references to Io in the *Aegimius* of Hesiod (or Cercops); see Hesiod fr 186 (R): here Zeus' naming of Euboea 'after the heifer' must refer to a part of Io's wanderings. The accounts in Apollodorus and Hyginus include wanderings in Scythia and across the (eponymous) Bosporos, though in Apollodorus (as at Aesch. *Suppl.* 544–6) it is the Thracian Bosporos, in *Prometheus Bound* the Cimmerian Bosporos, which Io crosses. (The former joins the Euxine, the Black Sea, to the Propontis; the latter joins Lake Maeotis, later the Sea of Azov, to the Euxine.) The valuable and well-supported suggestion that the *Arimaspea*, ascribed to the mysterious, shaman-like (seventh-century?) poet Aristeas, may have been Aeschylus' source for some of the northern geography (and related mythology) involved in his account of Io's wanderings has been developed by Bolton, in *Aristeas of Proconnesus* chapter 3, pp 45–64 (see pp 63–4 for a summary of his tentative conclusions on this point). Cf below, chapter 3, n 47.

latter fled with his family to Egypt (after whom that country was named) but returned to Argos when his sons had grown up. Danaos, in fear for his kingship, arranged a treacherous marriage pact between his own and his brothers children, bidding his daughters slay their bridegrooms under penalty of death. (The rest of the myth, including the list of Hypermnestra's descendants, continues as we have already indicated).

Just when the Egyptian connection of Io herself came into the myth has been the subject of much interesting dispute.[30] The lost epic *Danaides*, belonging to the seventh or sixth centuries,[31] is generally regarded as the major, perhaps the first, source joining the Io and the Danaid legends in their final form. Thus Mazon's suggestion[32] that Io legends first reached Egypt through Argive Rhodian colonists in the seventh or sixth centuries seems a reasonable guess. On the other hand Roscher, noting Herodotus 2.41 ('for the statue of Isis is as a horned maid, just as the Greeks depict Io'), dates Io's Egyptian connection with her earliest tragic representation (as a horned maid instead of as a cow)[33] early in the fifth century. However, Roscher's dating of Io's Egyptian connection seems unreasonably late; nor need the identification of Io and Isis depend on the image of the horned maid.[34]

Finally, the return of Io's descendants from Egypt to Argos, so essential to the theme of Aeschylus' *Suppliants*, is given a new significance in *Prometheus Bound*. Just as Aeschylus is probably the first to blend the myths of Io and Prometheus, so too he is probably the first to have Herakles, son of Zeus and descendant of Io and Zeus, appear as the liberator of Prometheus (prophesied at *PV* 770 ff and 871 ff)[35] –

---

30 This question has been discussed recently by Garvie *Aeschylus' Supplices* pp 172–80; see also various references and authorities there cited.

31 *I.G.* xiv. 1292. fr II 1.10.

32 Mazon *Eschyle* I² '*Les Suppliantes,*' *Notice* p 4.

33 Roscher *Lex.* col 271.

34 Cf also Apollod. II. 1.3 (Frazer), where Io is said to have dedicated a statue to Demeter, 'called Isis by the Egyptians, as they called Io herself.'

35 That Prometheus is not freed in Hesiod seems clear from *Theog.* 616 (μέγας κατὰ δεσμὸς ἐρύκει). This is also the view of Wilamowitz (*Interpretationen* p 130) and of West (*Theogony* p 313, note on vv 523–33). West follows the view of Sittl here that this does not contradict *Theog.* 526–8 where 'Hesiod does not say that Herakles released Prometheus from his chains, only that he killed the eagle and delivered Prometheus from his torment.' Note, too, West's reference to Pherecydes 3 F 17 where Herakles' role is similarly limited, though Prometheus is clearly grateful for the release. Wilamowitz, however, regards the passage about Herakles (*Theog.* 526–34) as a later addition to the *Theogony*, since he believes that it *does* contradict v 516 (= 515 in Wilamowitz' reference).

and this, as we shall see, is to have great significance in the development of the trilogy. The liberation of Prometheus is, in turn, to be closely associated with Prometheus' use of the secret which he holds over Zeus. Now the secret of Prometheus and the Io myth have, of course, no connection whatever in the mythological tradition. Nevertheless, it is fitting that we should have discussed them both in the same section of this introductory chapter, for in this connection, also, the poet exploits the career of Io in a completely novel way. The visit of Io to Prometheus is intimately related to the dramatic deployment of Prometheus' secret, just as the prophesied consummation of Zeus' love for the human Io is thematically related to the secret of Zeus' future dangerous and unconsummated love. Thus the treatment of the Io theme in *Prometheus Bound* provides the crowning example of Aeschylus' brilliant adaptations of the mythological tradition to his own dramatic and thematic needs.

CHAPTER TWO

Prometheus Bound: introductory comments

1 Some problems and assumptions

The discussion of *Prometheus Bound* presents major problems which should, perhaps, be stated at the outset. The first of these is the question of presentation, for here one faces a recurrent dilemma: various critical statements which need to be made about the play will inevitably involve opinions about related problems some of which, in turn, require prior knowledge of the play for their discussion. It seems best, then, to state these problems initially, to accept certain (I think reasonable) opinions and even assumptions concerning them, and then to review those assumptions later, when a proper basis has been established by discussion of the play.

One problem of this latter kind concerns the actual authorship of *Prometheus Bound*, which has been called in question in modern times. However, despite the serious doubts which have been expressed, the majority of classical scholars still accept the Aeschylean authorship of the play (which was not questioned in antiquity), and we shall proceed on this assumption in our study of the play. The pros and cons of this particular debate have been rehearsed in several specialized studies; for our purposes, it must suffice to review the main arguments on the matter in an appendix.[1]

A second problem concerns the connected trilogy (which we may call for convenience the '*Prometheia*') of which *Prometheus Bound* formed a part. As in the case of *The Suppliants* of Aeschylus and, to a

---

1 See below, appendix 1, pp 141 ff. (Since the above paragraph was written, the alleged 'majority' view favouring Aeschylean authorship may have declined as a result of some of the work to be considered in this appendix.)

lesser degree, his *Seven against Thebes*, our understanding of the theme and meaning of *Prometheus Bound* is limited by the loss of the two related plays, and our interpretation must be coloured in part by what we guess about their contents. In the case of *Prometheus Bound* the problem tends to be particularly acute and tantalizing: first, because we have more evidence, of one kind or another, concerning the lost plays than in the case of the other truncated trilogies; secondly, because the major interpretative problems of *Prometheus Bound*, specifically those concerning the nature of Zeus and the ultimate significance of Prometheus' struggle with him, are closely bound up with the mysteries of the missing plays. Here again, a few generally accepted assumptions (together with one or two certainties) may be stated at the outset. In *Prometheus Bound*, we see the rebel god Prometheus bound on a Scythian mountain range for his defiance of Zeus in stealing fire for mankind. One of the lost plays of the trilogy is named *Prometheus Unbound* (*Prometheus Luomenos*) and so we may safely state that it followed the *Prometheus Bound*. The name of the other play is generally thought to be *Prometheus the Firebearer* (*Prometheus Purphoros*) (though we shall see there are grounds for some uncertainty here); it is usually assumed that the name refers in some way to the Torch-festival in honour of Prometheus at Athens and therefore that this play was the third in the trilogy, dealing with events after Prometheus had been released and was reconciled with Zeus. So much, then, we may set down in the way of preliminary information and assumptions about the trilogy: we postpone further consideration of these matters until our discussion of the fragmentary evidence about the trilogy and of the interpretative problems related to it.[2]

The lack of any didascalic information (ie, information about the play's date, connected and competing plays, prize-winners in the dramatic festival concerned) appended to the Alexandrian *Hypothesis* (or preliminary summary) of our manuscript of *Prometheus Bound* has opened the door to considerable speculation concerning both the date and the place of its performance. Arguments in the past for a fairly early date (eg, c 470) for this play rested on very insubstantial evidence, and more recent scholarship (supported, to a degree, by *some* earlier opinions) has probably been justified in placing the '*Prometheia*' among the latest, possibly the last, of Aeschylus' works, between the *Oresteia* of 458 and the poet's death in 456/5.[3] Perhaps the surest arguments for a

---

2 See below, chapter 5.

3 For arguments in favour of this later dating of the *Prometheia*, see Herington *The Author of the 'Prometheus Bound,'* passim; cf also Herington 'Some Evidence for a Late

late date are metrical and stylistic ones,[4] but they have been supported also by comparison of the subject matter and possible use of the trilogy form in the '*Prometheia*' with what we know of other trilogies (the '*Suppliants* trilogy,' the *Oresteia*) known to belong to the last ten years of the poet's life.[5] We shall find, too, that certain features of the thought and language of *Prometheus Bound* (such as the interest in civilization myths, the prominence of medical metaphors, perhaps, even, the overtones in the use of the word σοφιστής) must surely belong to the later period of Aeschylus' life, if they are to be accepted as Aeschylean at all. From all this, it will be seen that the question of the date of *Prometheus Bound* soon becomes involved with questions concerning the reconstruction of the trilogy and even concerning the authenticity of the play. Assuming, as we have, its Aeschylean authorship, we must, I think, accept a late date for *Prometheus Bound* (probably between 458 and 456/5) as most probable, though readers will want to weigh the general arguments put forward as we study the play's ideas and their dramatic formulations.

Dating of the *Prometheus Bound*' and 'Aeschylus: The Last Phase.' Among earlier scholars, Thomson, Rose, and Méautis have all agreed to this approximate dating of the *Prometheus*. For a summary of their arguments, and of other, differing ones, see Podlecki *The Political Background of Aeschylean Tragedy* appendix B, pp 144–7. See also below notes 4–8. Previously, arguments for an earlier date for the *Prometheus*, eg, in the 470s or shortly thereafter, had been based mainly on the possible influence of the eruption of Mount Aetna (in 479 or 475 BC) on the description of Typho's punishment at *PV* 351–2; cf Pindar *Pythian* I (dated at 470) 15–28, which deals with the same subject matter. See, among others, Wecklein's introduction to his edition pp 25–7 and references there given. The earlier date also fits the approximate time of Aeschylus' first visit to Syracuse in the late 470s. (See *Vit. Aesch.* 9–10; cf Diodorus 9.48 and Podlecki *The Political Background* pp 142–7, who, however, rightly resists these arguments for an early date for *Prometheus Bound*.) Wilamowitz *Interpretationen* p 242 and n 2, who alleges signs of Sicilian influence on the language of the play, suggests 469 or 468 as possible dates. But these and other arguments for 'Sicilian aspects' of the production (see below, n 7) could apply as well to Aeschylus' second visit to Sicily at the end of his life.

4 Eg, the metrical arguments of Yorke, Ceadal, and Denniston referred to by Podlecki *The Political Background*, p 144 and notes *ad loc.* Cf Herington 'A Unique Technical Feature in the *Prometheus Bound*' pp 5–7, and 'Some Evidence for a Late Dating of the *Prometheus Bound*' pp 239–40, who adds valuable formal and verbal observations on the *PV* in support of the metrical arguments for a date late in Aeschylus' career for this play. (Herington's observation of the high incidence of choral quatrains in the *PV* as a sign of comparatively late date is particularly interesting.)

5 Cf especially Herington 'Aeschylus: The Last Phase,' who believes that Aeschylus' *Suppliants*-tetralogy, *Oresteia* and *Prometheia* (which he dates between 458 and 456/5) – in that order – form a compact group of works at the end of the poet's career. This view of Herington's, which goes rather beyond the present point at issue, will be considered later (see below, chapter 5).

The assumption of a late date for *Prometheus Bound* leads in turn to the question of its place of production, for if the play was produced after the *Oresteia* and still in Aeschylus' lifetime, it may have been produced in Sicily, where Aeschylus is alleged to have spent the last two years of his life.[6] This possibility of a Sicilian production of the *Prometheus Bound* has, in turn, been used to explain other features, both of form and content, which one critic or another has found remarkable in the play. The relative poverty of the choral lyrics (in length, in grandeur, in complexity of thought, expression, and metre) has been mentioned by several critics, and the reasonable explanation has been advanced that Aeschylus did not have available in Sicily the well-trained *choreutae* capable of performing, in song and dance, his usual demanding choral lyrics.[7]

The 'Sicilian explanation' has also been used (less convincingly, in my opinion) in connection with the tyrannical characterization (off-stage) of Zeus in *Prometheus Bound*.[8] Now it is true that, as these critics have pointed out, many of the words and phrases used to describe Zeus' attitudes and actions concerning Prometheus, Io, and mankind

6 See *Vita Aesch.* 10–11. As Podlecki has noted, *The Political Background* p 5, the *Vita* fails to distinguish between the Sicilian visit (apparently to Gela, where Aeschylus allegedly died) during the last two or three years of his life and what must have been an earlier visit to Aetna in the 470s, when Hieron 'founded' Aetna and Aeschylus produced *The Aetnaean Women* to congratulate its inhabitants (*Vita* 9).

7 See Focke, 'Aischylos' *Prometheus*,' who, however, assigns the Sicilian production of the *Prometheus Bound* to Aeschylus' visit to Hieron's court at Aetna in 470/69. Cf also Focke's references to Wilamowitz' and Robert's more extreme views on the limitations of the Chorus in *Prometheus Bound*. Griffith 'Aeschylus, Sicily and Prometheus', pp 105–39, has argued, for the most part convincingly, against signs of Sicilian influence in the style and language of *Prometheus Bound*. He is, perhaps, less convincing in his reasons (pp 120–1) for rejecting the view that Aeschylus may have shortened and otherwise adapted the choral portion of *Prometheus Bound* to suit Sicilian production – a very different kind of argument (though still quite hypothetical) from those urging (on very slender evidence) Sicilian influence on style, vocabulary, or thought. However, Griffith does well to remind us (p 124) that it is difficult (though not perhaps impossible) to believe in the Sicilian production of *Prometheus Bound* while also acknowledging that its sequel probably linked Prometheus closely to the Prometheus of Athenian cult, especially in the alleged representation of the founding of the Prometheia, the torch festival in honour of Prometheus, in the second or third play of the trilogy. See below, chapter 5, note 23.

8 See Méautis, who regards *Prometheus Bound* as a play with a political sub-plot ('un arrière-plan politique') written in and for Sicily, at the end of the poet's career (p 8). For a balanced assessment of this and other political interpretations of *Prometheus Bound*, see Podlecki *The Political Background* pp 107 ff. Podlecki devotes the latter part of his chapter (pp 115–22) to a sane exposition of his own view that 'in the *Prometheus Bound* [Aeschylus] has formulated the specific charges which the maturing democracy was

are ones which can and have been used to describe tyrants of the more despotic kind in the Greek world. That Aeschylus himself was aware of this and even that he expected his audience to be reminded of tyrants who have appeared in the context of human politics also seems reasonable. But that the poet intended this description of Zeus in relation to his opponents and subjects to be applied to a particular human tyrant (such as Hieron at Syracuse) is surely a gratuitous assumption. The theme and the dramatic conception of the play (and, as far as we can tell, of the trilogy) provide quite sufficient explanations for the political aspect of this impression of Zeus; nor need we regard this picture as so contradictory to the Zeus of other Aeschylean plays as to require extra-dramatic apology.[9]

2 Prophecy and tragic action: a synoptic view of the play

In most Greek tragedies words (including how and why they are said) are action, and in Aeschylus, where actual events in causal sequence are minimal, this is particularly true. In *Prometheus Bound*, we should be especially attentive to certain verbal sequences, specifically those which refer, in progressively differing ways, to future events affecting Zeus and Prometheus. For *Prometheus Bound* is, in all the more obvious ways, surely one of the most static of Aeschylean plays: not only is its central figure fixed in at least an illusion of permanence in the centre of the stage, while all other figures, dramatic and choral, move in and out or to and fro before him; but also the conflict between Prometheus and the off-stage Zeus provides at least an illusion of the immovable object assailed by irresistible force.

Now it is true that much of our interest in the play derives from the ever-expanding revelations which Prometheus makes, in response to the stimuli of various 'visitors,' concerning his quarrel with Zeus and his services to man which first occasioned it. But as far as plot progression or evolving action is concerned, the one dynamic element, the one

laying at the door of the form of government from which it had evolved' (p 121). If there is a contemporary political 'message' in *Prometheus Bound* (subordinate, I would argue, to the specific dramatic theme and mythological context of the play itself), then it is surely best formulated in these general terms.

9 Cf Lloyd-Jones 'Zeus in Aeschylus,' especially the conclusions at pp 65–7. It is possible, however, that these well-documented conclusions overstate the case for the consistency of the Zeus of the Prometheus with the impressions of Zeus to be gleaned from the other plays and fragments of Aeschylus. We shall return to this major question in a later chapter on the play and trilogy. (See below chapter 6.)

feature of the situation with any potential for change or dramatic movement, resides in the secret knowledge (and the use to be made of it) which Prometheus holds over Zeus. Prometheus' prophetic utterances about Zeus and himself undergo a gradual and significant change, involving in the end an actual reversal, between the Prologue and the final episode. This change is, I believe, dictated by a change in the attitude of Prometheus to his situation, a change induced by the effect of his visitors (both choral and dramatic) upon him. In this change and its catastrophic result lies the tragic action of the play.

If this is true, then the relations between Prometheus and Zeus (rather than, say, the celebration of Prometheus as a civilization *daimon*) is the *central* issue of this play and possibly (though we cannot, of course, be at all sure of this) of the trilogy as a whole. This is not to say that the themes of Prometheus' services to mankind and of Io's wanderings and future progeny are either minor or irrelevant.[10] Mankind is the essential third element in the triangle which expresses the destinies of Zeus and Prometheus in *Prometheus Bound*. The account of the civilizing of man by Prometheus expounds the symbolic meaning of Prometheus and of his initial quarrel with Zeus. The story of Io and her descendants is likewise essential to the understanding of Zeus in his relations (present and future) with mankind and, ultimately, with Prometheus himself. Yet these great narrations (however germane to these larger meanings) must, as far as the tragic *action* is concerned, be regarded as subordinate to the issue of the Zeus-Prometheus conflict.

The structure of the play, regarded as the sequence in which themes are introduced and the dramatic 'justifications' of that sequence, supports the view that it is the struggle between Prometheus and Zeus

10 Cf Karl Reinhardt's long and interesting answer (*Aischylos* pp 74–6) to the question whether the *Prometheus* is (as it has been taken to be) 'the tragedy of human culture.' Reinhardt has definite reservations, eg, 'In the essential nature of the divine, there is a dissension or cleavage (*Entzweiung*) which extends down into the human element and which has gone on from primitive times right up to the present [ie, up to the dramatic date of this trilogy].' Thus Reinhardt suggests that the unending struggle between the Titanic and Olympian opposites (which he regards as implying and completing one another) is extended, after the expulsion of the Titans, to men and Earth. This seems a useful correction of more simplistic views of the *Prometheus Bound* as primarily a celebration of Prometheus as civilization *daimon* or as symbolizing 'the crucifixion of intellectual man' in the world. (See Havelock *Prometheus* preface and essays in part I, passim.) George Thomson, though he expounds well the 'divine' aspects of the play and the trilogy, also tends at times to see Prometheus exclusively through humanist or, in this case, Marxist eyes, which is not, perhaps, entirely appropriate to the poet's own conception. (See George Thomson *Aeschylus, The Prometheus Bound* introduction, passim. eg, pp 6 ff.)

which is the major dramatic concern. George Thomson's view of the structure as divided into four 'movements' – present, past, future, present – is excellent from a formal point of view,[11] but the larger thematic units which I would like to suggest will cut across these neat temporal divisions. The first third of the play, up to the first stasimon (1–396), deals mainly with Prometheus and the gods (their treatment of him; his treatment of them); the second third, to the end of the Io episode (397–886), deals with the relations of Prometheus and Zeus with human beings – and with the effect of these relations on their own related destinies; the final third of the play deals (almost to the exclusion of all human interest) with the relations of Prometheus and Zeus, seen now as a power struggle in which as one god prophesies the other's destruction, he is overwhelmed for refusing (at this point) to avert it.

This 'gods-man-gods' sequence clearly indicates the direction of the play's dramatic action. That action begins with the impalement of a silent and apparently helpless Prometheus by Zeus' minions; travels in retrospect through both divine and human spheres (Prometheus' services to both Zeus and man; Zeus' involvement with the human Io, ancestress of Prometheus' liberator) and returns to present actuality with a restatement, very different from the statement of the Prologue, of the Zeus-Prometheus struggle. Before considering specific dramatic effects within the play, let us take a slightly closer look at the overall structure just indicated and at the dynamic devices by which the plot is made to serve the theme.

Throughout the impalement scene of the Prologue, Prometheus is silent before his divine gaolers, Kratos and Hephaistos. In the final scene of the play with Hermes, another lackey of Zeus, Prometheus

---

11 Thomson summarizes his analysis of the play's structure as follows: '... the main subject of the first movement is the binding of Prometheus – the present; of the second, the history of gods and man – the past; of the third, the destiny of Io and the birth of Heracles – the future; and the fourth movement, with its increase of the penalty, balances the first.' These time elements are interwoven (both in the larger structure and within each of its parts) in such a way that 'our attention is thrown with increasing emphasis upon the future' (Ibid pp 14–15).

Thomson might also have noted that this interweaving of 'time elements,' which he so skilfully delineates, also suggests the great stretches of time involved in the Zeus-Prometheus struggle, just as the wanderings of Io in this play and of Herakles in the next (see frr 109–112N) suggest the vast extent, over the whole known world, of Prometheus' and Herakles' civilizing process. Thus Thomson's temporal scheme for the play's structure can be related, in a general way, to the main themes of the play and the trilogy; it is in no way contradicted by the more specific suggestions concerning plot development and theme to be expounded in the present study.

indulges in torrential speech. This movement from silent self-containment to vociferous defiance indicates the main dynamic flow of the play, the ever-expanding revelations by Prometheus which are the principal effect of his visitors upon him.[12] *Pari passu* with these experiences moves Prometheus' changing attitude not toward Zeus but toward his struggle with Zeus and to that secret knowledge which is his sole resource.

Prometheus' first revelations are made in soliloquy, to the natural elements (88 ff) which surround him, but here his situation and his knowledge of Necessity are expressed, after a struggle with his self-imposed silence (106–7), in the most terse and general terms (101–13). With the arrival of the sympathetic Chorus, Prometheus makes his first overt references to the secret which he holds over Zeus and prophesies his liberation *and reconcilement with Zeus* through use of it (167 ff, 186 ff). To the Chorus' further invitation that he reveal the cause of Zeus' harsh punishment, Prometheus replies instead with a long account (197 ff) of his services to Zeus and of Zeus' base ingratitude. Only at the end of the speech (234 ff) and in the brief enigmatic passage of stichomythia with the Chorus-leader which follows it, does he say anything of his services to man. So, too, Prometheus puts off further questions about the possible end of his punishment with the cryptic clausula, 'Only when it seems best to Zeus' (258).

The intervention of Ocean (298–396) ends this first movement of the play. Ocean's attempt to reconcile Prometheus with Zeus, and Prometheus' answer, are both concerned exclusively with the *natures* of the two warring gods (note especially 309 ff, 320–4, 333–4), and the two cautionary tales (Zeus' punishments of Atlas and of Typho, 347–72) remain on the same divine or Titanic level. Again Prometheus describes the end of his woes in terms of Zeus' future disposition ('... till Zeus' mind be lightened of its wrath,' 376). Again the scene ends with an enigmatic passage of dialogue (377–96), this time on 'sick minds' and their treatment, though whether of Zeus, Prometheus, or even Ocean remains obscure.

The second movement of the play opens with a choral ode (the first

---

12 This development is, of course, obvious enough and has been noted in one way or another by various critics. See, for example, Garzya 'Le Tragique du *Prométhée enchaîné*,' pp 117 ff, who expresses the changes in Prometheus from mute endurance through bitter plaints and proud self-vindication to confidence in ultimate victory. I do not, however, agree with Garzya that this indicates a process of 'self-enrichment' through suffering. Nor, of course, do I wish to suggest that these dramatic changes imply any change in Prometheus' nature.

stasimon, 397–435) expressing the sympathy not only of the Chorus but of all the neighbouring races of men, and of all nature, with Prometheus and his dishonoured kin. Prometheus responds (after a third struggle with his brooding silence, 436 f), this time with his first full account (436–71; 476–506) of all the practical arts by which he raised men from a brutish to a civilized existence. In between these two speeches, the Chorus-leader likens Prometheus (significantly, in view of his last exchange with Ocean) to a doctor who cannot heal himself (472–5). In the dialogue which, as usual,[13] concludes the scene, the Chorus-leader returns to the question of Prometheus' liberation. Prometheus (for the first time since his Prologue soliloquy) refers to Necessity, as somehow limiting both his bondage and Zeus' freedom (514–18) but remains tight-lipped ('In no way is it timely to speak of this,' 522–3) about the secret knowledge which lies behind this reference. Once again, Prometheus is clearly in control, waiting for the right moment (καιρός, 523) to reveal his secret.

The Io episode (561–886) forms the second and major portion of the human theme in the play. It is related to the divine theme by Zeus' cruel courtship of the persecuted wandering maiden and by Prometheus' prophecies of Io's destiny as the ancestress of his own saviour, Herakles. The long Io scene is enclosed by two brief odes, the one anticipating (albeit unconsciously), the other reflecting on the mating theme involved therein.[14] In the first of these odes (526–60), the Chorus insist on their own pious observance, in contrast to Prometheus' boldness, of Zeus' power (κράτος, 528) and Zeus' order (ἁρμονία, 551) and dwell nostalgically on the happy wedding day of Prometheus and Hesione. In the second ode (887–907), the Chorus, moved by the terrors of Zeus' courtship of Io, hymn the wisdom of 'marriage at one's own level' and pray that the eye of Zeus may never light on them.

The Io episode is fundamental to the structure and theme of the play and (as far as we can guess) of the trilogy as a whole. It begins with the paradox that Zeus, the would-be destroyer of the human race, is here presented as the relentless lover of the human maiden Io, and ends with the paradox that Zeus, the persecutor of Prometheus, appears as the ancestor (in Prometheus' prophecy) of Prometheus' liberator. So it is that the divine and human themes are inextricably interwoven in a scene which provides, moreover, the crucial turning-point in Prome-

---

13 Cf vv 242 ff, 377 ff.
14 Cf Herington in his introduction to *Prometheus Bound*, translated by Scully and Herington, p 10; Herington also comments on the striking metrical links, complementing the thematic links, between the two odes.

theus' attitude to his struggle with Zeus and to his prophetic knowledge of their linked destinies. Discussion of this change and of the
ironies involved in it must await detailed analysis of the play; for the
purpose of this structural outline, two preliminary points should be
made. It is in this scene that Prometheus begins to separate his 'secret,'
earlier envisaged (167 ff, 186 ff) as a means of honourable reconciliation
with Zeus, from his own liberation. Now the possibility of Zeus' *fall*
and the *subsequent* liberation of Prometheus is, for the first time, envisaged (755 ff), though a saving qualification of this possibility is introduced briefly (770) a few lines later. Secondly, it is in this scene that
Prometheus loses for good (as far as this play is concerned) that
vacillation between self-confidence (eg at 167 ff, 186 ff), fearful uncertainty (115–27; 267–9), and almost despairing resignation (258) which
has marked his earlier reactions. The Prometheus who shouts his
defiance at Zeus at the beginning of the play's last movement has
undergone a fatal change of attitude.

In the final movement of the play, we return again to present
actuality, to the struggle between ruler Zeus and rebel Prometheus.
Notice has been served even in the early parts of the play that the secret
knowledge which Prometheus holds over Zeus will somehow equalize
the intolerably unbalanced situation of the Prologue, but we have been
given to understand by Prometheus himself (...σπεύδων σπεύδοντι,
192) that the resolution, the use to which this playing of the secret
trump card will be put, will be one in which both antagonists eagerly
acquiesce. Now all that has changed. The separation of the secret
(involving Zeus' possible overthrow) and the liberation of Prometheus, a separation subtly introduced toward the end of the Io scene, is
now restated more violently in Prometheus' speech of outright
defiance against Zeus at the beginning of the final scene. Now for the
first time Prometheus actually describes the fall of Zeus, and the
unknown agent of that destruction, in unconditional terms (915–27),
though he still prefaces that description with the statement that he
alone of the gods would be able to show 'the way out' (ἐκτροπή) from
that disaster (913–14).

Thus it is Prometheus' clear prophecy of Zeus' fall which brings
Hermes from Zeus to learn the details of the fatal secret. Our *sympathy*,
of course, remains with Prometheus in his heroic defiance of the bully
Hermes and the all-powerful Zeus: the consistent loyalty of the Chorus, along with the various role-assignments and the rhetoric of the
play throughout, makes sure of that. Nevertheless, amid the cosmic
atmospherics which herald the final cataclysm, the hurling of Prome-

theus to Tartaros, we are left in no doubt that it is this new intransigence of Prometheus, born of the action of the play, which has brought about the fatal confrontation.[15]

'With mind diseased I hear you raving' declares Hermes, reviving a fear first raised by Ocean and the sympathetic Chorus.[16]

'Diseased I might be,' replies Prometheus, 'if to hate one's foes be a disease.'

15 Even this preliminary structural outline of *Prometheus Bound* must lead us to question the various critical strictures wich have been made concerning the lack of organization and even of thematic unity in this play. See, for example, Snell *Aischylos und das Handeln im Drama* p 213; Focke 'Aischylos' *Prometheus*' pp 261–2; Smyth *Aeschylean Tragedy* pp 99–100; Rosenmeyer *The Masks of Tragedy* pp 53–5.
16 Cf 337 ff, 472–5.

CHAPTER THREE

Prometheus Bound:
detailed commentary

1 The Prologue (vv 1–127)

As the play begins, the silent Prometheus is being chained to a
Scythian mountain by the minions of Zeus. Kratos (Power), who
directs the work, and Bia (Force), who stands silently by, are in one
sense allegorical figures representing the harsh discipline of Zeus, the
new ruler of the gods. However, they have, in this context, a specific
mythological significance as well. As the children of Styx they were
made permanent members of Zeus' household from the time when
Styx became the first volunteer to fight on Zeus' side against the Titans
(Hesiod, *Theog.* 383–403): thus their position is to be contrasted sharply
with that of Prometheus, another ally from the old days of Zeus'
struggle for power. It is Kratos who states Prometheus' offence
(ἁμαρτία) in stealing 'the flash of all-contriving fire' (παντέχνου πυρὸς
σέλας) for men and the necessity of his punishment (7–11), who
declares the absolute supremacy of Zeus' rule (10–11, 50), and who
despises all sympathy (36 ff, 43–4) in urging on Hephaistos in each
particular of the binding (52–80: Kratos' admonitory couplets, from vv
40 ff, alternate with the gentler one-verse answers of the blacksmith-
god). Hephaistos, related to Prometheus by both kinship (cf συγγενῆ
θεὸν ..., 14) and function, represents in his sympathy for Prometheus
something of the latter's own sympathy for man. Thus Hephaistos
mournfully prophesies the prisoner's age-long sufferings (21 ff), be-
wails his own enforced handiwork (45, 48), and deprecates the harshness of Kratos (42, 78) and even of Zeus himself (34–5).

Equally important are the atmospheric effects of this powerful Prologue:

To earth's most distant stretch we come, to this Scythian waste, unmanned and desolate. (1–2)

These opening lines, starting with the word Χθονὸς ... (Earth), provide the elemental setting, the cosmic loneliness in which this struggle of the gods will take place. The marked remoteness from mankind contrasts sharply with Prometheus' own involvement with the human race which is mentioned twice (8, 11) by Kratos as the cause of his punishment. These elemental 'atmospherics' are continued in the descriptions, by both Kratos and Hephaistos, of Prometheus' impalement. He is to be bound 'to lofty-cliffed rocks [πρὸς πέτραις / ὑψηλοκρήμνοις ...] in unbreakable fetters of adamantine chains' (6),[1] to be scorched by day beneath the blazing sun and chilled by bitter frosts at night (22–5). All this is to take place 'far from the sight and sound of man' (21) and over apparently endless stretches of time, 'for the one who will free you has not yet been born' (27).

Here, albeit unwittingly, Hephaistos gives us the first of several hints of Prometheus' ultimate liberation, for the speech is true in the literal sense in which the speaker does not mean it.[2] It has been further suggested that the sympathetic tone of Hephaistos, and the submissive tone of Prometheus' 'ally,' Okeanos, a little later (307 ff), are meant

1 Dumortier *Les Images dans la Poésie d'Eschyle* pp 57 ff describes the depiction of Prometheus throughout as that of 'a charger proud and constrained' ('fier coursier entrave', which he regards as the dominant image of the play. Dumortier begins his illustrations (some more convincing than others) of this image with vv 4–6, but while ἀρρήκτοι πέδαι may be used of horse fetters (Dumortier suggests that the expression here and at v 19–20, δυσλύτοις χαλκεύμασι, is derived from *Iliad* 12. 34–8, where the hobbling of Poseidon's horses is described) it is not, of course, limited to these. Certainly other words in the Prologue 'binding-scene' (ψάλιον, 'curb-chain,' 54; νασχαλιστήρ, 'chest-strap,' 71; λχφάω, 27 – of Prometheus' putative 'unyoking') and elsewhere (χαλινός, 'bridle,' 562; στόμιον, 'bit' and ἡνίαι, 'reins,' 1009–10), all used of Prometheus, do support Dumortier's conception. Dumortier finds that this image sequence reaches its climax with Hermes' insult to Prometheus at vv 1009–10: 'Biting the bit like some newly-yoked colt, you fight and struggle against the reins.' (It should be noted, however, that when a similar image is used of the compulsion of Inachos, it is the harshness of the *rider* which the metaphor, 'the curb of Zeus,' emphasizes.)

2 All that Hephaistos means, of course, is 'the man able to free you has not been (and never will be) born,' that is, he 'means' the expression in the same conventional sense as Macbeth fatally misunderstood that other conventional expression, 'No man born of woman ...' and the same sort of irony is involved. (Schol M compounds the literal fallacy by his paraphrase of ὁ λωφήσων of v 27: ὁ ποιήσων σε λωφῆσαι Ηρακλῆς. Sikes and Willson in their note ad loc. set this right, but fail to comment on the irony involved.) Cf vv 1026 ff, where Hermes describes another apparent 'impossibility' relating to Prometheus' freeing, with comparable ironic effect.

to indicate the kind of modulations by which the Zeus-Prometheus conflict will be resolved.[3] But far in the future, in the last fragment of *Prometheus Unbound* which we possess, Prometheus addresses Herakles as 'Beloved son of a father whom I hate!' (fr 201 N) and in the present play, neither of these 'mitigators' are shown to have the slightest effect upon the deadlock between Prometheus and Zeus. 'Strike harder, bind him, don't let up!' urges Kratos (58), 'Drive through his breast the adamantine wedge!' (64–5). And Hephaistos, for all his expressions of kinship and sympathy with the victim, accomplishes the deed with reluctant efficiency (45, 60, 63, 75).

There is, however, another sense in which Hephaistos, or rather Hephaistos' *art*, may be said to indicate, symbolically and ironically, the route to liberation which Prometheus will follow. Prometheus shares in the art ($\tau\acute{\epsilon}\chi\nu\eta$) of Hephaistos; indeed it is as the supreme artisan that he is to base his claim to be champion of man. In the Prologue, Hephaistos' art provides the apparently invincible barrier to Prometheus' escape, though later (514) Prometheus is to remind us that that art (like Prometheus' own) is 'weaker than Necessity.' Hephaistos' art or skill is a special form of knowledge: it will be overcome, in turn, by some special knowledge on Prometheus' part. All this, too, is heralded, if obscurely, in this opening scene. Kratos, who has already (62) sneered at Prometheus as a helpless $\sigma o\phi\iota\sigma\tau\acute{\eta}s$ (one possessed of special knowledge),[4] finally indulges in the punning taunt that Prometheus will indeed need 'foresight' ($\pi\rho o\mu\eta\theta\acute{\epsilon}\omega s$, 86) to extricate himself from Hephaistos' handiwork. It is fitting that Prometheus' gaolers should retire with this ironic heralding of Prometheus' prophetic power, for this is to govern both the (putative) resolution of the conflct (in the trilogy) and the tragic action of the present play.

> O divine ethereal fire and swift-winged winds and primal springs of rivers
> and many-twinkling smiles of ocean waves and earth all-mothering and

3 Cf Rosenmeyer p 60.
4 $\Sigma o\phi\iota\sigma\tau\acute{\eta}s$ was originally used of an expert in a particular craft (see LSJ *s. v.* 1); though by Aeschylus' time it could also be used of one with a reputation for wisdom or cleverness in general, in the present context the word may well carry something of the overtone of 'the expert.' Commentators regularly warn us, of course, against taking $\sigma o\phi\iota\sigma\tau\acute{\eta}s$ to mean 'teacher' or 'Sophist' (with or without pejorative overtones) before the time of Socrates. Nevertheless, it could have, as here, the invidious note so often used of clever people when they are discomfited, without the sophistic overtone. Cf, for example, Eur. fr 905.

all-seeing eye of sun, on you I call. Look upon me and see what kinds of outrage a god from other gods does suffer. (88–92)

So Prometheus breaks his long silence (itself a powerful statement while his torturers were present) with this invocation to the natural elements[5] and to the all-seeing sun which looks upon his suffering. Immediately, the restrained dignity of these opening lines is interrupted by a passionate outburst, in anapaests, against his outrageous punishment and a despairing question as to how long it must be suffered (93–100). Passion, in turn, gives way to resignation, self-rebuke even, as Prometheus (returning to measured iambics) answers his own question:

Yet what am I saying? Of all that will come I have foreknowledge, in every detail [σκεθρῶς] ... The fate ordained one must bear as easily as possible, knowing Necessity [ἀνάγκη] is invincible. (101 ff)

Here follows Prometheus' first struggle between speech and silence[6] which he resolves with the briefest statement of his situation:

For mortals I provided the gift of fire, teacher of all men's arts. In punishment for this offence, I'm riveted aloft in public servitude. (107–13, paraphrase)

5 The possible significance of this invocation to the elements by Prometheus, in some sense an 'elemental' god himself, has been raised in ancient as in modern times. See schol. M to *PV* 88 μεγαλοφυῶς δὲ τὰ τέτταρα στοιχεῖα ἐπικαλεῖται; Adams 'The Four Elements in the *Prometheus Vinctus*' pp 97 ff; Herington 'A Study in the *Prometheia*. I: The Elements in the Trilogy,' pp 180 ff. (Herington's elaborate argument concerning this passage and the possible place of the elements in the trilogy will be discussed later, in chapter 5.) However, the frequency of such appeals to the elements in Greek literature (for a list of such conventional invocations in Greek tragedy, see W.S. Barrett's note on Euripides' *Hippolytus* 601 in his edition) should lead us to be cautious about too special an interpretation of this passage.
6 'To speak or to be silent about these woes: both choices are impossible!' (106–7); cf 197–8, 436–7: these are Prometheus' own allusions to his 'speech or silence' dilemma, which is, however, obvious from many other passages in the play. Cf also 379–80 and 522–5, passages where Prometheus gives specific reasons (apart from his own brooding bitterness) for silence with regard to Zeus and their related future fates. Cf also Taplin 'Aeschylean Silences and Silences in Aeschylus' especially pp 59 ff, who distinguishes Prometheus' silences preceding vv 88 ff (during the enchainment) and 436 ff (as well as several other 'silences in Aeschylus') from the kind of 'Aeschylean silence' (eg, those of Achilles and Niobe in the lost plays, *Phrygians* and *Niobe*, respectively) to which Aristophanes is referring at *Frogs* 911 ff.

Again, Prometheus' mood and metre change;[7] apprehension, then fresh indignation seize him as he hears the rustle of unseen visitors:

> What sound, what fragrance (source unseen) approaches? Divine? mortal?
> mixed of both? comes it to spy upon my woes? See me, ill-fated prisoner
> god, hated of Zeus ... for too great love of men. Alas ... the air rustles with
> the beat of wings. All that approaches is a source of fear. (115–27, in part)

Does Prometheus, with his prophetic knowledge, fear the approach of the eagle which aeons later (cf *PV* 1021 ff) is to come and gnaw his liver? Though commentators are divided on this point, both Prometheus' language and, as we shall see, the ironic alleviation of his fear suggest that this is so.

The 'Prologue soliloquy' of Prometheus which we have just reviewed is a passage of great dramatic power. Nevertheless, the god himself has shown us, by the tight-lipped nature of his revelations and by the unexpected chinks appearing in the armour of his resolution, how far he still must travel before becoming the vaunting 'hero' of the final scenes. The dramatic action, and something of the tragic meaning of the play, will be seen to reside in this journey of Prometheus.

2 The Parodos (vv 128–92)

The fluctuating moods which we have noted of Prometheus in his opening speech continue, in some degree, until the entry of Io; from that point on, Prometheus' tone grows steadily more confident until, at the end of the scene, and more so after the departure of Io, Prometheus' increasing confidence and indignation reach an extreme of defiance against Zeus. It is these changes of mood, in relation to changing dramatic contexts, which seem to account for the variety, almost to the point of inconsistency, of Prometheus' disclosures about Zeus' future and his own. The first of such revelations from Prometheus occurs in the epirrhematic parodos, for the winged visitor whom Prometheus senses at the end of the Prologue turns out to be the

---

7 At vv 115–19, Prometheus mingles bursts of song (115, 117) with iambic (spoken)
   metre; at 120–7, he returns to anapaestic chant. Many readers will, of course, have
   noted these metrical changes accompanying Prometheus' sudden changes of mood.
   Cf Thomson's note to vv 88 ff and, on the speech as a whole, Herington, introduction
   to *Prometheus Bound* p 13. As Herington notes, this passage is 'metrically unparalleled
   in all Greek drama.' Cf also Tracy '*Prometheus Bound* 114–117,' who comments particularly on the dramatic reason for this unique 'lyric interruption' of the iambic passage
   in these lines.

Chorus of Okeanids in their winged chariot whose gentle sympathy provides a nicely ironic response to Prometheus' fears. (The question whether, and if so how, the winged chariot appeared on-stage will be considered later, along with other problems of staging.)[8]

The epirrhematic form of the parodos (in which the Chorus sing and the actor chants in response to one another) is ideally suited to the dramatic need of 'drawing out' the suffering god. The Chorus blend sympathy for Prometheus' hideous punishment ('withering away on this rocky crag,' 147) with gentle warning of the lasting quality of Zeus' anger (163–6). Each statement results in the expansion by Prometheus of certain terse comments in his Prologue soliloquy. In that speech, Prometheus had complained in one word ($\dot{v}\pi\alpha\dot{\iota}\theta\rho\iota o\varsigma$, 113) of the public nature of his shameful punishment. In response to the Chorus' sympathy, he now expands this complaint to a whole stanza (152–9): he had rather been hurled down to Tartaros than suffer as an ethereal phantom ($\alpha\dot{\iota}\theta\dot{\epsilon}\rho\iota o\nu$ $\kappa\dot{\iota}\nu\nu\gamma\theta$, 158) for his enemies to laugh at. So, too, when the Chorus warn:

> Zeus will not cease from anger till his heart be sated ... or till, by some device, some one should seize his power, so hard to seize (165–6),

Prometheus picks up the unconscious cue which the Chorus have provided and expands on his Prologue hint (105) about Necessity:

> He'll need me yet, I tell you, will that great lord of gods forever blessed – yes, *me*, tormented as I am by heavy chains about my limbs – to show him the new scheme by which he'll have his sceptre and prerogatives torn from him. And in no way will he beguile me then, with honey-sweet persuasive charms, till he release me from these savage bonds and promise recompense for outrage done. (167–77)

The Chorus, shocked at Prometheus' persistent boldness, add further warning of Zeus' unchanging ways; this leads to Prometheus' first clear prophecy of reconciliation between himself and Zeus:

> ... he'll be mild of mood, I think, when he's crushed by the threat I've spoken of. Then smoothing his implacable anger, eagerly [$\sigma\pi\epsilon\dot{\upsilon}\delta\omega\nu$] will he come into harmony and friendship with me, eager alike [$\sigma\pi\epsilon\dot{\upsilon}\delta o\nu\tau\iota$] to receive him. (188–92)

Here, then, Prometheus unequivocally prophecies the reconcilia-

---

8 See appendix 2, pp 175 ff, 'Notes on the Staging of *Prometheus Bound*.'

tion of himself and Zeus, when he has saved Zeus from destruction: a prophecy which is to be all but reversed in the final scene of the play (cf 918–27).

3 The first episode (vv 193–396)

πάντ᾿ἐκκάλυψον ..., the Chorus-leader bids Prometheus, at the beginning of the first episode, 'Reveal everything! Tell us the whole story of your offence against Zeus ...' (193 ff). However, this is a play in which answers are continually being postponed on one pretext or another or else (as here) on none at all. Prometheus chooses to tell first not the cause of Zeus' anger with *him* (which must involve an account of his services to man) but the cause of *his* anger with Zeus. The sequence is indicative of the play's priorities and perhaps those of the trilogy as well. At any rate, as far as *Prometheus Bound* is concerned, we begin and end with Prometheus' sense of outrage against Zeus.

When the gods were choosing sides (Prometheus tells the Chorus, 199 ff) on the eve of Zeus' struggle with Kronos, Gaia foretold to Prometheus in what way the future would be brought to pass:

... that not by strength nor by might but by guile [δόλῳ] was it fated that the winners [τοὺς ὑπερσχόντας] should prevail. (212–13)

The Titans, offered 'first refusal,' as it were, of the services of Prometheus (here representing 'guile'; see vv 206 ff), reject him and are defeated; Zeus accepts Prometheus and wins:

By my counsels the black depths of Tartaros hides Kronos, the ancient born, with all his allies. (219–21)

Next, Prometheus, in turn ('for somehow it is a taint of tyranny not to trust one's friends,' 224–5), is punished when he saves men from the destruction planned for them by Zeus (231–8).

There are two points in Prometheus' account of 'the past of the gods' which shed light on the future destinies of Zeus and Prometheus and on Prometheus' prophecies (both previous and forthcoming) about them. (Both points are, as far as we can tell, Aeschylean; at any rate neither occurs in anything like the same form in Hesiod.)[9] The first is

---

9 It is possible, of course, that the points to be mentioned *may* have occurred in the (putative) lost *Titanomachy* to which reference has already been made (above chapter 1, n 8). But since both points are inextricably bound up with the new emphasis on Prometheus in the battle with the Titans, I am inclined to attribute them to the author of the present play.

the obvious one that Gaia's prophecy as to 'how the future will be brought to pass' (211) is clearly conditional in that it involves a choice: had the Titans (the implication is) chosen Prometheus (or 'guile'), they need never have been defeated. Zeus, by the simple addition of guile to his side, prevailed.[10] The second (and related) point is the strongly 'political' flavour of the whole passage: the change in the destinies of the gods is seen to depend on a change in alliance, with Prometheus crossing from one side to the other. So, too, Prometheus' own fall from power is due in part (according to his account, 224–5) to a tyrant's occupational mistrust of friends. The Titans, Prometheus' brothers and former allies, languish in Tartaros by Prometheus' own counsels; Prometheus too, we are soon to learn, will spend a period in Tartaros at the tyrant's pleasure – and the Titans will be restored to favour while *he* still languishes. The point to be made from this passage is that the destinies, or the changing fortunes, of the gods (including Zeus) seem here to be dramatized in terms of practical politics, power, and situation: the changing of an alliance, the acquisition or neglect of some valuable asset or even of some crucial piece of advice. Nor (as a few perceptive critics have observed) is Prometheus himself as completely above the vicissitudes of power (including the victimization of former allies) as his more romantic admirers would have us think. The overtones, at least, of political pragmatism are present in Prometheus' account of his decision: 'Of the available choices [$\tau\hat{\omega}\nu\ \pi\alpha\rho\epsilon\sigma\tau\acute{\omega}\tau\omega\nu$] the best course seemed to me ... to side with Zeus' (216–18), and Prometheus' political involvement with the new régime appears later in his boast that he helped set up Zeus' tyranny (305) and actually allotted to the new divine rulers their various prerogatives (439–40).[11] Nevertheless, while we should not ignore the political tone of these passages (an element which will continue to be important in the struggle for freedom and survival, respectively, between Prometheus and Zeus), we should not forget that what Prometheus brought to Zeus before (and what he may bring to him again) is not merely a new 'super-weapon' (as was the case with Zeus' 'Hesiodic' allies, the Cyclopes and the Hundred-armed ones) but *intelligence*, in however limited a sphere. This is what gives significance to Gaia's prophecy and to Zeus' victory,

10 Contrast the Hesiodic version of Gaia's prophecy and its denouement at *Theog.* 626–8.

11 Cf Herington, introduction to *Prometheus Bound* p 8, on this role of Prometheus as 'King-maker' and (p 14) as organizer of the new power structure. Cf also Podlecki 'Reciprocity in the *Prometheus Bound*' on the general point (repeated by Herington) that most of the characteristics attributed to Zeus by Prometheus are also attributed to Prometheus himself by the Chorus or by other characters in the play.

and this too may be what will raise the ultimate 'solution' of the trilogy above the considerations of power politics with which so much of the struggle on the way to this goal is necessarily concerned.

It is in the light of these observations about Prometheus' account of the Titanomachy and its sequel that we should consider both Prometheus' prophecies about Zeus' future and his own and the ways in which the resolution of the conflict may come about. Prometheus' prophetic knowledge on this score is contingent on future decisions (by both Zeus and himself), just as his prophetic knowledge about the outcome of the Titanomachy was contingent on the choices of the Titans and of Zeus, respectively, to heed his counsels. If and when Prometheus himself abandons this 'contingent element' in his present prophecies about Zeus and himself, and says, in effect, that such and such *will* happen, then we may suspect that he is overstepping his prerogative.

Secondly, it has often been argued that for any reconciliation between Zeus and Prometheus to take place, the nature of Zeus must change.[12] Other critics, well versed in Greek views about the gods, have argued that the idea of an 'evolving Zeus' is unacceptable.[13] While we need not, at this point, make up our minds between these opposing views, we may, in the light of the foregoing discussion, make some preliminary observations. Just as the changes in the divine dynasties and fortunes of the past have been seen to come about by such means as changes in alliances and circumstances, so also changes in the present harsh tyranny of Zeus, and in Zeus' relations with the Titans, Prometheus, and man, may also be effected, at least initially, by similar external factors. (An analogous line of argument may, perhaps, be applied in evaluating the numerous references to the *newness* of Zeus' rule, which some critics have taken as a clear indication of a subsequent change in Zeus' nature.)[14]

There is one further, though less certain, inference which might be drawn from this passage on the past history of the gods. If Gaia's prophecy that 'not by power ... but by guile are the conquerors to prevail' continues to have validity in the present struggle, then Zeus' policy in *Prometheus Bound*, as indicated by the presence of Kratos and

12 See below, nn 14 and 15, for references to a few of the critics holding this view. We shall, however, return to a fuller discussion of this problem later; see below, chapter 6.
13 See, for example, Schmid *Untersuchungen zum gefesselten Prometheus* 89; Farnell 'The Paradox of the *PV*' pp 47–8; Lloyd-Jones 'Zeus in Aeschylus.'
14 See, for example, Todd 'The Character of Zeus in *Prometheus Bound*,' who cites (pp 62–3) the various suggestions in the play of the newness of Zeus' rule as an indication of a coming change in his nature.

Bia in the Prologue and by the cataclysm with which the play ends, must surely change drastically if he is to survive. Since we know that he does survive, it seems unlikely (again if Gaia's prophecy continues to be valid) that he gains the knowledge of his danger purely by *force majeure*. Further than this we are not prepared to go, at this stage in our discussion. The absolute equation of the Zeus of the *Prometheus Bound* with Power and Prometheus with Intelligence, which some critics have made, is, surely, a shade simplistic:[15] it suggests a more allegorical conception of the play than the speeches of Prometheus, both here and later, justify, and besides (as other critics have indicated) neither Zeus nor Prometheus has exclusive claims on the two attributes described.[16]

Only toward the end of the first episode does Prometheus return to the Chorus-leader's original question as to the actual offence (αἰτίαμα, 194) for which Zeus is punishing him. Even here, his three brief explanations take a very different form from his long account of himself as 'father of the arts' in the next episode.

The first of these explanations comes as a sort of footnote to the account of the Titanomachy ... and incidentally gives us our first hint of the new order planned by Zeus:

> To the various gods he distributed various powers ... but of wretched men he took no account; instead, he wished to reduce the whole race to nothingness and beget another one. (229–33)[17]

15 See, for example, Kitto 'The *Prometheus*,' especially p 19: '... the slow coalition of power and intelligence typified in the reconciliation of Zeus and Prometheus ...' Cf Golden *In Praise of Prometheus* pp 110 ff. Cf also Case 'On *Prometheus Desmotes*, Lines 980–81,' who cites with approval the early German adherents (such as Dissen and Caesar) to the view of an undeveloped Zeus who evolves toward Promethean wisdom. Reinhardt *Aischylos* agrees in many passages (see especially pp 57, 68–74) with this polarization of Zeus' power and Prometheus' intelligence but in resisting the simplistic 'evolutionary' theory of Zeus in the trilogy makes some important distinctions of the kind which we have been seeking to make here; according to Reinhardt, 'new,' in connection with Zeus' tyranny, does not refer to Zeus' age but to the newness of his rule over the 'old' powers ... not to potential growth and maturity but to the ways of power which new tyrannies show in politics (p 69). We shall return later to Reinhardt's view of the possible 'change' in Zeus later in the trilogy, but we should note his declaration here on one essential point, 'That Zeus changes or matures is a conception which contradicts the whole of Greek belief.'

16 Cf above (n 11 to p 39) and references to Podlecki and Herington there given. For indications that Zeus stands for more than just 'power' in this play, see the brief suggestions of Zeus' 'new order' implied in vv 228–32 and 551 (τὰν Διὸς ἁρμονίαν). As we have already noted, Prometheus himself has had a hand in this new order. (Cf vv 439–40.)

17 Thomson in his note *ad loc.* (vv 247–8 in his edition) refers to Pindar fr 107, 17–18, and to Apollod. 1.7.2. He thinks that 'Aeschylus was probably thinking of the flood' (to

Prometheus alone (by what means we are not told) protected men and saved them from destruction (234–6). Here Prometheus breaks off with a fresh outburst of indignation against Zeus, which is still his dominant concern at this moment of the play. The second revelation in this series is again prompted by the Chorus-leader:

– You did not, I suppose, go a little further than this?
– Well, yes: I stopped men from foreseeing their fated end [μόρον].
– What sort of cure for this ill did you find?
– I placed in man blind hopes. (247–50)

Here, for a moment, Prometheus' gifts to man are allowed to soar beyond the merely technological: freed from too acute awareness of his limitations, man's reach will exceed his immediate grasp: the key to all true advances in 'civilization.' But it is indicative of the mood of the god (and the intention of the poet) that this rich theme is merely touched on in the elliptical manner of the stichomythia. Instead, Prometheus proceeds, at last, to name his particular gift to man for which we know (from the Prologue) that Zeus has punished him:

– In addition to these other matters, I bestowed (ὤπασα) on them the gift of fire.
– And do creatures of a day now possess flame-visaged fire?
– Yes, and from this they will learn many arts. (252–4)[18]

Here, however, the gift of the arts (to be so richly developed in the next episode) is restricted to this one brief reference, as once again the Chorus' and Prometheus' interest switches to Prometheus' punishment:

– Is there no end of suffering laid down for you?
– None other save when it seems best to Zeus. (257–8)

which these two passages refer), but there is no indication of this. Ἀιστόω (232), moreover, suggests a more immediate and ineluctable disposal of the human race. (The obliteration of the human race by Zeus was not, of course, a completely novel conception. According to Hesiod *Erga* 137 ff, Zeus hid the race of silver beneath the earth, before creating the race of bronze.)

18 The impressive word ὤπασα ('I bestowed,' 252) and the surprise of the Chorus (253) emphasize the Aeschylean originality of this claim. (Cf Sikes and Willson, introduction xviii, and n 5). Previously, in Hesiod (*Theog.* 562 ff), Prometheus had merely stolen back the fire of which Zeus had already deprived man in punishment of Prometheus' trick over the food offerings on their behalf. On this point, as well as on the treatment of 'Hope' in Hesiod, see above, chapter 1, section 3.

This statement, in which the possibility of Prometheus' freedom is linked to neither the threatened nor the actual downfall of Zeus, sounds (for the Chorus at any rate) the nadir of Prometheus' situation, present and prospective, in the play. The same seems true of Prometheus, for he answers their gentle rebuke, 'Do you not see that you have erred [ἥμαρτες]?' with the passionate (and puzzling) cry:

> Willingly, aye willingly, have I 'erred' [ἥμαρτον], I'll not deny it ... (266)
> Yet not with such penalties as these, at least, did I expect to be wasted against these lofty cliffs. (268–9)

(It is idle to reduce, as some editors have done, the meaning of ἥμαρτον in this passage to 'I have made a mistake in judgment.' One does not 'willingly' make a mistake in judgment and to take the emphatic ἑκών, ἑκών ... with anything but the emphatic word which follows it is fatuous and destroys the fine defiance of the line.)[19]

What are we to make of οὐ μήν τι ... ᾠόμην ... (268: 'yet in no way did I expect ...') in this passage? Either Prometheus did not, and does not,

19 Rackham, in his note to vv 265–81, makes this (in my opinion) erroneous decision, explaining (in an extension of Wecklein's slightly ambiguous note), 'he [Prometheus] did make a mistake insofar as he did not expect the penalty to be so severe.' Most editors, however (eg, Paley, Sikes and Willson, Thomson in his translation), appear to agree with the translation which I have given.

Garzya 'Le Tragique du *Prométhée enchaîné*' pp 124–5 interprets ἑκών ἑκών ἥμαρτον in accordance with Aristotle's sense of ἁμάρτημα, a 'culpable error' (lying between ἀτύχημα, on the one hand, and ἀδίκημα, on the other), where the injury is done 'not contrary to reasonable expectation ... but without evil intent (*EN* 1135b17–18).' But this interpretation, though interesting, surely involves ethical distinctions not suitable to the dramatic context or, perhaps, even to the historical date of the play; cf also Stinton's subtler treatment of Aristotle's distinctions in this passage ('*Hamartia* in Aristotle and Greek Tragedy' pp 223–31), and his tracing of these distinctions back to sophists and rhetoricians of the second half of the fifth century.

Bremer *Hamartia* p 47 points out that there is also (ie, in addition to the uses emphasizing miscalculation of some kind) 'widespread use of *hamart*-words to decry serious offences. From Homer onwards (... *Od*. 13. 214) they are found denoting evil deeds for which divine revenge is expected or accomplished ...' Bremer aptly cites (n 65) Kratos' reference to Prometheus' *hamartia* (here his theft of fire) and its consequences (*PV* 9–11) in this connection. Even the sympathetic Hephaistos agrees that Prometheus is being punished by Zeus for bestowing prerogatives on man 'beyond what is right' (πέρα δίκης, 30). It is possible, then, that there is something of this meaning in the Chorus' present, repeated use of the term at v 260; if so, Prometheus' answering cry would be a sarcastically emphatic agreement: 'Oh, I offended, right enough, and willingly too!' – an admission which he immediately justifies with θνητοῖς ἀρήγων ('by helping mortals'). (It is curious that Bremer does not discuss this rather vexed passage in *Prometheus Bound*.)

have the detailed knowledge of the future which here (265) and earlier (101 ff) he has claimed,[20] or else self-pity and indignation are here to be regarded as vying with that claim and the knowledge which should attend it – and *does* attend it in more sober moments. In either case, we have, in these impressions of Prometheus early in the play, a god and (in the dramatic sense) a 'hero' whose spirit, fluctuating between resignation, confidence, and fear (cf 124–7) does not match its later sustained and confident defiance of the tyrant Zeus.

The entry of Okeanos, unannounced, conveniently postpones till 'the right moment' the fulfilment of Prometheus' promise to tell his story 'right through to the end' (273).[21] This sudden and strange apparition of one of the 'primal' Nature gods, appropriately equipped and masked and riding a hippocamp, must have added to the eerie atmosphere already created by the outlandish setting and the exotic Chorus in their winged car.

Much critical ink has been expended on the characterization of Ocean as a time-saver, a political trimmer whose sincerity Prometheus doubts and who is easily frightened off from his attempts at reconciling Prometheus with Zeus.[22] There is, indeed, some support for this view: Ocean's initial professions of sympathy and friendship (288–97) strike the modern ear at least as a shade fulsome, and there are, perhaps, touches of sarcasm (331, 343) and eventually of asperity (374, 383) in Prometheus' treatment of Ocean's professed good offices. However,

20 Cf also οὐκ ἠξιώθην ... 240, which, in the context of Prometheus' previous indignant outburst, also seems to suggest that he failed to anticipate his precise punishments. Cf, in this connection, Sikes and Willson's note on v 874: 'Both here (874) and in 209 ff., Prometheus definitely acknowledges that his insight into the future is due to his mother Earth. Indeed, it is quite true that his prophetic powers are limited ...' Sikes and Willson further contrast Prometheus' boast of complete foreknowledge of his sufferings at 265 with his admission of ignorance at 268. 'Aeschylus [they add] seems to represent Prometheus as inspired by Gaea, just as the Pythian priestess was from time to time inspired by Apollo; he only knows her "oracles" (χρησμόν, 873).'

21 This is the first of many such postponements in the play. (Cf 379–80, 522–5, 624, 631–4, 776, 782–5, 823–8.) With the Chorus, Prometheus has been becoming increasingly expansive; with Ocean, he now tends to reserve again, at least about his own affairs.

22 Cf especially Thomson's edition pp 10, 150 and note on vv 358–9 (=OCT 342–3). Lloyd-Jones 'Zeus in Aeschylus' p 66 and n 40 has properly corrected suspicions of the 'sincerity' of Ocean's offer to intercede with Zeus. Lloyd-Jones adds: 'What else he could have done, I cannot see. When his offer is rejected, there is nothing left for him to do but to warn Prometheus to moderate the violence of his utterances ...' This is not, perhaps, quite true, since Ocean could have stayed and suffered with his friend, as the Okeanids do, even though they give him the same advice. But there is no real reason at this point in the play to expect him to do so.

the main dramatic effect of Ocean's abortive intervention is the additional light which it throws on Prometheus and his situation.[23]

Prometheus' complete rejection of Ocean's temporizing approach shows us the absolute nature of the confrontation between Prometheus and Zeus: not until the situation *changes*, ie, until the apparently invincible Zeus is forced by dint of Prometheus' saving secret to restore the Titan's honour, will reconciliation be possible. (Prometheus with his knowledge of what is fated knows this; Ocean does not.) Supporting this impression are Prometheus' two terrifying paradigms of Zeus' power, the punishments of Atlas and especially of Typho by which he warns Ocean of the kind of risks rebellious encounters with Zeus involve. The passage provides some of the finest intimations of cosmic struggles in the play:

> ... (Typho)
> who stood 'gainst all the other gods
> with fearful hissing from his awful jaws
> and Gorgon-flashes from his eyes,
> seeking by might to overthrow
> the tyranny of Zeus.
> Then on him came the sleepless bolt of Zeus,
> straight downward, shooting flame with thund'rous blast,
> to smite the big-voiced boasts quite out of him.
> Smashed in his being's very core,
> all strength was burned and blasted out of him.
> Pressed down 'neath Aetna's mighty roots,
> he lies, a helpless sprawling mass,
> beside the narrow gateway to the sea. (354–65)

Typho is the rebel incarnate, the rebel (unlike Prometheus) without a cause, save to overthrow the supreme ruler. His brute strength (βία, 357), without Promethean knowledge, is useless against Zeus. The moderate, 'sensible' reaction of Ocean to the object lessons (Atlas' and Typho's fate) of Zeus' awesome power plays up the important dramatic point that it is only a rebel of heroic stature such as Prometheus who

---

23 The Ocean episode has not fared well with the critics. Stoessl *Die Trilogie des Aischylos* p 118 quotes with approval Schmid's view that it in no way moves the action forward and could easily be omitted in the structure of the play. Later (p 124) Stoessl even suggests that the only explanation of the scene's inclusion is for the sake of its putative counterpart (presumably the intervention of Gaia) in the following play of the trilogy. A similar explanation is given (though without the severe criticism of the scene) by Owen (*The Harmony of Aeschylus* p 58).

will continue to shout his defiance at Zeus. But it is significant that Prometheus does not reveal to Ocean (who does not understand the situation) a hint of his own secret knowledge. Only the Chorus and the audience understand the veiled meaning of his gloomy forecast:

> I'll drain to the last my present fate until the mind of Zeus be lightened of its wrath. (375–6)

It is in this connection, too, that Prometheus' answers to Ocean, at the end of the scene, must be understood. In a brief, dialectical exchange (which contrasts nicely with the terms of the power struggles just narrated), Ocean tries arguments based on medical metaphors: 'Words are healers [$ἰατροί$] of a sick temper [$ὀργῆς νοσούσης$]' (378): language which might well be expected to appeal to the clever Prometheus. Prometheus replies in the same terms, with the important addition (indicative of his sense of 'timing' throughout) that one must apply medicine 'at the right moment' ($ἐν καιρῷ$, 379). Ocean's intervention he reduces to 'empty-headed folly'; Ocean replies with the most 'sophistic' lines in the play:

> Then let me be ill with that illness [$τῇδε τῇ νόσῳ νοσεῖν$] since 'tis an advantage for the truly intelligent [$εὖ φρονοῦντα$] not to *seem* so. (384–5)[24]

Once again Prometheus tops Ocean's clever *mot* by declaring, with justice, that the description applies rather to himself. Nevertheless, however sound Prometheus' timing and his confidence in his hidden knowledge, there is in this exchange an irony at his expense as well. The medical imagery and the allusions to sick passions are to recur in contexts less favourable to Prometheus.[25]

With the withdrawal of Ocean, unsuccessful in his premature attempt at reconciling Prometheus with Zeus, we have reached the end of the play's first phase in which we have seen Prometheus mainly in relation with his fellow gods, both new and old. With his divine jailors in the Prologue, he has maintained his silence and integrity. Alone, he calls on the divine elements and all-seeing sun to witness his suffering;

24 On the dangers of having a reputation for wisdom, cf also Eur. *Med.* 294 ff.
25 Cf vv 472–5 and 977–8 and discussions of these passages in the present chapter. See also appendix (2) to this chapter (p 80).
    Cf also Fowler 'The Imagery of the *Prometheus Bound*,' who comments on the specific application of the various medical terms used in the play and the varying degrees of metaphorical and literal meaning involved both in *Prometheus Bound* and in other near-contemporary occurrences.

in a soliloquy which fluctates between outrage, foresighted resignation, and foresighted fear, he briefly reveals his offence of stealing fire and gives his first indication of his knowledge of Necessity, of all that must happen in the future. To the sympathetic Chorus, he gives his first hints of the secret he holds over Zeus (167 ff, 186 ff). Becoming gradually more expansive in his indignation, he expounds his past services to Zeus and, more briefly and enigmatically, his services to men. Despite his foreknowledge, a certain inconsistent amazement and lack of confidence (268 ff, cf 258) seem to adhere to his cries. In the scene with Ocean, this passionate expansiveness, with its untimely disclosures, disappears; here Prometheus' heroic resolution and his grasp of the realities of the situation (witness his account of other Titanic punishments) contrast sharply with the political temporizing of the weaker god.

4 The first stasimon (vv 397–435) and the second episode (vv 436–525)

The first stasimon, a beautiful ode in the Ionic metre, ushers in the second phase of the play. In it, the Chorus begin by expressing their own sympathy ('shedding a tearful stream from my eyes, moistening my cheek from their watery springs') for Prometheus and the whole race of the Titans dishonoured by Zeus 'whose rule's a law unto itself' (ἰδίοις νόμοις κρατύνων, 403). But soon (and more significantly – for we now take the Chorus' sympathy for granted), they add the sympathy of mankind – 'the whole world mourns …' The exemplars of the human race which follow are, it is true, all barbarian, including the Amazons of Colchis, the Scythians around the outermost stretches beyond the Maeotic Gulf (the Sea of Azov), and the martial flower of Arabia 'who inhabit the steep citadel near Caucasus.'[26] There are several possible reasons for this exclusively barbarian list: Prometheus is bound in Scythia and so it is fitting to have these and neighbouring barbarians mourn for him; also the unfamiliar non-Greek names will

26 The 'Arabian' situation of dwellers near the Caucasus (which has puzzled critics from the Scholiast on) has been explained as a result either of textual corruption ('Αβασίας and 'Αρίας have been two unsatisfactory suggestions for 'Αραβίας) or of Aeschylean geographical vagueness. The latter explanation seems the more likely, particularly in view of the unsatisfactory attempts at emendation. Note also Paley's interesting quotation of Plautus *Trin.* 934: '*Omnium primum in Pontum advecti ad Arabiam terram sumus, CH. Eho, an etiam Arabia est in Ponto?*' Could this be a reflection of ancient ridicule of this Aeschylean passage? (Sikes and Willson note further that the [Greek] scholium on this line is in the iambic metre, which suggests that the ridicule may have come originally from Greek New Comedy.)

suggest to the audience the broad extent of human sympathy, far beyond their own people, and will add to the remoteness and foreignness of the play's atmosphere; finally, the lands mentioned anticipate, to some extent, the wanderings of Io, soon to be described. In the epode, the Chorus return briefly to the sufferings of Atlas, as the one god comparable to Prometheus in his imprisonment. The passage ends with a fine sonorous lament from all the watery element:

> The waves of the sea cry out
> and with them moans the surging deep.
> In Hades' caverns dark, their cries resound.
> And pure and sacred river streams
> together mourn the piteous woe. (431–5)

– a splendid instance of the pathetic fallacy becoming fact, for it is the very daughters of earth-encircling River Ocean who convey the message to Prometheus.

The Chorus' expression of human sympathy for Prometheus provides the cue for Prometheus' full revelation of his services to man, an account which forms the first part (the Io episode being the second) of the 'human phase' of the play. And just as the human element has obtruded significantly into the divine conflicts of the preceding passages, so too, in the present movement, the divine element, represented by Prometheus and Zeus, vitally affects the human experiences and destinies now to be described.[27]

In each of the two great speeches in which Prometheus expounds his gifts to man, (*PV* 442–71; 476–506), a series of practical arts is enumerated in ascending order. The first list concerns shelter (at least by implication) and agriculture; calculation and writing; the adaptation of animals (first for practical, then for 'luxurious' purposes, 446);

---

27 Unterberger *Der Gefesselte Prometheus des Aischylos* p 70 also comments on the division between the world of the Olympians and the world of men in the first two episodes of the play, and further observes that Prometheus' ἁμαρτία was required to establish the connection between them. Without this, the world of Zeus was still no 'Kosmos,' no ἁρμονία, and human existence, which would have perished before divine indifference, survives only through self-assertion. (Unterberger, it is true, tends to equate Prometheus' intervention with human self-assertion: it might be more precise to say that the former led to the latter.) Note also Unterberger's observation that at v 436 (the beginning of the second episode) Prometheus' mood begins to change from complaint to anger. Her comment here (' ... the emotional change is, in conjunction with the "secret", the bond which holds together the scenes between the Prologue and the Exodos,' p 69) is very much in sympathy with the analysis attempted in the present chapter.

finally, sailing, as the first stage in commerce with people across the seas. In the second speech (476 ff) Prometheus begins his catalogue (perhaps in ironic response to the Chorus-leader's comment about his being a bad doctor, who cannot cure himself, 472–5) with medicine (by which one cures afflictions) and augury (by which one may forestall them). Last comes the discovery of metals (bronze, iron, silver, and gold, in that order) beneath the earth. Once again, the ascending order is observed: as in the first list chariot horses, 'an adornment of wealthy luxury' (466), and ships for commerce, were mentioned only after the more basic essentials of civilized living, so here metals (especially silver and gold, the last ones mentioned) as ὠφελήματα (501) will be relevant only to a more advanced stage in civilization.

There are several interesting features of this account of Prometheus' gift of the arts. First, the ascending order which I have indicated suggests an evolutionary sequence, as if each new art were discovered in response to the new needs of a higher level of civilization, once the needs at the lower, more pressing level had been met. Such a sequence (we shall see) is normally descriptive of *man's own* ingenuity in meeting each new challenge. (One is reminded for example, of Sophocles' *secular* account of man's ascending series of accomplishments in the so-called 'Ode to Man' in *Antigone*, 332 ff).

Next we may note what appear to be merely stylistic variations, which do, indeed, relieve the account of tedium, but which may reflect something else as well. In Prometheus' first speech on the arts, after his general claim to have made men intelligent when, previously, they had been witless, we find the following introductory passage:

> In the beginning, then, men had eyes but saw not and hearing did not really hear; rather, like shapes of dreams, all their life long they confused all things at random. They knew nothing about building houses of brick, facing the sun; they knew nothing of wood-working; rather, like little ants, they lived underground in sunless caves. Nor did they know any sure boundary mark [τέκμαρ] of the seasons, neither of winter nor of blossom-bringing spring nor fruitful summer, but kept doing everything without thought or plan *till I showed them the risings and the settings of the stars*, so hard to understand.
> (447–58)

Thus Prometheus' first list of his gifts is introduced by a description of man's *state of need* (eg, of proper housing, of knowledge of the agricultural seasons) which goes on for some dozen verses (447–58) before Prometheus mentions any contribution from himself – and this despite the fact that at least one art (house-building) and the beginnings of a second (field husbandry) are implied before Prometheus comes in with his claim to have indicated the seasons to men by teaching them the difficult art of astronomy. We *infer*, of course, that Prometheus taught them what they needed to supply these lacks, but stylistically the passage is quite different from what follows: from here on (with one slight exception), Prometheus stakes his claim immediately and emphatically, with no preliminary description of the state of *need*, as soon as each successive art is mentioned. Thus:

> And further, *counting* [ἀριθμόν] ... I discovered for them and the putting together of letters ... And I first yoked monsters ... etc. (459 ff)

The other slight exception to this procedure comes at the beginning of the second speech of Prometheus' gifts. Here again, before Prometheus' claim to the invention of medicine, there is another description (this time much briefer) of the state of need preceding the discovery:

> ... if anyone were to fall ill, there was no alleviation, no herb nor ointment, no trusty cure but rather, in the lack of any drugs, men kept perishing, until I showed them the mixings of gentle remedies ... (478–82)

Now the description of the state of need (of which we have here suggested two vestiges in Prometheus' account of his gifts) is, as we shall see, another feature of ancient evolutionary accounts of civilization in which *man* (sometimes with a vague initial reference to divine guidance) gradually discovers the arts to meet the successive exigencies of life.

Another stylistic feature of Prometheus' speeches on the arts is the *selection* of one art, in each of the two lists, for more detailed treatment. The second of these two selections (the description of various kinds of augury, vv 484–500)[28] is, perhaps, a reasonable one in view of the 'Promethean' attribute of the speaker (though it is not, of course, by these routes that Prometheus knows the future). As for the first selection for some detailed treatment, that of adapting animals to man's use

---

28 Cf Sansone *Aeschylean Metaphors for Intellectual Activity* pp 43–4, who suggests that prophecy as a form of ἐνθουσιασμός is omitted from the various mantic arts listed here because it is a gift of Apollo or of Zeus, rather than of Prometheus. Also, Sansone observes, the kind of prophecy which Prometheus did give was 'that which was learned ... For Prometheus did not give direct knowledge but showed the way (v. 498).' (Ενθουσιασμός does not, in any case, involve a τέχνη – cf Cic. *de div.* i – and it is with τέχναι that Prometheus is here concerned.)

(462–6), I know of no particular reason why this should be given prominence. Conversely, two arts which are given particular pre-eminence, *number* (ἀριθμόν), ἔξοχον σοφισμάτων (459), and *writing*, μουσομήτορ᾽ ἐργάνην (Stobaeus; ἐργάτιν codd.), 'Muse-mothering worker' (461), are given the briefest possible descriptions. One is tempted to explain both anomalies (the extended description of two of the arts, and the apparently truncated description of arts rather ill-suited to Prometheus) in the same way: perhaps Aeschylus is adapting material from some other (evolutionary?) account of the origin of the arts which provided a fairly extended treatment of each of them?

Whatever the explanation of these curious features in the passages just discussed, the materialistic emphasis in Prometheus' account of his gift of the arts to men cannot be denied.[29] The point is worth stressing if only to correct the impression so often given by critics of this play (as encouraged by romantic treatments of the Prometheus myth) that the Aeschylean Prometheus is to be regarded as *daimon* of civilization in the broadest sense. Not only the fine arts but also the political arts are omitted from the god's claims in these two speeches. Of the arts which are mentioned, the two which gave most opportunity for development beyond the practical level (number and especially writing) are not so developed, and it would even be possible to argue that, in the context, the two descriptions of writing, μνήμην ἁπάντων (which suggests 'recording') and μουσομήτορ᾽ ἐργάνην (where the businesslike noun 'worker' somewhat reduces the creative epithet, 'Muse-mothering') lead us back in the same practical direction. Augury and medicine, sailing (for commerce), and mining may all be regarded as essentially practical in their purpose and effect, and in the case of the arts to which more than a few phrases are allowed (e.g., animal husbandry and augury) it is the practical and technical details on which Prometheus dwells.

The exclusive concentration on the practical arts in the specific list which Prometheus retails does contrast slightly with his larger claims elsewhere in the play; on the other hand, the frame in which the list is enclosed (viz, 'I made men intelligent and endowed them with wits,' 442–4, and 'All arts came to mortals from Prometheus!' 506) is more in keeping with this picture of Prometheus as man's 'civilizer' (eg, at 110–11, 252, 254) and, indeed, saviour and protector (eg, at 235–6,

---

29 Cf George Thomson *Aeschylus and Athens*[3] p 306, who comments on this feature with the enthusiasm of the dialectical materialist. Solmsen, on the other hand (*Hesiod and Aeschylus* pp 142–3), seems to find the exclusively materialistic features of these passages an embarrassment, 'almost un-Aeschylean.'

250). Furthermore, the omission of fire from this list of Prometheus' specific gifts is curious in a somewhat different way. It might be argued that fire can now be taken for granted, since it has already been treated as a sort of generic symbol of Prometheus' gifts. Even so, one would expect, in this selected list of *practical* arts, at least some mention of certain fire-related ones.[30] Thus the omission of any mention of fire in this passage remains odd, especially in view of the earlier emphasis on the theft of fire as the essential breach of the divine prerogative (see vv 7, 30, 109–11, 252–4). This problem leads, in turn, to the related question, why this particular selection of arts at all? Some are reasonably 'Promethean' – but why, for example, describe sailing and omit the potter's art? One might say, perhaps, that Prometheus claims 'all the arts' and that some selection has to be made in the detailed treatment. But both the selection and the treatment seem, in the various ways I have mentioned, to fit some independent evolutionary account better than they do the specific claims of the culture-*daimon* Prometheus.[31]

I have already commented, in my introductory analysis of the play, on the significance of the concluding dialogue (506–25) of this scene. Here the Chorus' concern for Prometheus' liberation becomes subtly converted into the question of *Zeus'* freedom and its possible limitation – a question which, in turn, is broken off by Prometheus' warning that it is not yet time to speak of this. This conversion (so vital to the tragic theme) of interest in Prometheus' future to interest in *Zeus'* future is enhanced by certain complementary effects. The Chorus-leader has begun by warning Prometheus not to go 'beyond the right point' ($\kappa\alpha\iota\rho\sigma\hat{\upsilon}$ $\pi\acute{\epsilon}\rho\alpha$, 507) in his aid to man. Prometheus, in encouraging the Chorus in their hope for his freedom, reminds them that Art ($\tau\acute{\epsilon}\chi\nu\eta$) is weaker than Necessity ($\dot{\alpha}\nu\acute{\alpha}\gamma\kappa\eta$, 514). In the context, it is probable that Prometheus means that his own bonds, the result of Hephaistos' art, will be loosed by Necessity. Nevertheless, there is a touch of ambiguity

30 See, for example, Unterberger's explanation (*Der Gefesselte Prometheus* p 71) of the absence of fire and of the fire-based arts in these two speeches of Prometheus: namely, that these arts are so obvious as to need no demonstration, but that Prometheus (in his role as founder of the arts) *does* need to establish specific claims to other arts against rival claimants in mythology. Unterberger's further argument that the poet wishes to emphasize the 'spiritual-intellectual' aspect of Prometheus' inspiration of man, as distinct from his merely physical provision of fire, is weakened by the fact that few of the arts mentioned in these two speeches are really better suited to this emphasis than are the 'fire-based' ones.

31 The general question concerning the possible sources and influences on these passages (442–71; 476–506) of *Prometheus Bound* is discussed in the following chapter.

in the statement at v 514: the audience will remember that Prometheus has just declared himself to be the originator of all the arts (τέχναι, 506); thus the statement may suggest a limitation of Prometheus' powers as well. In response to a question from the Chorus-leader, Prometheus names the Moirai and the Erinyes as 'the helmsmen of Necessity.' 'Is Zeus weaker than these two?' the Chorus-leader asks. Prometheus answers with a sort of qualified affirmative: 'He may not, at any rate (γε), escape from what is fated' (518). Now the one thing which we know, in this play, to be 'fated' is that if Zeus makes a certain 'fatal' marriage he will be overthrown by the resultant offspring. That is all that Prometheus is talking about here, and the Chorus-leader (taking the point more successfully than some commentators) immediately asks the relevant question: 'Is there, then, something besides ruling forever in Zeus' fate?' Prometheus, showing the same wisdom here as he did when he reminded Ocean (379–80) that it was not the right moment to soften Zeus' wrath with words (λόγοι), refuses further information at this point: '*Not yet* may you gain information on this point' (τοῦτ' οὐκέτ ἄν πύθοιο); 'don't ask me further' (520). Thus at the end of this passage, Prometheus (unlike the more outspoken Prometheus of the parodos, still more unlike the vaunting Prometheus of the final scene), wisely draws in his horns. In his concluding quatrain (in what modern critics would term 'ring composition'), he reverts to the Chorus' own warning (v 507, in the initial quatrain of the dialogue) about καιρός, which he now applies to 'the right moment' to be awaited before further revelations about Zeus' future.

This seems to me to be all that it is necessary to say about the meaning of vv 507–25 in their dramatic context. However, the passage has been much debated in connection with other passages involving 'Fate' in Aeschylus.[32] (Sikes and Willson, for example, find it inconsistent with several passages in Aeschylus' *Suppliants*, where, it is alleged, Zeus is 'above Fate'; they conclude, then, that Prometheus, the enemy of Zeus, is simply wrong in his present statements on the matter.) A fruitful discussion of the whole problem is to be found in Fraenkel's note to *Ag.*, 1535 ff. With regard to *PV* 517, Fraenkel argues

32 References for the views mentioned in the present discussion are (in the order mentioned) as follows: Sikes and Willson *Prometheus Vinctus* p 113, in their note to *PV* 514–22; Fraenkel, ed *Aeschylus, Agamemnon* III (Oxford 1950) 727–30, esp 729; Wilamowitz *Interpretationen* p 123 and n 1; Lattimore *The Poetry of Greek Tragedy* p 48 and nn 25, 26; Kranz *Stasimon* p 46; George Thomson *Promethus Bound* pp 159–60; cf also Thomson *Aeschylus and Athens* pp 50 ff. For further discussion of various aspects of this problem, see also W.C. Greene *Moira* (Harvard University Press 1944) esp p 124 on *PV* 515 ff.

that Zeus is weaker (ἀσθενέστερος) than the Moirai and the Erinyes in that no more than any human being can he escape the consequences of his actions. Wilamowitz adopts a similar position warning us against regarding the Moirai and the Erinyes as personal deities rather than the moral order of the world to which the gods must submit.

Now Fraenkel is surely right in criticizing scholars who seek to work out 'a complete theological hierarchy ... a matter with which Aeschylus was not concerned at all' instead of looking at the peculiar *function* of the Moirai and the Erinyes in such passages as *PV* 511 ff and *Ag.* 1535 ff. Both Fraenkel and Wilamowitz are also right in depersonalizing the Moirai and the Erinyes in such passages so that the temptation to hierarchical evaluation (between them and Zeus) may be properly resisted. (It is to be noted that Prometheus' answer to the Chorus takes the same line.) Where Fraenkel's and Wilamowitz' view is harder to accept is their insistence on the *moral* aspect of the Moirai's function: while the moral connotation is clearly present at *Ag.* 1535 ff (the passage from which Fraenkel's argument begins), it is hard to see how Zeus' potential marriage with Thetis is to be regarded as 'a deed of guilt,' as Fraenkel clearly says it is. It seems better to regard the Moirai and their associates 'the Erinyes of long memory' as fulfilling the natural order of things, 'the way things are and must be.' (Compare Lattimore's translation of ἀνάγκη as 'nature' or 'natural force' and his comment on the depersonalizing quality of the participial phrase τὴν πεπρωμένην ... at *PV* 518.) When Zeus himself is *not* involved in such fatal sequences, he may indeed be spoken of as 'directing fate' and the like, as at Aesch. *Suppl.* 673, αἶσαν ὀρθοῖ ... (cf also *Suppl.* 815–16, 822–4, 1047–9: it is to be noted, however, that in such passages Aeschylus replaces Moira and the Moirai, when a word for 'fate' is needed, by αἶσα, *Suppl.* 673, and ὅ τί ... μόρσιμόν ἐστιν, *Suppl.* 1047). But Zeus himself, once he puts on the yoke of Necessity (as Fraenkel observes, borrowing the phrase applied to Agamemnon at *Ag.* 218) by some fatal deed is not free of the inevitable consequences of that deed.

These considerations lead us to reject (as Fraenkel does) another fairly prevalent view, expressed by Kranz and later in a more extreme form by Thomson, that Zeus in Aeschylus was at first inferior to the Moirai while later, by the time of the dramatic date of the *Oresteia*, 'the will of the Fates is at one with the will of Zeus' (Thomson). Zeus has to face only one such crisis (the danger of the fatal mating), which he survives (just as his predecessors faced one such crisis, the danger of begetting an overthrower, but perished), and it may reasonably be assumed, mythologically speaking, that the danger from that kind of hurdle will not recur. Indeed, it is not to be expected, again 'mythologically speaking,' that Zeus will ever be presented at risk again. But this is far from saying that, from now on, Zeus is ('theologically speaking') 'above Fate.'

5 The second stasimon (vv 526–60); second episode (Io episode, vv 561–886); third stasimon (vv 887–906)

The Chorus, recoiling a little from the subversive overtones of the last exchange, now affirm their own piety and fear of Zeus. This is the first of the two odes encircling the Io episode. Both odes express awe before the power of Zeus, but in the second ode we will find a certain modulation of that piety, after the terrors of the Io scene. Both odes also treat the theme of divine marriage: the first one briefly, at the end of the ode, in unconscious anticipation of the coming action; the second one at length, and again the intervening Io scene effects a significant change in treatment.[33]

The second stasimon begins, then, with a quiet affirmation of the Chorus' piety and fear of Zeus and goes on, in the first antistrophe, to contrast the life of peaceful submission with the rebellion, and its attendant sufferings, of man-loving Prometheus:

> Sweet it is
> to sustain a long life with cheerful hopes
> and keep the spirit bright
> with food of happiness.
> But I shiver when I see you, Prometheus,
> wasted with ten thousand pains,
> because, with judgment all your own,[34]
> you grant to mortals too much honour
> and tremble not before the name of Zeus. (536–44)

The second strophe expresses a firmer admonition of Prometheus:

> Come, friend, how was your 'favour' *truly* one?[35]
> What help comes now from creatures of a day?

33 Cf Herington, introduction to *Prometheus Bound* p 10.
34 ἰδίᾳ γνώμᾳ (543) … in contrasting balance to ἐμᾷ γνώμᾳ (527) in the first strophe, where the Chorus pray that their judgment may never be in rivalry with Zeus' power. However, this reading at v 543 is uncertain because of the failure in metrical responsion which it involves.
35 Literally: 'How was your favour truly a favour … ?' Here I translate Headlam's text at v 545 (φέρε πῶς χάρις ἁ χάρις …;) which is the only one which does not substantially

Did you not see the dreamlike feebleness
To which the race of mortals is enchained?
Never will plans of mortals override
the all-composing law of Zeus. (545–52)

... πῶς χάρις ἀ χάρις (545): a cold view, perhaps, of Prometheus' service
to men, but one which reminds us sharply of the peculiarly Greek
concept of χάρις in the sense of 'favour' in which some element of
reciprocity is so often involved. (Hence Prometheus' favour to mankind was not really χάρις in the full sense of the word at all.)

In the final antistrophe, the Chorus look back to happier times: the
wedding of Prometheus with their divine half-sister Hesione. 'How
different then the songs I sang! ...' Different too will be Zeus' harsh
courtship to Io which this wedding motif anticipates.

The long Io episode forms the central portion of the play. Its complex
structure and skilfully interwoven themes, relating the destinies of Io,
Prometheus, and Zeus himself, mark it as the most significant part of
the play and, perhaps (for here we can only guess), of the trilogy as a
whole. Humankind has been the cause of the original breach between
Prometheus and Zeus; now through Io, the only human character in
the play, the quarrel is to reach its climax and, perhaps, its eventual
resolution, later in the trilogy.

The relations between the Zeus-Prometheus *muthos* and the Zeus-Io
muthos are of several kinds. One consists of the obvious parallel between Prometheus and Io as fellow victims of Zeus' tyranny: one the
victim of Zeus' enmity, the other of Zeus' love. Thus a stronger bond
exists between Prometheus and Io than between Prometheus and any
other of his visitors, including the Chorus. Another equally obvious
relation between the two stories lies in the identity of Prometheus'
liberator who is to be revealed as a descendant of Zeus' and Io's
offspring. Finally, the manner of Zeus' liberation of Io may provide a
hint concerning the ultimate reconciliation of Zeus with Prometheus.

As a theatrical effect, the sudden entry of the horned maid, lost,

change the MSS reading (... χάρις ἄχαρις). Triclinius' ἄχαρις χάρις is attractive in that
it reproduces the oxymoron implied in typically Aeschylean fashion (cf *Ag.* 1545,
Choeph. 43, *PV* 903), but the linguistic difficulties involved are too great: φέρε (which
would become φερ' in Triclinius' text) would have to mean 'see,' which it cannot; or
else πῶς would have to be exclamatory, which it never is in classical Greek. For the
reciprocity so often involved in χάρις cf χάρις ἀντὶ χάριτος (Eur. *Hel.* 1234) and χάρις
χάριν φέρει (Soph *O.C.* 779); cf also *LSJ* s.v. II. 1 and 2.

exhausted, and leaping madly from the gadfly's stings, must have been the most startling apparition in a play already rich in spectacular effects. The opening passages of the episode, like those at the beginning of the Cassandra scene in *Agamemnon*, present the crazed and hysterical aspect of this object of divine passion. The wildly racing figure provides a violent contrast to the bound Prometheus; so, too, the account of Io's wanderings, past and still to come, will suggest the vast dimensions, in time and space, of the cosmic struggles with which this trilogy is concerned. Language, metre, and movement are effectively combined in this introduction of the tortured Io. First there are wild questions, chanted in anapaests, about the land and people she has reached and the fellow sufferer she sees before her; then the gadfly's sting brings on a rush of leaping and trochaic cries; finally, the gadfly itself gives place, in Io's imagining (in excited dochmiacs), to 'the image of earth-born Argus'; though slain by Hermes, the monstrous herdsman seems still to reappear and plague her (561–73).

The nightmare rhythm of these opening cries continues into Io's monody (574 ff)[36] as she hymns an accompaniment to the gadfly's drone, assails Zeus with plaints (as Cassandra assails Apollo), and, like Prometheus before her (cf 582 ff and 152 ff), begs to be hurled to the depths rather than endure her present torture. 'Do you hear the cry of the horned maid?' Only at the end of the strophe does Io thus break out of her private world and elicit Prometheus' reply:

> Full well I hear you, child of Inachos, fly-driven maid. The heart of Zeus burns with love and now, pursued by Hera's hate, she roams perforce in frenzied flight.

Recognition gradually quietens Io. Now (in the antistrophe, 593 ff), questions about Prometheus' identity and about her own future sufferings begin to replace her anguished cries. Prometheus promises clear answers 'such as friends should receive' and reveals himself as 'Prometheus, giver of fire to men' (609–12).

In the short dialogue which follows (613–30), the fates of Prometheus and Io are interwoven, this time in purely formal fashion: a two-verse question from Io about Prometheus' 'crime and punish-

---

36 Io's formal monody consists of the strophe at vv 574–88 and antistrophe at 593–608; between strophe and antistrophe comes Prometheus' four-line iambic answer to the question at the end of the strophe. The metres of the ode are mostly dochmiac (with some cretic additions) and trochaic, thus continuing in more formal lyric fashion the metres introduced in the second part of Io's opening plaints (566–74).

ment' is followed by seven lines of stichomythia (single-verse exchanges) 'debating' this question; then a second two-verse question
from Io, this time about her own future, is followed by another set of
seven stichomythic lines. Despite Prometheus' repeated promises
(609, 617, 626) to tell all, each sequence is neatly rendered unproduc-
tive, the first by Prometheus' refusal to repeat the tale of his 'offence'
(621), the second by the interruption of the Chorus-leader, who asks
(631–4) that Io should first relate her previous sufferings. The passage
provides a nice example of procrastination, an element used skilfully in
this play.[37] In the present scene it is one of a series of devices by which
the poet is to deploy the coming revelations in a complex pattern
interweaving the past, the present, and the future of Io's and (eventually) Prometheus' and even Zeus' destinies.[38] A brief summary will
indicate the schematic outline of this pattern.

In vv 640–86, Io narrates her own past, from her first dream-
warnings of Zeus' love to her expulsion from her father's home in
Argos. In vv 700–41, Prometheus prophesies the first stage in Io's
wanderings, from her present stop in Scythia to her crossing from Asia
to Europe at the Cimmerian Bosporos. Here the account of Io's
wanderings is interrupted by another passage of dialogue (742–81)
interweaving, this time in more significant fashion, the destinies of Io
and Prometheus in relation to their 'persecutor,' Zeus. After another
'postponement device' by the poet (this time delaying the revelation of
Prometheus' liberator),[39] Prometheus resumes his prophecy of Io's
wanderings, bringing her now (786–818) from her crossing of the
Cimmerian Bosporos to her arrival at the Delta of the Nile, where she
and her descendants are destined to found a distant colony. Revelation
of Prometheus' own liberation is again postponed (819–26) by a token
account (829–43) of that part of Io's past adventures (her journey to
Prometheus' Scythian rock) which has not yet been told. (Here Prometheus, like Cassandra in *Agamemnon*, is providing his credentials as a

37 ὁ καιρός ('the timely,' 'the right moment') is, as we have seen in the case of earlier
   postponements of crucial answers, a major constituent of this play, since it is crucial
   to the careers of both Prometheus and Zeus (cf comments on vv 193 ff, 273 ff, 379, and
   522 ff; only in the last two of these passages is the word actually used). It is by such
   postponement devices as that just noted that the poet calls attention to the thematic
   importance of 'the right moment.'
38 George Thomson's analysis of the Io episode is excellent on this point; the present
   discussion is indebted to it. See pp 14 and 17 of the introduction to his edition.
39 See vv 778–85. Again it is the Chorus-leader whose intervention is exploited by the
   poet; cf 631–4.

prophet.)[40] Finally (844–76), Prometheus reaches the climax of his prophecies. He reveals the rest of Io's future (her gentle release and impregnation by Zeus) and the future destiny of her descendants down to the 'bold and famous bowman' (Herakles) who will free Prometheus himself from his woes. This whole long passage (640–876) is a *tour de force* of complex design, interweaving the great stretches of present, past, and future time involved in the trilogy and reserving for its climax the final coalescence, long heralded, of Prometheus' and Io's destinies.

Let us now look more closely at certain key passages in the Io scene. The first of these is Io's own account of the beginnings of her troubles with Zeus. Like several of Prometheus' prophetic passages, part of Io's account is given in vivid detail, while other parts are so ellipticial as to defy close analysis of causation and events alike. The details of Io's dream (the apprisal of Zeus' love, the instructions to go to Lerna's meadow 'that Zeus' passionate gaze might be relieved,' the warning, in words already suggestive of Io's coming bovine form, 'not to kick away'[41] Zeus' amorous assault) all receive most explicit treatment (645 ff). So, too, do its results: Io's consultation of her father, *his* consultation of oracles and consequent expulsion of Io, lest he earn Zeus' wrath, to wander at large to the farthest boundaries of the earth (656 ff). Now in all this, it should be noted that neither Io nor her father *rejects* Zeus' suit; indeed, the very expression used of Io's exiled wandering, ἄφετον ἀλᾶσθαι (666), is the expression used of sacred animals regarded as being under the patronage of a god.[42] Moreover, Io herself (admittedly crazed by her sudden bovine transformation) rushes straight to the very spot ('the spring of Lerna,' 676–7) whither she had been bidden in the dream; however unwilling (ἄκουσαν ἄκων, 671), neither father nor daughter seems to have resisted the compelling 'curb of Zeus' (672). It is at this point that the narrative (reasonably enough, considering Io's at least partial transformation) becomes

---

40 Cf *Ag.* 1184–97. In the present passage Io would be able to verify the truth of Prometheus' supernatural knowledge of her experiences, just as the Chorus in *Agamemnon* would be able to vouch for Cassandra's extraordinary knowledge (as a foreigner, cf *Ag.* 1199–1201) of the past of the house of Atreus, well-known to Argive citizens.

41 μὴ 'πολακτίσῃς: the bestial connotations of the term are noted by schol. м to v 651. Might there also be some echo here of versions of the myth in which Zeus actually 'approached' Io in the form of a bull *in Argos*, after she had been transformed into a cow by Hera? (cf Aesch. *Suppl.* 300–1).

42 See Sikes and Willson's note *ad loc.* and references there given.

rapid, elliptical, and obscure. We are not here told who caused the transformation (673), nor who sent first the watchful Argos (674 ff) and then the gadfly which replaced him. Hera's role in all this is here left unexpressed.[43] In the play as a whole, it might be claimed that, statistically, the blame is almost equally divided between Hera and Zeus.[44] Nevertheless, there is no doubt that both by the omission of any reference to Hera at this important point (673 ff) in Io's story, and by Prometheus' repeated promptings of Io's hatred for Zeus in this connection (735–8, 757–9), it is Zeus rather than Hera who takes the brunt of the blame for Io's suffering. This emphasis, in the face of the more casually mentioned facts of the matter, is surely significant, particularly in view of the denouement, Zeus' gentle delivery of Io (848–9). Here, surely, is a case where one extreme view of a situation is presented where the opposite view is also possible (and indeed is actually taken in Aeschylus' *Suppliants*),[45] a state of affairs ripe for the kind of reversal of perspective observable elsewhere in Aeschylean trilogies.[46]

43 Compare the more explicit account at *Suppl.* 295 ff. Cf above, chapter 1, p 17 and notes *ad loc.*
44 Io, in her first, raving description of her sufferings (566–88), makes no mention of Hera and does explicitly blame Zeus at vv 576–8. At vv 590–2, Prometheus gives Hera's anger as the cause of Io's suffering and Zeus' love as the cause of that anger. At vv 600–1, Io blames her suffering on 'the vengeful plots of Hera,' if Hermann's almost certain emendation of v 600, following the scholiast's explanation of these lines, is correct. At v 704 (at the beginning of Prometheus' first prophecy about Io), Hera is again mentioned as the source of Io's suffering. At vv 735–8, we find the most emphatic blame of Zeus by Prometheus for Io's troubles, followed later (758) by a further reminder to Io of her enmity for Zeus; with this Io emphatically agrees, since she 'suffers evilly' from Zeus (759). Finally at v 900, in the concluding choral 'frame' to the episode, Hera is again mentioned as the cause of Io's wanderings.
45 At Aesch. *Suppl.* 584–7, Zeus is glorified for his gentle delivery of Io, '... for who else could have relieved the afflictions due to the assaults of Hera?' As we have seen, the earlier phases of Zeus' *amour* in *The Suppliants*' account are more explicitly physical than in that of *Prometheus Bound*; yet nowhere (for obvious dramatic reasons) is Zeus ever spoken of in opprobrious terms in connection with Io and her sufferings.
46 In *Agamemnon*, the first play of Aeschylus' *Oresteia* trilogy, the 'justification' of Agamemnon's death is allowed to appear in many passages; in *The Libation Bearers* (the second play), however, where it is the vengeful Clytemnestra who is now to suffer just punishment, Agamemnon is seen entirely as the wronged King. In *The Suppliants*, the Danaid Chorus appear as wronged victims of their cousin suitors, whereas by the third play of the same trilogy it seems likely (cf fr 144 [N]) that Hypermnestra is defended for sparing one of these vicious suitors for the sake of fructifying love. Some such shift in perspective (without any change in the facts) with regard to Zeus *may* have taken place in a later play in the present trilogy. With regard to Zeus' treatment of Io, there is, perhaps, an anticipatory hint of such a shift (though it is not so recognized by Prometheus) at *PV* 848–9.

With the details of Io's wanderings and encounters (as prophesied by Prometheus, 700–41; 786–812; 823–76), we shall not here concern ourselves: detailed comments on the confused geography of the account and of the mythological peoples and monsters (similarly confused in their locations) abound in various editions of the play and elsewhere.[47] One or two essential points must, however, be kept in mind. First of all, Io's travels after she leaves Prometheus' place of punishment in northern Scythia on the unmapped and mysterious verge of Ocean (the Ocean nymphs hear Hephaistos' hammering from the oceanic depths, 133–5) are all eastward and southward until she reaches Egypt: it is probable that the account is complemented by the description later in the trilogy (cf frr. 109–12) of Herakles' travels and encounters in the north and the west.[48] Thus, in these two sets of spacious wanderings, Aeschylus covers the whole known ancient world (however vague the geographical details) and so provides a magnificent panorama as a background to the cosmic struggle he depicts. The general direction of Io's wanderings needs to be stressed since various localities are misplaced (eg the Caucasus, which is placed too far to the north-west as Io approaches it in skirting the Black Sea) and various mythological tribes and monsters (eg, the hideous crones of Cisthene, 703 ff, the Gorgons, 799, the Griffins, 803–4) are placed in the east, after Io has crossed into Asia, whereas other ancient writers situate them in the north and west. Some commentators have gone to extraordinary lengths to explain these mythological difficulties, imagining textual *lacunae*, intercontinental leaps by Io, or both, to resolve the apparent confusion of east and west.[49] Such theories, however, would destroy the symmetry of the complementary travels of Io and of Herakles (suggested above) and would, moreover, introduce far greater confusion into Io's travels than already exists. It is surely better to assume 'a vagueness and freedom on the part of the poet in dealing with a mixture of half-known fact and fable'[50] (consistent with the geographical vagueness which Aeschylus has already shown). It may

47 See especially Sikes and Willson's edition, appendix II, pp 180–3 (as well as their detailed notes on specific passages) and the notes in Wecklein's edition. However, the most detailed and interesting discussion of the whole account is to be found in Bolton *Aristeas of Proconnesus* chapter 3, pp 46–54, to which reference has already been made (above, chapter 1, n 29) concerning Aeschylus' sources.

48 Cf Sikes and Willson p 183; Havelock *Prometheus* pp 59–62; Thomson, introduction to his edition, pp 25–30.

49 See, for example, the editions of Paley (on v 812–793 OCT) and of A.O. Prickard on v 790.

50 Sikes and Willson, appendix II, p 183.

indeed be largely a matter of dramatic convenience, aided by the poet's geographical insouciance, which occasions the importation of these displaced monsters; such encounters are an essential part of Io's harrowing journey, just as the far-shooting nomad Scythians (709–12) and the inhospitable Chalybes (715–16), everyone, indeed, except the man-hating Amazons (723 ff), present dangers which she must circumvent.

At the end of Prometheus' first prophetic speech, the main thematic line of the Io episode makes its second overt appearance.

Here Prometheus pauses to remind Io (735–41) of the harshness of Zeus' courtship, for her troubles have just begun. As in their earlier exchange (613–30), the close relation between the destinies of Io and Prometheus is precisely indicated by the formal pattern of the dialogue: a five-verse complaint from Io (747–51) over her woes is followed by a five-verse statement from Prometheus concerning his own more desperate plight (752–6); then in a passage of stichomythia (757–79) their two destinies, and that of Zeus as well, are intertwined, in substantive as well as in formal fashion. The possibility of Zeus' fall (raised by Prometheus at vv 755–5) is the common point at which Prometheus' and Io's interests meet (755–60). The first part of the stichomythic treatment of Zeus' future leads to the prospective freeing of Prometheus, presented as 'a way out for Zeus' (770); the second part of the stichomythic treatment of the future (771–75) is again related to Io, through her descendant, Herakles. At each crucial moment in the revelations (at 769 ff and 775 ff), the subject is abruptly changed and more final answers postponed.

There are several striking features in Prometheus' prophetic utterances in this passage. The first comes in the god's contrast of *his* lot with that of mortal Io:

... for *me* there is no end of woes laid down until Zeus falls from power (755–6)

– a statement which is almost the exact reversal of his despondent prophecy at v 258 '(for me) there is no end of woes, till it seems best to Zeus.' Just as the earlier statement seemed to imply (to those knowing about 'the secret') that Prometheus would have to save Zeus before 'it seemed best' to Zeus to free Prometheus, so now the present statement seems to imply that Prometheus will *fail* to save Zeus – and that Prometheus will then be freed.

Prometheus' apparent certainty about Zeus' fall continues into the first part of the stichomythia (757–68), in which this fall is even offered to Io as a cause of rejoicing and in which its actual nature is for the first time revealed, save for the identity of Zeus' mate whose son will overthrow him. Half-way through the stichomythic passage, this sequence of future 'certainties' is changed to another sequence, which depends on the denial of the preceding one. The change is triggered by Io's question (769): 'Is there no turning aside of this fate for Zeus?' The 'way out' for Zeus now reappears (770) as dependent on the liberation of Prometheus, whereas at v 258 (in a sentence of similar structure) the liberation of Prometheus has appeared as dependent on the will of Zeus.[51] Thus in fifteen verses (756–70), the situation seems to have been reversed from 'no freedom for Prometheus until Zeus *falls*' to 'no *safety* for Zeus until Prometheus is freed.'

Further paradoxes are in store in the second prophetic sequence (770 ff), which concerns the freeing of Prometheus. Io, as the ancestress of Prometheus' liberator (772, 774), will be the indirect cause of Zeus' safety (cf 770), though his *fall* would give her joy (758–60). (Zeus, in turn, will be revealed later[52] to be the ancestor of Prometheus' liberator, thereby forestalling his own fatal (divine) union and overthrow.) A final touch of confusion is added by Io's question:

Who, then, is the one who will free you, with Zeus unwilling? (ἄκοντος Διός, 771),

for the phrase 'with Zeus unwilling' is not rejected by Prometheus in his answer. More than one view is possible here, but it seems wisest, given a later hint of corroboration of Io's phrase, to accept it as one more obscure paradox with which the poet invests the final outcome at this point.[53]

51 See appendix (1) to this chapter where key passages containing Prometheus' prophecies relating to Zeus' future and his own are collected.
52 That Zeus will be the ancestor of Prometheus' liberator through his impregnation of Io is not to be revealed until Prometheus' last speech of prophecy about Io (see especially 848 ff, 871–3). That Zeus is also to be the immediate father of that liberator (Herakles) will not be revealed till later in the trilogy (cf fr 201 of *Prometheus Luomenos*). Thus the full paradox of Zeus' twofold engendering (direct and indirect) of Prometheus' liberator is but gradually revealed as this and the following play of the trilogy progress. Save for Prometheus' intervention (see *PV* 231–6), the mortal women essential to this process would never have been born.
53 Some editors seem to think that Io has simply misunderstood Prometheus' statement at v 770 and that Prometheus does not take the trouble to correct her. See, for example, Wecklein's and Rackham's editions ad loc. Long *Notes on Aeschylus' 'Prometheus Bound,'* in his note on v 770, cites vv 177, 192, 258, 771 in his demonstration of an alleged contrast between Prometheus' and Io's views on the flexibility of Zeus' will. (The possible 'corroboration' of Io's phrase, 'with Zeus unwilling ...?', to which I have referred above, appears, of course, in fr 201 of *Prometheus Luomenos*, where Prometheus' description of Herakles as 'beloved son of a hated father' suggests that at least Herakles' slaying of the eagle gnawing at Prometheus' liver may occur before Zeus and Prometheus are reconciled.

What are we to make of these ambiguities, in contrast to Prometheus' earlier prophetic statements (167 ff, 187 ff) about his own and Zeus' futures? It might be argued that, in view of the contingent nature of this (as of most) Greek prophecies, no absolute contradiction is involved. Zeus' future safety (according to Prometheus' earlier statements) depends on the freeing of Prometheus and the reconciliation of the two gods, with full satisfaction being paid to Prometheus. The earlier prophecies, especially 187–92 (with its unconditional future statements about the reconciliation) regard those conditions as certain of fulfilment; vv 755 ff, on the other hand, appear to exclude that possibility. However, at this point in the play, Prometheus is saved from this (implicit) contradiction concerning the future fulfilment of his conditions by the fact that he reintroduces the possibility of his being freed (and so, then, of saving Zeus) at v 770. Later, as we shall see, at a more intransigent moment in his defiance of Zeus (989 ff), he seems to abandon for a time all such thoughts of reconciliation.

Io is, of course, the occasion of Prometheus' changing attitude toward the future destinies of himself and Zeus. As victim of Zeus, she whets his indignation against the tyrant; as ancestress of his deliverer, she fills him with new confidence against his enemy. But it is ironic that Io, in her own career and that of her descendants, appears ultimately as a symbol of reconciliation in the larger framework of the trilogy.

Prometheus' final prophecies about Io and her descendants suggest, without Prometheus seeming aware of it, some hope for the resolution of his own struggle with Zeus. The most striking feature of Zeus' deliverance of Io in Egypt is its gentleness ('Zeus will make you sound of wit again, childing you by harmless stroke of hand' 848–9), in contrast to the violence of his pursuit. So, too, while the flight of the gentle Danaids (Io's descendants) from their hawk-like cousin suitors (853 ff) recapitulates the bitter tale of Io's flight from Zeus' love, the fertile marriage of Hypermnestra, the one Danaid whom love softens (865 ff),[54] provides a similarly gentle ending. Prometheus, to be sure, dwells (in a grimly vivid passage)[55] on the hideous murder with which

---

54 865: μίαν δὲ παίδων ἵμερος θέλξει (Hypermnestra is not mentioned by name). It seems better in the context to take παίδων as partitive genitive with μίαν rather than as objective genitive with ἵμερος. Moreover (cf also Thomson's note *ad loc.*) Aphrodite's later defence of Hypermnestra (if we are justified in supplying this context for *Danaides* fr 44 [N]) suggests that it was love of Lynceus rather than longing for children which stayed Hypermnestra's hand.

55 '... when the husband-suitors have been subdued by the night-time daring of their murderous wives' (860–1): the vividness of the effect is in direct relation to the word-straining economy (with attendant ambiguity) of the style; translation cannot really do justice to θηλυκτόνῳ / ᾿Άρει δαμέντων νυκτιφρουρήτῳ θράσει ...

the other Danaids greet their unwelcome bridegrooms. 'May love so violent come upon my foes!' (864): in Prometheus' mind, this marriage stands, perhaps, as a sort of paradigm for the fatal marriage which Zeus is to fulfil. For Prometheus himself, on the other hand, the long distant τέλος of the bitter struggles of Io and of the Danaids is his own liberation by the 'bold and famous bowman,' their descendant (871–3). For the first time, Prometheus makes no mention at all of Zeus or of 'the secret' which, in all his earlier utterances, have sooner or later appeared as linked with his own freedom. Ironically, even as Prometheus omits this element, the nature of his other prophecies (the gentle liberation of Io by Zeus, the fruitful resolution, by love, of the Danaids' bitter struggles) leads us to anticipate a similar reconciliation between Prometheus and Zeus.[56]

The ode (887–906) following the long Io episode complements, in more ways than one, the ode preceding it. Most obvious is the ironic relation between the happy memory of Prometheus' marriage briefly recalled at the end of the earlier ode (553–60) and the terrified deprecation of marriage above one's station which forms the major theme of the present ode. The maidens of the Chorus begin with this minimum generalization ('Wise indeed was he who ... first declared that marriage at one's own level was best by far,' 887–90), but in the antistrophe (894–900) their concern grows more explicit: fear (for themselves) of a marriage such as Io's with Zeus, with all its attendant suffering. This, in turn, reminds us of the major theme of the earlier ode, where the Chorus' timid piety ('May I never cease approaching the gods with reverent sacrifices ...' 529–30) has contrasted with the dangerous 'humanism' ascribed to Prometheus (542–4). But where the previous ode had deprecated Prometheus' alliance with mortals and urged awareness of Zeus' new 'world-order' (τὰν Διὸς ἁρμονίαν, 551), the present ode shudders at union (for the Chorus as for Io) with any of the Olympians (897) and ends by expressing helplessness before the guile (μῆτιν, 906) of Zeus. Thus, though the themes of the two odes are complementary and there is no overt contradiction between them, the tone and the attitude to the gods on high are subtly different, now that the Chorus have seen the maid Io, suffering from Zeus' love and the weary roaming imposed by Hera. True, the Chorus retain, almost to the end of the play (see vv 1036–39), a certain mediating ambivalence between sympathy for Prometheus and fearful respect for Zeus' power. But the implicit criticism of Zeus in the present ode prepares us for the Chorus' bold decision (1063 ff) at the final climactic moment.

56 Cf below, n 69 and reference to Dawson 'Notes on the Final Scene of the *P.V.*' *ad loc*.

6 The final scene (vv 907–1093)

The last scene of the *Prometheus Bound* returns to the central issue of the drama: the confrontation between the wills of Zeus, the ruling god, and Prometheus, the rebel god. Io is forgotten except in so far as her destiny, along with that of her descendants, is a part of Prometheus' now exuberant confidence; even the original cause of the divine conflict, Prometheus' championship of man, is now scarcely mentioned. Thus, at the crisis of the play, the conflict is stripped to its bare essentials: Prometheus with his knowledge, Zeus with his power,[57] fate which (in ways which are still obscure) will decide the ultimate issue, and the elements, once Prometheus' 'allies' (88–92), which will form the stuff of his immediate and imminent catastrophe. The time for 'meanings' – moral, sociological, theological – is over: all dramatic energy is concentrated on the intensification and resolution of the immediate issue of knowledge versus power.

The long episode, a sort of play in miniature within the larger framework of the whole, falls into three parts, each part contributing in a different way toward the total cumulative effect. In the first (907–43), Prometheus, now etching his rebellious will against the Chorus-leader who seeks to restrain him, reaches a new peak of certainty and confidence in his prophecies of Zeus' overthrow. In the second (944–1039), Hermes demands and Prometheus refuses (each with mounting threats and insults) the revelation of the secret to Zeus. In the last (1040–end: the switch to anapaestic metre indicates the heightened excitement), Prometheus himself prophesies and then describes (amid interruptions from both Hermes and Chorus) the details of the catastrophe which we must envisage as taking place before our eyes.

We have noted, throughout the gradually expanding revelations and increasing confidence of Prometheus, a corresponding decrease in overt suggestions of reconciliation between himself and Zeus.[58] In the

---

57 Cf Reinhardt's acute observations (*Aischylos* pp 57–8) about the final scene of open strife between Prometheus and Zeus, to the effect that the fate of the world depends on Prometheus here as it did on the Titanomachy before. Reinhardt also observes (as I have) that according to some passages Prometheus seems to want Zeus to fall but that there are others where he appears to be guarding his secret only until Zeus submits to his terms.

58 Thomson has well observed, in his note on vv 939–59 (=907–27 OCT): 'In 202–8 [=186–92 OCT] Prometheus spoke of his secret as a means to his ultimate reconciliation with his adversary, and in 538–41 [=522–25 OCT] as a means to his deliverance without mention of reconciliation. Now [907–28 OCT] he speaks of it solely as a means to his enemy's downfall. These changes in his attitude to the secret indicate his gradual loss of restraint.'

climactic speeches of defiance between the departure of Io and the arrival of Hermes, this tendency of Prometheus to treat the fall of Zeus almost as a certainty reaches its most extreme degree. In his opening prophecy in the final episode, Prometheus does, to be sure, make brief reference to the future gentleness of Zeus (Ζεύς ... ἔσται ταπεινός, 907–8) and to Zeus' future need of Prometheus as the only one of the gods who can warn him of his danger (907–9, 913–15); but sandwiched between these more hopeful indications, and somewhat qualifying their promise, is Prometheus' first allusion to the curse of Kronos which he sees as reaching its fulfilment (παντελῶς κρανθήσεται) with the fatal union Zeus is planning. From this point (913–15) until well into the altercation with Hermes (at 989–91), no further mention is made of any possible saving of Zeus by the freeing of Prometheus. Instead, the whole emphasis is on Zeus' danger and on Zeus' coming fall. Indeed that fall is now prophesied unconditionally, with the bold and repeated uses of future tenses.[59] Now, too, sarcastic taunts ('So let him sit confident in his lofty thunderings ... !' 915–17) replace veiled threats, and vivid descriptions of the physical power ('such a wrestler ... an irresistible monster ...' 920–1) and the superior weaponry ('greater than the thunderbolt,' 922) of the unborn overthrower convert the danger into a seeming actuality. The speech ends with Prometheus' first blunt statement, still unqualified by any 'saving' reference to himself, of Zeus' fall:

Then he will learn, when he has stumbled on this bane, how different ruling is from slavery! (926–7)

The faithful (but truthful) Chorus-leader is quick to note Prometheus' own fall from his properly prophetic role:

It is surely what you *want* to happen that you now declare in your boasting over Zeus! (928)

Prometheus is adamant:

I state what *will be accomplished* [ἄπερ τελεῖται] as well as what I wish to be accomplished. (929)

The Chorus-leader's attempts to qualify these statements and to tem-

---

59 See vv 910, 911, 922, 925, 926 for these future tenses and v 920 for a vivid present anticipating the future.

per the rebel's dangerous rage meet with scornful repudiation from Prometheus and still stronger statements of Zeus' certain fall:

Pray, wheedle, fawn upon the current ruler ... (937)
Let him rule as he wishes for this little spell, for he'll not rule the gods for long. (939–40)

At this point, then, Prometheus has reached the opposite pole, in his prophecies concerning Zeus' future, from his original clear prophecy (167–77, 188–92) of his reconciliation with Zeus when need forces Zeus to meet his terms. We have traced Prometheus' prophetic utterances about Zeus' future and his own through their various permutations, in response to different moments in the dramatic progression of the play. It is not until this final scene, before the entry of Hermes but after the full effects of Io's visit have been accomplished, that Prometheus makes these categorical statements about the fall of Zeus. This prophecy is not only false (for, as we all know, Zeus does not fall from power); it also represents a repudiation of that Necessity, of the linked fates of Zeus and himself, which Prometheus has hitherto, though with increasing reluctance, accepted.[60]

That we are, for the reasons just indicated, to regard these statements of Prometheus as implying if not *hybris* at least an overstepping of his *moira* seems an inevitable conclusion. Their immediate result – the arrival of Zeus' emissary, Hermes – bears this conclusion out. Hitherto, Prometheus has controlled himself to the extent of remaining silent about the content of his secret: only by waiting for 'the right moment' (ὁ καιρός), he knows, will he save himself (see vv 522–5). Now, his new intransigence – his unqualified assertions that as a result of a particular marriage Zeus will beget his overthrower, and his all-too-vivid descriptions of that overthrower – brings Hermes to wrest the secret from him. That Hermes arrives before 'the right moment' is clear: Zeus' danger is not yet imminent and he shows no sign of bargaining with Prometheus if threats (which are not idle ones) do not prevail. Thus it is Prometheus himself who has caused the untimely confrontation and the, now almost inevitable, catastrophe to which it

---

60 Stoessl *Die Trilogie des Aischylos* pp 125–6 also traces the various utterances of Prometheus about the outcome of the struggle between himself and Zeus, but shows curiously little awareness of the significant changes of attitude *on Prometheus' part* which appear to influence the views of the future expressed at different moments in the play. Rather, Stoessl tends to impute all the difficulties to the youth and arbitrary will of Zeus.

leads.[61] Certain features of this final encounter provide further illustration of this point.

With the abrupt entry of Hermes, we return to the atmosphere and the time sequence of the Prologue. Hermes' insulting tone and language remind us of Zeus' other bully, Kratos; so, too, his peremptory orders (947–8) and threats of immediate punishment (1014 ff) bring us back, after long journeys through past and future time, to the harsh realities of the present.[62]

The structure of the Hermes scene is carefully designed to fulfil its several purposes. First the confrontation, the ensuing quarrel, and the ultimatums from each antagonist are presented in three clearly distinguishable parts (944 ff, 964 ff, 987–1035). Hermes opens with a series of insults ('You teacher-fellow,[63] too clever for your own good ...'), presents Zeus' order to reveal the secret of the fatal marriage, and ends with a threat not to make him make a second journey; Prometheus returns the insults ('Pompous and lackey-like your words ... !'), spurns the command with fresh prophecies of Zeus' fall, and ends by mocking Hermes' threat ('Go back the way you came!' 944–63). Next (964–86) comes a passage of dialogue, the two-verse ripostes soon giving way to single-line exchanges as the quarrel becomes more lively. In this passage, the ponderous insults of the preceding speeches give way to more subtle scores, as, alternately, one god seeks to best the other by twisting each preceding thrust against his adversary.

Finally come the paired ultimatums. That of Prometheus is couched in a short speech (987–97); it contains as its kernel the last reference in the play to Prometheus' terms: his freedom for the revelation of the secret:

> Neither by torture nor by any other means will Zeus force me to utter these things, till these painful bonds be loosed. (989–91)

Hermes' (or, rather, Zeus') ultimatum requires a longer speech (1007–35), including, as it does, an outline of the whole course of Prometheus' future sufferings if he refuses to obey orders. Here for the first time a direct light is thrown on the background, at least, of the future

---

61 Again, Stoessl seems to ignore this point when he says (ibid): 'It lies in Zeus' power to do what he wishes with Prometheus ... the more difficult his terms for Prometheus' freeing, the more difficult his own rescue becomes as well, and the more insoluble the conflict of power.'

62 Cf Thomson, introduction p 14.

63 σοφιστής again; compare Kratos at v 63 (where also the word has pejorative overtones) and comments ad loc.

action of the trilogy; the cataclysmic descent of Prometheus in 'the rock's embrace,' to Tartaros; his return to the world of light, after long stretches of back-lagging time; the day-long feastings of the eagle on his liver. Hermes' final prophecy of the end of Prometheus' woes contains no hint of the reconciliation which Prometheus himself had once forecast:

> Of such woes expect no end till some god as successor appears, willing to go down to Hades, down to Tartaros' sunless depths. (1026–29)[64]

The presentations of Zeus' absolute tyranny and of Prometheus' heroic resistance are, no doubt, the major effects of this great quarrel scene. We have asserted that it was Prometheus' untimely vaunting of his secret (after his encounter with Io) and the new intransigence of his prophecies about Zeus' fall which have brought the action to its tragic crisis. Once that crisis is upon us, however, we can have little doubt of the justification of Prometheus in his fierce, even violent repudiation of Zeus' emissary. The harsh cruelty of Kratos in the Prologue, the unimpressive figure cut by the submissive Okeanos, and the sympathetic treatment of Prometheus throughout the play have prepared us for that conviction, and it is now further supported by the 'tyrannical' characterization of Hermes, fresh from the court of Zeus. Nevertheless, there is, in the present scene, a series of shortcomings and oversteppings alleged against Prometheus by Hermes, by the Chorus, and even, ironically, by Prometheus himself, which require careful interpretation, all the more so in that these descriptions of Prometheus' attitude are consistently couched in terms fraught with moral and tragic connotations.

The first of these terms occurs in a statement (unfortunately obscured by the almost certain loss of the verse preceding it)[65] in which

64 Some editors (eg, Sikes and Willson, Rackham) comment that Hermes would have regarded these conditions of Prometheus' release as impossible, or at least unlikely to be fulfilled. Possibly, but we cannot fail to regard these lines as at least an unconscious prophecy (which will be fulfilled) of the kind which Hephaistos makes in commenting on Prometheus' sad plight, 'For the one who will free you has not yet been born' (27).
65 Most editors accept Reisig's conjecture of a *lacuna*, before v 970, of one verse without which the specific point of v 970 is unclear. Manuscript attribution is missing for the speakers of vv 968 and 970; most editors give 968–9 to Hermes; 970 and presumably the missing verse preceding it will then go to Prometheus. Hermes' sarcastic remark at v 971 will then begin his series (971, 974, 977 etc) of *single*-verse ripostes. Not till 978 does Prometheus begin *his* 'one-liners'; from there on, the increasingly angry dia-

Prometheus appears to be justifying a particularly violent utterance:
' 'Tis right' (he declares) 'so to insult [ὑβρίζειν, treat with *hybris*] the
hybristic' (970). The second term is found in Hermes' description of
Prometheus' temper as 'no slight disease of madness' (οὐ σμικρὰν
νόσον 977), and in Prometheus' reply: 'I might indeed be ill if it be
illness to hate one's enemies!' (978). The third term occurs in the most
'sophistic' of the exchange of the quarrel scene. 'Not yet,' declares
Hermes, 'Have you learned σωφρονεῖν.' 'To show self-control' is what
Hermes means, but Prometheus chooses to understand the term in its
broader sense. 'True,' he replies, 'for if I *had* (shown sounder judgment) I'd not be talking to an underling like you!' (982–3). The arresting
feature of these three passages is that each involves the ironic acceptance (in one sense or another) by Prometheus of what would, in
normal circumstances, be regarded as a normally indefensible position: *hybris* and lack of *sophrosyne* are, in Greek tragedy, the almost
certain signs of imminent disaster for those displaying them, and *nosos*
has already been used three times in the present play[66] for a temperament unable to preserve itself by *sophrosyne*.

Hard on the heels of these indictments comes Hermes' ultimatum
with its detailed description of the particular quality in Prometheus
which (as with tragic figures generally) must spell his certain doom:

> Biting the bridle, you struggle and fight against the reins, like some colt new
> to the yoke. Too confident you are in the sickly power of devious cunning
> [σοφίσματι: a loaded word where Prometheus is concerned!]. Mere self-
> willed stubbornness [αὐθαδία] in a mind undisciplined [τῷ φρονοῦντι μὴ
> καλῶς] has no power at all. (1010–13)

and again, at the end of Hermes' speech:

> So take your bearings and think carefully whether you believe that self-

logue proceeds by single-verse alternations until Prometheus' short *rhesis* (or continuous speech) at 987 ff.
66 The tragic significance of lacking *sophrosyne* is well illustrated in Euripides' *Hippolytus*,
where we also find excellent examples of the two senses of *sophronein* (the infinitive of
the verbal cognate of *sophrosyne*) just noted at *PV* 982–3: cf *Hipp.* 667, where Hippolytus uses the term in alleging the need of Phaedra (and all women) to learn self-control
(in the limited sense here of 'chastity'), and *Hipp.* 731, where Phaedra, in turn, alleges
that Hippolytus needs to learn *sophronein*, ie, to show moderation, to exercise sound
judgment involving a balanced view of life. (It is an interesting coincidence that in the
same passage, Phaedra uses *nosos* of her own moral sickness: her inability to control
her passionate love for Hippolytus.) For a review of the various passages in
Prometheus Bound in which *nosos* is used, see appendix (2) to the present chapter.

willed stubbornness [αὐθαδία, again] is ever better than good counsel [εὐβουλία]. (1033–5)

This time it is the Chorus, Prometheus' allies, rather than Prometheus himself, who, echoing Hermes' own descriptions of the rebel, accept their accuracy.

To us also does Hermes' advice seem fitting [οὐκ ἄκαιρα]. For he bids you put aside your stubbornness [αὐθαδία] and seek out wise good-counsel [εὐβουλία]. Be persuaded, then. For 'tis shameful for a wise man so to err. (1036–9)

The last word (ἐξαμαρτάνειν) of the Chorus' warning reminds us of their earlier reproach – 'Do you not see that you have erred?' (ἥμαρτες, 260) – in connection with Prometheus' championing of men. There Prometheus proudly accepted the charge, 'Willingly, aye willingly, did I "err" … '(ἑκὼν, ἑκὼν ἥμαρτον, 266) and there, too, we saw that his 'error' was not an error in judgment, for he made it willingly, but an intentional wandering away from, transgression even, of the course set out by the Olympian power. So, too, must we accept, as Prometheus accepts, the literal truth of the indictments (*hybris*, *nosos*, lack of *sophrosyne* – here meaning compliant self-control). Here, too (as we did in the case of Prometheus' championing of men) we must accept these qualities as the right ones in the circumstances, albeit (as in more normal tragic circumstances), they must inevitably spell Prometheus' doom in the present tragedy. The times are out of joint: 'if it be sickness to hate such enemies as Zeus,' Prometheus told Hermes, in effect, at v 978 'then let me be sick!'

The Chorus have, up to this point, followed the proper role of even sympathetic Choruses: they have advised conventional morality that their friend may avoid the inevitable consequences of abandoning it. The superb answer of Prometheus to this advice, as to Hermes' warning, puts the matter in its true perspective:

To one who knows it all already has this fellow told his news! But that an enemy should suffer ill from enemies is in no way shameful [οὐδὲν ἀεικές]. (1040–2)

So, too, as long as this oppression lasts, Prometheus will make his enemy suffer, in the only way he can, by refusing to reveal the fateful secret. Once the matter is put in these absolute terms, *euboulia* (in the sense of conventional 'good counsel') has as little relevance to Prometheus' stand as fear of further punishment.

The quarrel is now over and the change of mood and metre (at v 1040, where Prometheus begins chanting in anapaests) quickens the pace for the tragic finale of Prometheus' noble rebellion. From this point on, Prometheus is concerned only with embracing in advance his cataclysmic punishment so that he can continue to shout over it his persistent defiance of Zeus. The final vindication of Prometheus' position comes (as Reinhardt has seen) with the Chorus' own indignant rejection of Hermes' advice, when he warns them to abandon Prometheus for fear of Zeus' thunderbolt:[67]

> Sing some other tune if you wish to persuade *me*! ... How can you bid me to practise baseness? With *this* one I wish to suffer what must be suffered. I have learned to hate turncoats and there is no disease [νόσος] which I reject more powerfully than such treachery! (1063–70)

Thus the Chorus put loyalty, however dangerous, above the safer conventional wisdom which they preached a moment earlier. The description of disloyalty as the worst kind of *nosos* significantly symbolizes their new position, for once the Chorus had described Prometheus (who saved men) as a bad doctor, unable to cure his own disease. Now they too abandon *euboulia* to stay with Prometheus (and presumably be hurled to Tartaros with him)[68] because they are his friends.

The final effects of this great play lie in the gradual and inevitable encroachment of the coming cataclysm upon the crucial conflicts of the action.[69] This impression quickens with Prometheus' abandonment of

---

67 Cf Reinhardt *Aischylos* pp 64–6, who contrasts the Chorus' relatively detached and even self-protective attitudes in the second and third stasima respectively (especially at vv 898–906) with this ultimate decision 'to go under' with Prometheus, and who concludes of the Chorus' final avowal that it, 'beyond all expectation,' justifies Prometheus.

68 For a discussion of different views as to what happens to the Chorus at the end of the play, see below appendix 2, pp 175 ff, 'Notes on the Staging of *Prometheus Bound*.'

69 Dawson 'Notes on the Final Scene of the *P.V.*' makes an interesting comparison between the language and imagery used in Prometheus' final speeches (1040 ff and especially 1080 ff) and those used in the description of Io's anguish in the third episode (eg, at vv 599 f, 675 f, 743, 883–6), and further compares the 'sea of ruinous woe' (746) which awaits Io with the 'boundless net of ruin' (1978) with which Hermes threatens the Okeanids if they remain by Prometheus. Finally, Dawson suggests that these parallels between the sufferings of Prometheus and Io may indicate that Prometheus, like Io when she receives Zeus' releasing touch, may also achieve a calmer frame of mind in reconciliation with Zeus. (Compare comments made earlier

argument as he begins his chants at vv 1040 ff. But there have been preliminary groundswells earlier. Prometheus (stealing, as is fitting, his adversary's thunder) is the first to hint briefly at the form the catastrophe will take, as he anticipates with characteristic arrogance Zeus' answer to his own ultimatum:

> So let the smoking bolt be hurled, with white-winged snow and earthy thundering let Zeus confound and mingle everything! (992–5)

Hermes, too, in his first warning of the same event, has given a brief and vivid preview of Prometheus as helpless victim:

> First the father, smashing this rocky crag with thunder and the lightning bolt, will cover up your body, and the rock's embrace will bear you off. (1016–19)

Again it is Prometheus who, in his last prophetic command, insists on the *elemental confusion* required to send him down to Tartaros:

> So let the jagged fork of fire be hurled at me, let the upper air [αἰθήρ] be set in turmoil by thunder and the wild winds convulsed. Let the blast shake the earth from its foundations, and mingle, with savage roar, sea's wave and heaven's stars. (1043–50)

Finally, Prometheus, now the play's 'Messenger,' as he has been his own prophet of doom, describes the cataclysm as it actually occurs. Once again, the confusion of all the elements (the fire of the thunderbolt, the dust raised from the earth, the winds set in strife against one another, and the sea now confused with *aither*) is elaborated, this time in more vivid detail (1082–8). Prometheus' last cry (1091–3), like his first (88–92), invokes the elements (specifically, his mother Earth, and *aither*, 'which revolves the common light of all')[70] to look upon him and his unjust sufferings.

in the present chapter in connection with *PV* 848–9.) For discussion of certain technical aspects of this scene, see appendix 2, pp 175 ff, 'Notes on the Staging of *Prometheus Bound*.'

70 See Herington's theory about this limited invocation of *two* (out of the four) elements ('A Study in the *Prometheia*' I, pp 182–3) and his discussion of the possible roles of Earth and *Aither* in the next two plays of the trilogy. (Cf below, pp 116–19.)

APPENDIX TO CHAPTER 3[1]

(1) Some prophetic passages in *Prometheus Bound*

A vv 167–77

Πρ. ἦ μὴν ἔτ᾽ ἐμοῦ, καίπερ κρατεραῖς
  ἐν γυιοπέδαις αἰκιζομένου,
  χρείαν ἕξει μακάρων πρύτανις,
  δεῖξαι τὸ νέον βούλευμ᾽ ὑφ᾽ ὅτου
  σκῆπτρον τιμάς τ᾽ ἀποσυλᾶται.
  καί μ᾽ οὔτι μελιγώσσοις πειθοῦς
  ἐπαοιδαῖσιν θέλξει, οτερεάς τ᾽
  οὔποτ᾽ ἀπειλὰς πτήξας τόδ᾽ ἐγὼ
  καταμηνύσω, πρὶν ἂν ἐξ ἀγρίων
  δεσμῶν χαλάσῃ ποινάς τε τίνειν
    τῆσδ᾽ αἰκείας ἐθελήσῃ.

Prometheus
Yes, there shall come a day for me
when he shall need me, me that now am tortured
in bonds and fetters—he shall need me then,
this president of the Blessed—
to show the new plot whereby he may be spoiled
of his throne and his power.
Then not with honeyed tongues
of persuasion shall he enchant me;
he shall not cow me with his threats
to tell him what I know,
until he free me from my cruel chains
and pay me recompense for what I suffer.

B vv 186–92

Πρ. οἶδ᾽ ὅτι τραχὺς καὶ παρ᾽ ἑαυτῷ
  τὸ δίκαιον ἔχων Ζεύς· ἀλλ᾽, [ἔμπας] ὀίω,
  μαλακογνώμων

---

1 The translations of these passages are taken from David Grene's *Aeschylus, Prometheus Bound*, reprinted in *The Complete Greek Tragedies* edd David Grene and Richmond
Lattimore vol I, *Aeschylus*.

ἔσται ποθ', ὅταν ταύτῃ ῥαισθῇ·
τὴν δ' ἀτέραμνον στορέσας ὀργὴν
εἰς ἀρθμὸν ἐμοὶ καὶ φιλότητα
σπεύδων σπεύδοντί ποθ' ἥξει.

Prometheus
I know that he is savage: and his justice
a thing he keeps by his own standard: still
that will of his shall melt to softness yet
when he is broken in the way I know,
and though his temper now is oaken hard
it shall be softened: hastily he'll come
to meet my haste, to join in amity
and union with me—one day he shall come.

C vv 257–8

Χο. οὐδ' ἔστιν ἄθλου τέρμα σοι προκείμενον;
Πρ. οὐκ ἄλλο γ' οὐδέν, πλὴν ὅταν κείνῳ δοκῇ.

Chorus
Is there no limit set for your pain?
Prometheus
None save when it shall seem good to Zeus.

D vv 515–25

Χο. τίς οὖν ἀνάγκης ἐστὶν οἰακοστρόφος;
Πρ. Μοῖραι τρίμορφοι μνήμονές τ' Ἐρινύες.
Χο. τούτων ἄρα Ζεύς ἐστιν ἀσθενέστερος;
Πρ. οὔκουν ἂν ἐκφύγοι γε τὴν πεπρωμένην.
Χο. τί γὰρ πέπρωται Ζηνὶ πλὴν ἀεὶ κρατεῖν;
Πρ. τοῦτ' οὐκέτ' ἂν πύθοιο, μηδὲ λιπάρει.
Χο. ἦ πού τι σεμνόν ἐστιν ὃ ξυναμπέχεις.
Πρ. ἄλλου λόγου μέμνησθε, τόνδε δ' οὐδαμῶς
    καιρὸς γεγωνεῖν, ἀλλὰ συγκαλυπτέος
    ὅσον μάλιστα· τόνδε γὰρ σῴζων ἐγὼ
    δεσμοὺς ἀεικεῖς καὶ δύας ἐκφυγγάνω.

Chorus
Who then is the steersman of necessity?

Prometheus
The triple-formed Fates and the remembering Furies.
Chorus
Is Zeus weaker than these?
Prometheus
Yes, for he, too, cannot escape what is fated.
Chorus
What is fated for Zeus besides eternal sovereignty?
Prometheus
Inquire of this no further, do not entreat me.
Chorus
This is some solemn secret, I suppose, that you are hiding.
Prometheus
Think of some other story: this one it is not yet the season to give tongue to, but
it must be hidden with all care; for it is only by keeping it that I will escape my
despiteful bondage and my agony.

E vv 755–75

(Πρ.) νῦν δ' οὐδέν ἐστι τέρμα μοι προκείμενον
        μόχθων, πρὶν ἂν Ζεὺς ἐκπέσῃ τυραννίδος.
Ιω.   ἦ γάρ ποτ' ἔστιν ἐκπεσεῖν ἀρχῆς Δία;
Πρ.   ἥδοι' ἄν, οἶμαι, τήνδ' ἰδοῦσα συμφοράν.
Ιω.   πῶς δ' οὐκ ἄν, ἥτις ἐκ Διὸς πάσχω κακῶς;
Πρ.   ὡς τοίνυν ὄντων τῶνδε γαθεῖν σοι πάρα.
Ιω.   πρὸς τοῦ τύραννα σκῆπτρα συληθήσεται;
Πρ.   πρὸς αὐτὸς αὑτοῦ κενοφρόνων βουλευμάτων.
Ιω.   ποίῳ τρόπῳ; σήμηνον, εἰ μή τις βλάβη.
Πρ.   γαμεῖ γάμον τοιοῦτον ᾧ ποτ' ἀσχαλεῖ.
Ιω.   θέορτον, ἢ βρότειον; εἰ ῥητόν, φράσον.
Πρ.   τί δ' ὅντιν'; οὐ γὰρ ῥητὸν αὐδᾶσθαι τόδε.
Ιω.   ἦ πρὸς δάμαρτος ἐξανίσταται θρόνων;
Πρ.   ἦ τέξεταί γε παῖδα φέρτερον πατρός.
Ιω.   οὐδ' ἔστιν αὐτῷ τῆσδ' ἀποστροφὴ τύχης;
Πρ.   οὐ δῆτα, πλὴν ἔγωγ' ἂν ἐκ δεσμῶν λυθείς.
Ιω.   τίς οὖν ὁ λύσων ἐστὶν ἄκοντος Διός;
Πρ.   τῶν σῶν τιν' αὐτὸν ἐγγόνων εἶναι χρεών.
Ιω.   πῶς εἶπας; ἦ 'μὸς παῖς σ' ἀπαλλάξει κακῶν;
Πρ.   τρίτος γε γένναν πρὸς δέκ' ἄλλαισιν γοναῖς.
Ιω.   ἥδ' οὐκέτ' εὐξύμβλητος ἡ χρησμῳδία.

(*Prometheus*)

        … but for me there is
no limit of suffering set till Zeus fall from power.

Io

Can Zeus ever fall from power?

Prometheus

You would be glad to see that catastrophe, I think.

Io

Surely, since Zeus is my persecutor.

Prometheus

Then know that this shall be.

Io

Who will despoil him of his sovereign scepter?

Prometheus

His own witless plans.

Io

How? Tell me, if there is no harm to telling.

Prometheus

He shall make a marriage that shall hurt him.

Io

With god or mortal? Tell me, if you may say it.

Prometheus

Why ask what marriage? That is not to be spoken.

Io

Is it his wife shall cast him from his throne?

Prometheus

She shall bear him a son mightier than his father.

Io

Has he no possibility of escaping this downfall?

Prometheus

None, save through my release from these chains.

Io

But who will free you, against Zeus's will?

Prometheus

Fate has determined that it be one of your descendants.

Io

What, shall a child of mine bring you free?

Prometheus

Yes, in the thirteenth generation.

Io

Your prophecy has now passed the limits of understanding.

F vv 871–4

(Πρ.) σπορᾶς γε μὴν ἐκ τῆσδε φύσεται θρασὺς
τόξοισι κλεινός, ὃς πόνων ἐκ τῶνδ᾽ ἐμὲ
λύσει. τοιόνδε χρησμὸν ἡ παλαιγενὴς
μήτηρ ἐμοὶ διῆλθε Τιτανὶς Θέμις·

(*Prometheus*)
but from her seed shall spring a man renowned
for archery, and he shall set me free.
Such was the prophecy which ancient Themis
my Titan mother opened up to me;

G vv 913–27

(Πρ.) τοιῶνδε μόχθων ἐκτροπὴν οὐδεὶς θεῶν
δύναιτ᾽ ἂν αὐτῷ πλὴν ἐμοῦ δεῖξαι σαφῶς.
ἐγὼ τάδ᾽ οἶδα χῷ τρόπῳ. πρὸς ταῦτα νῦν
θαρσῶν καθήσθω τοῖς πεδαρσίοις κτύποις
πιστός, τινάσσων τ᾽ ἐν χεροῖν πύρπνουν βέλος.
οὐδὲν γὰρ αὐτῷ ταῦτ᾽ ἐπαρκέσει τὸ μὴ οὐ
πεσεῖν ἀτίμως πτώματ᾽ οὐκ ἀνασχετά·
τοῖον παλαιστὴν νῦν παρασκευάζεται
ἐπ᾽ αὐτὸς αὑτῷ, δυσμαχώτατον τέρας·
ὃς δὴ κεραυνοῦ κρείσσον᾽ εὑρήσει φλόγα,
βροντῆς θ᾽ ὑπερβάλλοντα καρτερὸν κτύπον,
θαλασσίαν τε γῆς τινάκτειραν νόσων
αἰχμήν, τρίαιναν ἢ Ποσειδῶνος σκεδᾷ.
πταίσας δὲ τῷδε πρὸς κακῷ μαθήσεται
ὅσον τό τ᾽ ἄρχειν καὶ τὸ δουλεύειν δίχα.

(*Prometheus*)
                    ... no one
of all the Gods save I alone can tell
a way to escape this mischief: I alone
know it and how. So let him confidently
sit on his throne and trust his heavenly thunder
and brandish in his hand his fiery bolt.
Nothing shall all of this avail against
a fall intolerable, a dishonored end.
So strong a wrestler Zeus is now equipping

against himself, a monster hard to fight.
This enemy shall find a plan to best
the thunderbolt, a thunderclap to best
the thunderclap of Zeus: and he shall shiver
Poseidon's trident, curse of sea and land.
So, in his crashing fall shall Zeus discover
how different are rule and slavery.

(2) νόσος (sickness) sequences in *Prometheus Bound*

A vv 377–86

Ωκ. οὔκουν, Προμηθεῦ, τοῦτο γιγνώσκεις, ὅτι
    ὀργῆς νοσούσης εἰσὶν ἰατροὶ λόγοι;
Πρ. ἐάν τις ἐν καιρῷ γε μαλθάσσῃ κέαρ
    καὶ μὴ σφριγῶντα θυμὸν ἰσχναίνῃ βίᾳ.
Ωκ. ἐν τῷ προθυμεῖσθαι δὲ καί τολμᾶν τίνα
    ὁρᾷς ἐνοῦσαν ζημίαν; δίδασκέ με.
Πρ. μόχθον περισσὸν κουφόνουν τ' εὐηθίαν.
Ωκ. ἔα με τῇδε τῇ νόσῳ νοσεῖν, ἐπεὶ
    κέρδιστον εὖ φρονοῦντα μὴ φρονεῖν δοκεῖν.
Πρ. ἐμὸν δοκήσει τἀμπλάκημ' εἶναι τόδε.

Oceanos
Do you not know, Prometheus, that words are healers of the sick temper?
Prometheus
Yes, if in season due one soothes the heart with them, not tries violently to reduce the swelling anger.
Oceanos
Tell me, what danger do you see for me in loyalty to you, and courage therein?
Prometheus
I see only useless effort and a silly good nature.
Oceanos
Suffer me then to be sick of this sickness, for it is a profitable thing, if one is wise, to seem foolish.
Prometheus
This shall seem to be my fault.

B vv 472–5

Xo. πέπονθας αἰκὲς πῆμ᾽ ·ἀποσφαλεὶς φρενῶν
     πλανᾷ, κακὸς δ᾽ ἰατρὸς ὥς τις ἐς νόσον
     πεσὼν ἀθυμεῖς καὶ σεαυτὸν οὐκ ἔχεις
     εὑρεῖν ὁποίοις φαρμάκοις ἰάσιμος.

Chorus

What you have suffered is indeed terrible. You are all astray and bewildered in
your mind, and like a bad doctor that has fallen sick himself, you are cast down
and cannot find what sort of drugs would cure your ailment.

c vv 977–8

Eρ. κλύω σ᾽ ἐγὼ μεμηνότ᾽ οὐ σμικρὰν νόσον.
Πρ. νοσοῖμ᾽ ἄν, εἰ νόσημα τοὺς ἐχθροὺς στυγεῖν.

Hermes

Your words declare you mad, and mad indeed.
Prometheus
Yes, if it's madness to detest my foes.

D vv 1068–70

τοὺς προδότας γὰρ μισεῖν ἔμαθον,
κοὐκ ἔστι νόσος
    τῆσδ᾽ ἥντιν᾽ ἀπέπτυσα μᾶλλον.

I have learned to hate all traitors: there is no disease I spit on more than
treachery.

CHAPTER FOUR

Prometheus' speeches on the arts: some comparisons and speculations

In the preceding chapter, we noted several curious features in Prometheus' two great speeches on the arts (436–71; 476–506) which seemed to fit better with some independent 'evolutionary' account than with Prometheus' own claims here and, especially, elsewhere in the play. It seems probable, from what has been said, that in these two speeches Aeschylus is excerpting and adapting passages from other more extensive and perhaps more 'secular' accounts of the origin of the arts. Were these 'traditional' accounts, in circulation from the archaic period onwards, or were they more recent formulations, belonging to early sophistic thought on these matters? Or does Prometheus' account, with its curious selectivity and more curious variations in style and emphasis, reflect some kind of compromise between the two? Here we run into considerable difference of opinion among scholars as to the kind (and the date) of anthropological speculation which Aeschylus is here reflecting, and indeed not all the scholars agree about the evidence for the kind of adaptation at which I have been hinting.

Reinhardt and Dodds are both firm in their conviction that there is nothing properly speaking evolutionary or sophistic in the Aeschylean Prometheus' account of the origin of the arts. Indeed, for Reinhardt, the striking feature is the lack of suggestion (as he claims) of any natural development, eg,

'With seeing eyes, they saw not – until *I* showed them the rising and the setting of the stars'. There is no change which does not manifest itself in the contrast between intelligence and stupidity [von Geist and Dummheit]. The idea of reversal belongs to old myth and not to the sophistic idea of gradual development [Das Schema der Umkehr ist alte mythische, nicht das sophistische des Stuffenweisen Anstiegs].[1]

E.R. Dodds agrees with Reinhardt in describing the *Prometheus'* anthropological speeches (*PV* 442–506) as 'decidedly archaic and pre-sophistic.'[2] To the point that there are no *stages* of evolution marked he adds the point that there is no recognition of the decisive influence of food-producing techniques (cattle-herding and agriculture) and no reference to the origins of communal life. Technology, Dodds points out, takes a minor place and the Aeschylean emphasis is on intellectual progress rather than on economic necessity.

Dodds' observation of the limitations of Aeschylean anthropology provides a useful warning against linking it too closely with the more extensive accounts of cultural evolution such as we find in Diodorus 1. 8, and other late sources which some scholars trace back to fifth-century influences.[3] Nevertheless, both Reinhardt and Dodds seem too conservative in their estimate of Prometheus' account. In the first place, the denial by Reinhardt and Dodds alike of any hint of evolution in Prometheus' account is, perhaps, contradicted by the suggestion of an ascending order which we have observed in men's acquisition of the arts as Prometheus describes it. Granted the lack of any clear-cut stages in technological evolution, there is at least a hint of a specific advance from cave-dwelling to house-dwelling, with the implied discovery of brick-building and woodworking (*PV* 449–53) and of a like advance from random livelihood (*PV* 449–50) to the implied discovery of the seasons (essential for agricultural lore) through Prometheus' lessons in astronomy (*PV* 454–8). So, too, the yoking of beasts for heavy labours is specifically mentioned among Prometheus' discoveries for men (*PV* 462–5); indeed, mention of this technological advance is the only one which happens to be supplemented by a similar claim (now extended to horses, asses, and bulls) on Prometheus' part at fr 108 of the *Luomenos*. Finally, Dodds tends, perhaps, to see Prometheus as too

---

1 Reinhardt *Aischylos* pp 50–1.
2 Dodds *The Ancient Concept of Progress* p 5.
3 See Cole *Democritus and the Sources of Greek Anthropology* who develops and extends the arguments of Reinhardt 'Hekataios von Abdera und Demokrit' *Hermes* 47 (1912) 492–513. Neither Cole (cf p 50 n 8) nor Reinhardt, to be sure, regards the passages on the arts in the *PV* as having any systematic connection with Diodorus and the other later anthropological accounts; however, as we shall see, Diodorus 1.8 is sometimes cited for comparison with the Aeschylean passages.

purely 'the symbol of reason,'[4] when one considers the specific gifts of this passage; indeed, the significant omission of any mention of communal life (elsewhere, eg, Sophocles, *Antigone* 354 ff, regarded as a sort of pinnacle of intellectual advance) rather underlines the limitation of Prometheus' claims (for reasons yet to be discussed).

Dodds does mention Xenophanes (whom Aeschylus could have known as an old man in Sicily) as a possible influence on this passage, but feels that no particular source or special knowledge was really needed for its contents. However, if (as seems reasonable) we do think of Xenophanes in this connection, we must also think of him as marking the division (as Edelstein has observed)[5] between the depiction, in the old cult legends, of the arts and crafts as 'presided over by the gods,' and 'co-eval with the world,' and the idea of progress which began to develop in pre-Socratic literature. Xenophanes tells us:

> Not all things, by any means, did the gods show to mortals; rather, as time went on, men found improvement by constant searching. (Xenophanes B18, D–K)

This is admittedly a far cry from the way in which Prometheus puts the matter. Nevertheless, the list of arts which he produces is not one which (leaving aside his final generic claim at 506–7) one would expect to find attributed to any individual culture-*daimon*.

W.K.C. Guthrie also sees 'the idea of progress' as originating with Xenophanes and adds, 'By the mid-fifth century we find scattered hints that a rationalist view of man's development was being taught by the natural philosophers.'[6] Guthrie finds Aeschylus to be very much part of this development: though Aeschylus gives credit for human progress to Prometheus, Guthrie thinks that to a Greek ear Aeschylus is describing, through the name of Prometheus, the benefits that men owe to forethought, and wonders 'how far the poet knew that he was using mythological terms to describe a natural and purely human process.' This seems to me to put the question the wrong way around. Aeschylus seems here very much *au fait* with the evolutionary views which replaced the conception of a golden age followed by a period of degeneracy. But for Aeschylus, it is the dramatic concept of Prometheus, what Prometheus does in his relations with man and with Zeus,

---

4 Dodds *The Ancient Concept of Progress* p 6.
5 See Edelstein *The Idea of Progress in Classical Antiquity* pp 3 ff, esp p 6.
6 Guthrie *In the Beginning* p 84. For the comments cited on Xenophanes and Aeschylus, see pp 82–3.

which is primary, both here and throughout the trilogy (as far as we can know it). Thus I would prefer to think of Aeschylus as using contemporary evolutionary material, in which the role of the gods and even of culture-heroes was (as we shall see) gradually being phased out, but adapting it, in some places imperfectly, to the dramatic claims of Prometheus at which we have been looking.

The tentative conclusions so far advanced find some general support in the research and arguments of E.A. Havelock, whose discussion of pre-Socratic anthropological speculation and of the Greek dramatists' relation to it are indeed most relevant to the present study. It may be useful, therefore, to indicate certain points both of agreement and of difficulty which I find with Havelock's treatment. First of all, Havelock does, in my view, succeed in establishing that there was, at least by the mid-fifth century, a strong 'scientific' tradition among the Greeks which treated the history of civilization in rationalistic and evolutionary, as opposed to mythological and theistic terms.[7] Furthermore, Havelock also argues (as I do) for a close relation between this 'scientific' tradition and the account of the origin of the arts in *Prometheus Bound*.[8] However, Havelock does not distinguish between the way this subject is treated in Prometheus' two great speeches at 442 ff and 476 ff and the way it is treated in his other claims about the gift of fire and of the arts in general elsewhere in the play. Secondly, Havelock regards the historical process presented in *Prometheus Bound* as complete and fails to notice the significant omission of the civic arts from Prometheus' list[9] – an omission which (as I shall suggest later) *may* have implications for the subsequent development of the trilogy.

7 See Havelock *The Liberal Temper* chapter 5. That 'the main outline of this design' [for a 'scientific' anthropology] had already been sketched by the end of the sixth century, as Havelock also suggests (p 106), seems less certain. The slender evidence concerning Anaximander's and Xenophanes' views on the matter (quoted by Havelock, 104–6) does not really support this, even as a tentative conclusion, though there are hints (as we have already seen in the case of Xenophanes) of preliminary speculation along these lines. However, Havelock's strongest and best-supported statements on pre-Socratic anthropology are based on fragments quoted from Anaxagoras, particularly 59B4 (D-K) which, he declares, 'certainly establishes as the doctrine of Anaxagoras the naturalist and genetic conception of civilization and its institutions, including the city-state, as part of the continuous cosmic development' (p 111).

8 Ibid chapter 3, pp 52–81.

9 Ibid 60–1. Indeed, Havelock seems rather to overstress (p 62) the social aspects of Prometheus' gifts to man. So also, he argues later (pp 79–81), from very slender evidence in Prometheus' speeches, that the social cohesion and co-operation which are so much a part of the development of the arts in the later anthropologies (eg in Diodorus) are reflected in Prometheus' account as well.

Finally (and herein lies my major disagreement), Havelock seeks to identify Prometheus with man himself or, at least, with human intelligence, although he is careful to indicate that this identification cannot be made too explicit in the dramatic context.[10] That 'the dramatist's scientific source did not utilize a divine apparatus at all ...' we may, perhaps, agree, but to suggest that Prometheus is merely 'equivalent to the fire he gives and ... his instruction only a concrete symbolization of the process of self-instruction employed by men' is to import into the play a humanism alien to its theme. Nor (for there is no 'poet's view' beyond what the poet allows to appear in the play) can Prometheus be reduced to such a symbol: there are indications throughout the play and the fragments of the trilogy that the struggle between the gods is as thematically important as the fate of man from which that struggle began.

Among the scattered hints of a fifth-century view of progress in civilization, 'theistic' and 'rationalistic' explanations appear to have existed side by side. As we shall see, various similarities, however elliptical owing to the often fragmentary nature of our sources, between these accounts, suggest that most of them were influenced, in their form if not always in their conclusions, by some common tradition on the matter which gained increasing currency during the latter half of the century. Sometimes the gods are prominent in these explanations of human progress; sometimes they are not. Is there any reason, then, for suggesting that the underlying doctrine is rationalistic and secular and that when gods are mentioned in such accounts they are being inserted (whether for pietistic or dramatic reasons, or for both) into alien soil; that, in effect, an incipient secular tradition is being 're-mythologized'? There are, perhaps, no infallible guidelines by which we can establish this, but I would suggest (as I have already ventured to do in the case of *Prometheus Bound* 442–506) that when there are signs in the account of an ascending sequence of arts or of other means (social as well as technological) to civilized living, then we are in the shadow, as it were, of the 'scientific,' evolutionary approach, even if the gods (or some one of them) are given credit. Among the earlier philosophers, it is in the fragmentary tradition on Anaxagoras that we catch the clearest glimpse of a scientific, evolutionary sequence involving first plant and animal life[11] and later the use of human as distinct from animal intelligence in the various skills and techniques

10 Ibid 63–6. (For the two quotations which follow, see pp 64 and 65, respectively).
11 See passages selected from the accounts and fragments of Anaxagoras by Havelock (ibid 107–9) for illustration of this and the following point.

required for civilized existence.[12] The reason for regarding such 'ladder' sequences, in histories of man's acquisition of the arts, as primarily scientific and secular in nature is twofold. First, they continue in the same vein the scientific accounts of man's physical evolution; second, they suggest the laborious human process of fulfilling each need or lack ($\chi\rho\epsilon\iota\alpha$) as it occurs and as it becomes, in turn, most pressing, at each successive stage. (The essentially *human* process of inventive activity in response to need becomes, as we shall see, much clearer when it is spelt out more fully in later cultural anthropologies such as that of Diodorus.) Other signs of specific adaptations of originally secular accounts may well appear (as I have suggested in the case of the *Prometheus* passages concerned) in various individual instances. But it is this general feature – *some* sign of an ascending sequence and of successive needs successively fulfilled – which seems, from the evidence of accounts sustained enough to illustrate them, to indicate the scientific, secular nature of the common tradition for which I have been arguing.

We may now proceed to examine the various passages which bear some comparison, from one aspect or another, with the Aeschylean Prometheus' account of his gift of the arts to men.[13] In the Homeric *Hymn to Hephaistos* (xx. 3–7), it is Hephaistos who is credited with transforming men's lot by his teaching of the arts; the account is brief but the reference to the improvement of man's beast-like and cave-dwelling existence reminds us of *PV* 447–52. (The date of this hymn is unknown but the similarity with this and other tragic passages to be cited suggests the mid-fifth century BC.) More purely rationalistic (like the approach of Xenophanes) are the hints in Anaxagoras B21 (where men are said to make use of experience, memory, widsom ($\sigma o \varphi \iota \alpha$) and skill ($\tau \epsilon \chi \nu \eta$) in taking things such as milk and honey from beasts and insects), and in Democritus B154 (where men's imitation of other creatures – spiders for spinning, swallows for building, nightingales for singing – is stressed) and, indeed, in the 'evolutionary' passage in Sophocles' *Antigone*, 332–75. In the latter passage, as in *Prometheus*,

12 See especially 59A101, 59B21b, 59B4 (D-K).
13 Of the passages discussed below, for comparison or contrast with the account of the Aeschylean Prometheus, all except Sophocles *Antig.* 332–55 and Plato *Protag.* 321 c ff are cited by George Thomson in his edition to the *Prometheus Bound* in his note to vv 452–87 (436–71 OCT), though without detailed comparisons; all except the Homeric *Hymn to Hephaestus* (xx. 3–7) and the tragic fragments, *frg. adesp.* 470 (N) and Eur. 578 (N) are cited by Guthrie, though not in specific comparison with the *Prometheus* passage. Cf also Havelock *The Liberal Temper* chapters 3–5, where at least the major passages concerned are discussed.

men's achievements are detailed in an ascending order (though the sequence itself is not the same), and several of the achievements selected are identical or nearly identical: sea-crossing, use of animals as beasts of burden,[14] discovery of speech (it is 'writing' (γραμμάτων ... συνθέσεις) in the case of Prometheus), and, most significantly, the mastery of diseases. The significant *differences* are the inclusion in the Sophoclean passage of the 'civilizing dispositions' (ἀστυνόμους ὀργάς, 355, which, apparently, enable man to accept νόμοι and δίκη, 368–9) and the *omission* in the same passage of any credit to the gods in these achievements of man, with the possible exception of the last.[15]

In Euripides' *Supplices*, 195–213, Theseus outlines the basis of man's civilized survival in a passage that stands half-way between the Aeschylean and Sophoclean passages and indeed epitomizes the ambiguity between mythological and humanistic explanations of man's development characteristic of this period. In contrast to the Sophoclean passage, Euripides' Theseus insists on the divine provenance of man's civilization, but, in contrast to the Aeschylean catalogue of the arts, he keeps that provenance vague in the extreme: αἰνῶ δ' ὅς ... θεῶν ... : 'I praise whichever of the gods regulated our life' (in the way now to be described). Several features of King Theseus' list repeat, in somewhat different terms, the endowments of Prometheus: eg, the divine gifts of intelligence (*Suppl.* 203; compare *PV* 444); of speech (*Suppl.* 203–4; compare and contrast *PV* 460–1); of nourishment, τροφή, from the earth; of shelter (*Suppl.* 205–8; compare and contrast *PV* 450–8); of ships, specifically for trade in the Euripidean passage (*Suppl.* 209–10; compare *PV* 467–8); of augury by fire, by sacrificial entrails, and by flight of birds (*Suppl.* 211–13; compare *PV* 484–500, where there are both similarities and differences). Moreover, the basis of Theseus' optimistic claim that 'There are more good things than bad for mortals,'

14 The animals mentioned in this connection in the *Antigone* passage are the mule (so understanding ἱππείῳ γένει, *Antig.* 341, with Jebb) and, at *Antig.* 349–51, some 'free-ranging mountain beast,' the horse, and the mountain bull. At *PV* 462 ff such beasts 'enslaved to the yoke' are described simply as κνώδαλα (a vague term for large beasts), while the training of horses is restricted to more refined employment with chariots (465–6). In a fragment of the *Luomenos*, however, horses, asses, and bulls are all mentioned as the relievers of πόνοι supplied by Prometheus' gift. Democritus (A151) also draws attention to the way in which men came to breed mules from horses and asses. These and other coincidences are all suggestive of a common tradition, drawn on by poets from at least the 450s onwards, concerning the evolution of the arts.
15 The expression θεῶν τ' ἔνορκον δίκαν (which, as Jebb has rightly pointed out, means 'justice sworn to in the name of the gods') brings the gods into the picture, albeit indirectly.

namely that 'we would have perished otherwise!' may be compared with Prometheus' claim to have saved men from extinction (*PV* 231–6), for both claims are later substantiated by the gifts of intelligence and the arts.

The tone of Theseus' speech is admittedly much more optimistic than that of the Aeschylean Prometheus, implying as it does a sort of generalized divine benevolence in this world where τὰ χρηστά abound, if only men will take advantage of them. But this feature may be explained, at least in part, by the requirements of the dramatic theme, just as in the *PV* the championship of man *against* the divine rulers of the world is a special requirement of the theme. Nevertheless, the context which King Theseus provides for his optimistic statement ('more good than bad for mortals,' 199), namely that it has arisen out of debates with those holding the opposite view (195–9), is itself of some interest for our whole discussion. Since this is not the sort of circumstance readily associated with the legendary King Theseus, we may perhaps infer that the debates alluded to (ie, debates on 'civilization,' 'the sources of the arts,' and so on) were contemporary fifth-century ones. And this is just the sort of cultural climate we would expect for the conflicting and often paradoxical comments on the subject which we have been reviewing.[16]

16 Cf Guthrie *In the Beginning* p 83 and n 6, who also compares 'the progressive scheme of civilization' in the three tragic passages we have mentioned. Guthrie notes as well that 'as with Prometheus in Aeschylus, the first thing he ['the god' in the Euripidean passage] bestowed was σύνεσις, intelligence (line 203).' He also regards the Euripidean passage (presumably because of the vague 'background' nature of the anonymous god's role), as not 'more religious' than that of Sophocles.

   Guthrie does tend to rationalize the Aeschylean and particularly the Euripidean passages rather more than their expression warrants. After all, Theseus' description of 'the well-ordered universe' is expressed at least formally as a theodicy, despite the fact that there is (as in the Aeschylean and Sophoclean accounts discussed) a strong suggestion of that ascending order in the list of divine gifts which elsewhere we have suggested reflects the sequence of *human* accomplishments. Havelock (*The Liberal Temper* p 73) goes so far as to call the Euripidean passage 'a skilful rewrite,' an 'attempt to stand anthropology on its head,' and goes on to compare this device by which 'average orthodoxy tried to come to terms with the new teaching' with modern pietistic attempts to place Darwinian evolution under providential control. This formulation of the matter does perhaps polarize the theistic and the humanistic (or 'scientific') approaches rather more sharply than suits the cultural context (nor need we regard 'Theseus' as expressing Euripides' views), but I think that both Guthrie and Havelock are right in suspecting that the progressive scheme of civilization here attributed to the god's gifts does in fact reflect accounts in which the principal emphasis was on the gradual and increasing mastery of the environment by human intelligence.

One further, rather minor, similarity worth noting between the Euripidean and the Aeschylean passages is the mild coincidence of language and conception in the two descriptions of man's early existence: Theseus speaks of the god changing man's life ἐκ πεφυρμένου (sc. βίόν from βίοτον in the preceding line): 'from a confused and bestial existence' (201–2); Prometheus says men ... τὸν μακρὸν βίον / ἔφυρον εἰκῇ πάντα: 'confused all things at random throughout their long life' (*PV* 449–50), and he too goes on to make a subhuman comparison, in this case between early (cave)men and ants living underground (*PV* 452–3). Before dismissing the linguistic similarities (ἐκ πεφυρμένου sc. βιότου, Euripides; τὸν μακρὸν βίον, ἔφυρον, Aeschylus) as coincidence, one should note also the curious fact that the same word φύρω (confuse), in the same context of living in a confused and beast-like manner before the establishment of the arts, occurs in another tragic passage, *fr. adesp.* 470 (N):

> Then he took in hand [or 'directed,' 'managed'] the way of life of all Greece and its allies, a life which was formerly confused [πεφύρμενον] and beast-like. First, he discovered all-wise number, most excellent of the arts [ἔξοχον σοφισμάτων ...] ...

The subject of the sentence is almost certainly Palamedes, and the fact that the fragment is attributed by some scholars to Euripides' *Palamedes*, and by others, with more probability, to Aeschylus' *Palamedes*, underlines the verbal similarities among all three passages.[17] ἔχοχον σοφισμάτων (line 4 of the fragment) occurs as a description of number also at *PV* 459 (a form of εὑρίσκω is used in both cases), another indication that the *Prometheus* passage is perhaps based on some current or traditional account of the discovery of the arts. And before concluding that most of the similarities concerned are limited to the two Aeschylean passages, we should also consider Euripides fr 578 (N) (this time certainly from Euripides' *Palamedes*), where Palamedes' claim of the discovery of writing for men as a cure for forgetfulness is very reminiscent of the Aeschylean Prometheus' claim at *PV* 460–1.[18]

---

17 See the note ad loc. in Nauck *T.G.F.* In addition to the comparisons between this fragment and Aesch. *PV* 454–9 and Eur. *Suppl.* 201, Nauck notes Hermann's (less apt) comparison of our fragment with Euripides fr 578 (N) which I consider below.

18 Compare Eur. fr 578 1–3:
  τὰ τῆς γε λήθης, φάρμακ' ὀρθώσας μόνος,
  ἄφωνα φωνήεντα συλλαβὰς τιθεὶς
  ἐξηῦρον ἀνθρώποισι γράμματ' εἰδέναι ...
  and Aesch. *PV* 460–1:
  ... ἐξηῦρον αὐτοῖς, γραμμάτων τε συνθέσεις
  μνήμην ἁπάντων...

Turning again from the tragedians to the philosophers, we come next to Protagoras' formulation of the origins of the civilizing arts – if, indeed, we may take Plato's version (*Protagoras* 321 C ff) as a fair representation of it. According to the Platonic Protagoras, Prometheus (after Epimetheus had used up on the beasts of creation the various powers, δυναμεῖς, requisite for their survival), stole from Athena and Hephaistos 'the technical skills along with fire' (τὴν ἔντεχνον σοφίαν σὺν πυρί, 321 D) and gave these to man. 'Once man shared in the divine lot [θείας ... μοίρας] ... he soon articulated, through his art [τέχνῃ], speech and names for things and discovered for himself houses and clothes and footwear and beds and nourishment from the earth' (322 A). The language of 321 D makes it clear that fire is regarded in both a symbolic and a practical sense as the prerequisite of the arts. Protagoras says that one needs it both for the attainment and the use of ἡ ἔντεχνος σοφία, but it would seem that, beyond its application to the practical arts, fire is also the physical symbol of the divine lot of which man is now partaking: though fire is obviously needed for ἡ δημιουργικὴ τέχνη (322 B) in general, it is not needed in any practical sense for *all* of the skills (eg, speech) presented as the results of the new dispensation. (Fire is also, of course, treated in a similar way in the *PV*, at 7, 30, 109–11, 252–4, though not in the two great speeches at 436 ff and 476 ff). Indeed, it is this very ambiguity about fire as both a physical requirement for the practical arts *and* a symbol of the divine prerogative (θεία μοῖρα in the *Protagoras*; cf τίμας ... περὰ δίκης, *PV* 30, of Prometheus' gift of fire to *man*) which marks the blend of the rationalistic and the mythological in 'Protagoras'' account, for once man has the gift of fire, *his own discovery* of the individual practical arts follows. (In other, quite secular accounts of the origin of the arts, fire, now treated as a discovery not a gift, has the same primacy.)

This feature of the '*Protagoras* myth' gives a certain internal justification, in terms of the passage itself, to Guthrie's claim that, since elsewhere Protagoras appears as a self-confessed agnostic (*Protagoras* B 4), we may discount the divine elements in the '*Protagoras* myth.' 'What Protagoras seems to have done in this story,' Guthrie suggests, 'is to construct ... a rational account of human civilization, and graft on to it the tale of Prometheus and Epimetheus ...'[19] Similarly (as I have argued) Aeschylus, not as a rationalist but as a dramatist, may be

19 Guthrie *In the Beginning* p 88; cf p 84. Cf also J.S. Morrison 'The Place of Protagoras in Athenian Public Life,' esp pp 9–10, who seems to hold a similar view concerning the essentially rationalistic basis of the evolutionary theory of human society (at *Protag.* 321 C ff), a theory he regards as 'probably inherited by him [Protagoras] from the materialistic thought of the Ionian cities' (p 9).

adapting an essentially rationalistic account of the origins of civilization to mythological expression.

The '*Protagoras* myth' now goes on to expound in the same way the origin of 'the civic art' (ἡ πολιτκὴ τέχνη, 322 B, presumably the equivalent to the ἀστυνόμους ὀργάς of *Antigone* 355); indeed it is here that the adaptation of the naturalistic to the theistic or mythological explanation seems most transparent. In response to the danger from wild beasts, 'Protagoras' tells us, men banded together by founding cities, but, lacking the civic art, kept perishing in internecine strife until Zeus, through Hermes, distributed mutual respect (αἰδώς) and justice (δίκη) to each of them (*Protag.* 322 B–C). It is this most necessary crown to the civilizing arts which is conspicuously absent from the Aeschylean Prometheus' catalogue of gifts. Thus the grandiose claim to all the arts at the end of the speech (505–6) means all the *practical* arts, a limitation which Prometheus may not wish to make too explicit at this point. And this major difference (among, of course, many others) between the accounts in the *PV* and in the *Protagoras* makes particularly attractive the conjecture of Professor Lloyd-Jones that the trilogy may have ended with Zeus' gift of δίκη to man, as a quid pro quo for the revelation of the secret by which Prometheus, the champion of men, saves Zeus' rule.[20]

In addition to the classical sources which we have cited, Diodorus 1.8 1 ff is often cited by scholars (though usually without comment) for comparison with the account of the arts at *PV* 442 ff.[21] Much has been written concerning the possible fifth-century Greek sources of this and similar late accounts of the origins of civilization. However, if one studies Thomas Cole's excellent presentation of comparable passages from five such accounts (those of Diodorus, Vitruvius, Tzetzes, Lucre-

---

20 See Lloyd-Jones *The Justice of Zeus* pp 100 ff, and further references there given. Cf. below, chapter 5 n4.

21 Solmsen *Hesiod and Aeschylus* p 143 n 92, in connection with Werner Jaeger's view (*Paideia* I.337) that Prometheus' account of his inventions reflects the theories of progressive Ionian thinkers, suggests that this view may find support in the fact that these 'later philosophical descriptions [ie in Diodorus and Lucretius] of the growth of human civilization ... treat the evolution of civilization as the sequel to a κοσμογονία and ζῳογονία which are indeed subjects of long standing among the Ionian physicists.' However, Solmsen is undecided whether such evolutionary accounts of the origin of civilization stem from the Ionian physicists or from speculations by the tragic poets of Athens; he adds '... the absence of a definite pattern of gradual evolution in Aeschylus may favor the view that Aeschylus is not influenced by Ionian systems but is thinking in terms of the πρῶτοι εὑρεταί of human τέχναι ...' For a different view of the fifth-century Greek origins of these later evolutionary accounts (Diodorus, and others) – a view with which Solmsen disagrees – see the following note.

tius and Posidonius) one may well be convinced of their common origin, but one sees also their marked difference from the more restricted, less organized, and less 'evolutionary' account in our *Prometheus* passage.[22] (This, as we have seen, is substantially Cole's view of the matter also.) Nevertheless, since these accounts do provide us with our first complete examples of ancient 'histories of civilization' which are, for the most part, anthropological, ie, secular in the proper sense of the word, it may be useful to note a few general features in them which appear to support observations concerning the possible influence of embryonic scientific accounts, already current in Aeschylus' time, on these two speeches of Prometheus.

In this connection, we should note, first of all, that Diodorus' account begins with a description in some detail of the beast-like, random existence of man before the discovery of the arts; so, too, in Diodorus (and to some degree in the other anthropologies quoted by Cole), we find repeated examples of men learning to improve their lot by bitter experience or by their need of the successive improvements which the arts provide. (See, for example, Diodorus 1.8.2; 1.14.1; and, especially, 1.8.9 where need, χρεία, is clearly stated to be men's teacher; compare also Democritus B144, where it seems to be implied that Necessity, τἀναγκαῖον, created the earliest, ie, the practical arts.) I have commented on the presence of these features in two passages of Prometheus' speeches at *PV* 447–53 and, in more truncated form, at

22 See Cole *Democritus*, esp chapter 2, pp 26 ff, on whose quotations and references my subsequent discussion, except for my own comparisons with the *PV* passage, is based. Cole argues (chapter 3, pp 56 ff; cf chapter 9) that the common source of all these passages is Democritus; in this he develops Reinhardt's argument for the Democritean source of Diodorus 1.7 ff through Hecataeus. As Cole and Solmsen both note, Reinhardt's view has been resisted ('refuted,' according to Solmsen) by Dahlmann, who does, however, believe in pre-Socratic sources of these later evolutionary accounts of civilization.

The Democritean fragments which Cole cites in support of his view do show Democritus' interest in the origin of one or other of the arts and in technology in general. However, the evidence from direct quotations from Democritus seems a bit slender for the weight which Cole's view of Democritus' influence would put upon them.

Since (as I have indicated above) no *close* relation seems discernible between the later accounts of civilization which Cole would relate to Democritean thought and the *PV* passage under discussion, detailed discussion of the unresolved dispute over the sources of Diodorus 1.8 ff and the other passages cited seems uncalled for here. For other interesting discussions of the problem, see also Morrison 'The Place of Protagoras in Athenian Public Life' (cf below, n 24), and Vlastos 'On the Pre-History in Diodorus.'

476–81. Secondly, in all of the late accounts we note the familiar 'ascending sequence' of arts, often (in the case of the more primitive ones) with the same stages (cave-dwelling in four accounts; housing in two; crop-cultivation in four)[23] as those marked or implied in the early part of Prometheus' account (*PV* 450–8). (Agriculture is the only practical art which, in Diodorus' account, is attributed to divine intervention: Isis is responsible for the discovery of wheat and barley and Osiris for their first cultivation.)

Next, we may note a difference from the sequence of discoveries listed by Prometheus in the two great speeches: in four of the late anthropologies, the discovery of fire (by natural means) appears as an essential feature of the civilizing process; it comes in early, after the devising of shelter and clothing, and is marked by Diodorus (1.8.8) as a discovery which led to the various useful arts. (This, as we have noted, is true of Prometheus' statements elsewhere in the play, eg, at vv 109–11, 252–4, but is curiously absent from his present account.) Moreover, it is at the stage when fire is introduced in the late accounts that their difference from Prometheus' sequence becomes most marked. In three, it is after the discovery of fire that the definite *social* civilizing of men begins to take place. In two of these (Lucretius v.1011–27 and Vitruvius 33. 28–34.2) a specific connection is made between the discovery of fire and the beginnings of social covenants. In Diodorus, on the other hand, while the discovery of fire ensured the establishment of the practical arts, the divine establishment of law and justice is necessary (as in 'the *Protagoras* myth')[24] to ensure successful

---

23 For detailed references, see Cole *Democritus* chapter 2, pp 26 ff. The passages there cited are from Diodorus Βιβλιοθήκη 1.8 ff; Tzetzes as quoted in Diels-Kranz II, 68B5 (Democritus); Lucretius *De Rerum Natura* 5.932 ff; Vitruvius *De Architectura* 34.6 ff; Posidonius *ap.* Seneca *Ep.* 90.

24 The striking similarity between Diodorus and 'the *Protagoras* myth' on these points, and the difference to be noted in Lucretius (see vv 1011–27), seem the best arguments for regarding (with Morrison, cf above, n 22) Protagoras and not the Greek atomists as a possible source of Diodorus. Not only are fire and the technological arts separated in both Diodorus and 'the *Protagoras* myth' from the *divine* gifts of δίκη and αἰδώς needed for the civic arts; in both, also, the cause of men attempting the communal life in the first place is the same: the depredations of wild beasts (cf Protag. 332 B ff and Diodorus 1.8.2; contrast Lucretius v 982–7, where the fear of wild beasts is mentioned but not in connection with the first social covenants which are described at 1011–27). Morrison ('The Place of Protagoras' p 10, n 3) also cites a few similarities in language between the passages concerned in Diodorus and in the *Protagoras*, though these may be merely coincidental. In all of this, of course, the major question, 'How accurately does the Platonic account represent the actual formulations of Protagoras in these matters?' must still remain unanswered.

communal living. In both accounts, the discovery of fire seems to mark a significant watershed, either (as in Diodorus and 'the *Protagoras* myth') indicating the potential for the merely practical as opposed to the civic arts, or (as in Lucretius and Vitruvius) providing new circumstances propitious for the development of the civic arts as well. This division is, of course, lacking in Prometheus' two speeches on the arts where we have noted the omission of any claim to the civic arts, though his list, while it might be called practical, is by no means exclusively technological (note, for example, the brief references to 'calculation' and 'writing'). Once again we may ask whether the reason may be that the civic arts (ie, specifically, justice) are being saved as the gift of Zeus in the third play of the trilogy, as a possible conciliation to Prometheus, champion of men, after the earth has been rid by Herakles of the dangers of monstrous beasts.[25] It is possible, though one would not wish to press the point, that this may also explain the absence of any mention of fire in Prometheus' present speeches on the arts, for in the extant ancient accounts the introduction of fire and technology seem always to have been followed by the introduction of the civilizing virtues of justice and mutual respect, as the next stage.

For the rest, while there are, to be sure, several agreements (or coincidences) in the arts named by Prometheus and in those named in one or another of the late anthropologies (eg, mining, astronomy, animal training, and sailing), the contexts and sequence in which these arts are mentioned are so different that one can claim from such coincidences no similarity at all in evolutionary treatment. Once again, the lack of any mention of fire in Prometheus' account *could* help explain some of the differences. In Prometheus' account, we miss, for example, any enumeration of practical arts such as metal-working and tool-making, and when the discovery of metals *is* mentioned (*PV.* 500–2), it comes right at the end of the list (after medicine and augury) – not, as in several of the late anthropologies, in sequence with other practical arts related to the discovery of fire.

In sum, certain features of Prometheus' speeches on the arts seem, for one reason or another, odd or anomalous, and I have sought an explanation of these anomalies in the possibility that Aeschylus was adapting other material on the origins of civilization not completely

25 On this conjecture of Professor Lloyd-Jones concerning Zeus' subsequent gift of δίκη, cf above, p 92 and n 20. (For evidence that the wanderings and, presumably, the monster-destroying labours of Herakles were treated later in the trilogy, see fragments 195–9 (N) of the *Luomenos*. Fear of marauding beasts is, in Diodorus (1.8.2), the immediate cause of men's communal association for mutual protection.)

congenial to his drama or to the dramatic personality of his Prometheus. Lacking any clear evidence on these matters from the mid-450s (which, with Herington and others, I take to be the date of the *PV*'s composition),[26] I have reviewed various shreds of evidence of what poets and philosophers – some earlier, most a bit later – were saying along the same lines. Xenophanes, it was suggested, marked the beginning (as far as our evidence goes) of secular evolutionary ideas on civilization (without, however, cutting out the gods altogether), and Aeschylus could well have known Xenophanes in Sicily before the philosopher's death in about 460 BC. In Protagoras' civilization myth there are clear indications of evolutionary stages (eg, the technological stage followed by the sociological or civic stage) and the same blend of the evolutionary and the mythological as we find in Aeschylus' and in other, later accounts. (Protagoras may have begun teaching about 460 BC,[27] – though not at Athens until some fifteen years later – and it is quite possible that Aeschylus in his later years was aware of some of the intellectual currents begun by the early Sophists.) The same evolutionary strain appears in the Sophoclean and Euripidean passages reviewed: more markedly secular in the Antigone's 'Ode to Man' (c 441 BC), but returning, in the passage from Euripides' *Suppliants* (c 420 BC), to the familiar blend of the evolutionary and the vaguely mythological which here happens to suit the dramatic context. But perhaps the most interesting features of the comparison of these and other passages of tragedy with the *Prometheus* passage are the marked coincidence of the specific human accomplishments mentioned, and the occasional coincidence of vocabulary employed. It is this which renders particularly attractive the view that the Euripidean reference to disputes on these matters (*Suppl.* 195 ff) reflects, in a general and characteristically anachronistic way, recurrent discussions which had been going on among the wise since at least the time of Aeschylus.

Finally I have indicated that the late accounts of the arts are indeed of a different order from that given, or even reflected, in *Prometheus Bound*. Nevertheless, one or two features in Diodorus' account do suggest that, if the arguments for its fifth-century sources be sound,

26 For arguments in favour of dating the *PV* between the *Oresteia* in 458 and Aeschylus' death, 456/5 see above, chapter 2, pp 22–4, including notes and references there given.
27 Protagoras' exact dates are subject to some uncertainty (see the useful summary of conflicting evidence in Freeman *The Pre-Socratic Philosophers* pp 343 ff). If he really was old enough to be Socrates' father (*Protag.* 317C), then he cannot have been born much later than 490 BC.

the Aeschylean account, in that it reflects similar features, may too have been influenced by more secular 'evolutionary' accounts of the origin of the arts. These features are the descriptions of the early state of man and the early stages of his gradual civilization, the intrusion (though limited, in Diodorus) of divine provision into the sequence of human self-help, and the clear distinction (similar to that found in the Protagoras myth) between the practical and the civic arts.

The general tendency of the foregoing survey has been to nudge us, I think, toward a choice between two conclusions with regard to the cultural climate dimly reflected behind Prometheus' account of his gifts of the arts. One is that semi-rationalistic, 'evolutionary' views of man's gradual rise to civilization were already being worked out, in some detail, in the mid-fifth century, and that Aeschylus had already become familiar with them before composing *Prometheus Bound* within the last few years of his life. The other is the (to my mind less palatable) view that those who deny Aeschylean authorship to *Prometheus Bound* are right[28] and that the play is the work of an unknown, younger poet, composing slightly after the time of Aeschylus and more familiar than he would have been with the new currents of sophistic social thought which became prevalent in the second half of the fifth century BC.

28 See below, appendix 1, pp 141 ff.

The trilogy

1 Expectations arising from *Prometheus Bound*

Before considering the ancient evidence concerning other plays with which *Prometheus Bound* may have formed a connected trilogy, let us review briefly the various hints and expectations about the future course of events which we have noted in the surviving play.

First of all, there is the somewhat contradictory series of prophetic statements by Prometheus which has been discussed at length in our detailed analysis of *Prometheus Bound*. These statements veer from initial prophecies (167 ff, 186 ff) of reconciliation with Zeus and compensation for Prometheus (as the price of his 'saving secret') to the final prophecy (915–27), implying failure of these gods to come to terms, of Zeus' fall from power. The latter statement, however valid as a threat, cannot be true as a prophecy, for Zeus survives; nevertheless, it suffices to show that the road to reconciliation will be long and difficult and that we are further from this goal at the end of *Prometheus Bound* than at its beginning.

With regard to the liberation of Prometheus, we have heard two specific prophecies. First, Prometheus tells Io that his liberator will be one of her descendants, in the thirteenth generation after her (771, 773); a little later (871–4), the liberator is identified more precisely as 'a bold and famous bowman' (ie, Herakles), and the certainty of the prophecy is guaranteed by the reference to its source, Prometheus' mother Themis (=Gaia, cf 209–10). One further circumstance of the liberation is provided by Hermes (1026–9): it cannot occur until some divine successor of Prometheus' woes appears – one who is, moreover, willing to go down to Hades (ie, to yield up his immortality?). Still one more hint (though a more uncertain one) may perhaps be added concerning the liberation of Prometheus. It is suggested that it may take place 'with Zeus unwilling' (771): at any rate, Prometheus does not reject this phrase of Io's in his answer concerning the identity of his liberator. (One might be tempted to disregard this puzzling hint were it not for a corroborating hint which we shall see in fragment 201 of *Prometheus Unbound*.)

In addition to these specific prophecies, there are other more general indications in *Prometheus Bound* about the kind of reversals and resolutions which the rest of the trilogy may expound. One such hint of the future concerns the presentation of Io, whose treatment abounds in paradoxes. Portrayed, particularly by Prometheus, as the pitiable victim of Zeus' lust, she can also be viewed (at least at certain moments in the play) as the proffered, though reluctant, mate of Zeus whose flight in bovine form is due to Hera's machinations until Zeus frees her from them. Furthermore, on the one hand it is Io's presence that whets Prometheus' indignation and confident defiance of the tyrant, but on the other it is Io's future career and that of her descendant Hypermnestra that seem to point the way to peaceful resolution (for Prometheus as for these ancestors of his liberator) after many years of strife and suffering.

A hint of another kind concerning the future course of the trilogy (or at least of the succeeding play) is contained in the 'political climate' of *Prometheus Bound* and of the preceding power struggle among the gods described in it. In the first place, the frequent references which, with many critics, we have noticed to the *newness* – and the attendant harshness – of Zeus' rule surely cannot be accidental. This emphasis suggests the possibility of change, not necessarily in the *nature* of the gods concerned but in their *circumstances*, which may, in turn, affect their policies and attitudes, Prometheus himself has given clear evidence of this in his own case: he tells us that he left the side of the Titans to ally himself with Zeus by reason of certain circumstances (his acquisition of Gaia's prophetic advice and the Titans' rejection of it) which he makes quite clear. And just as the changing fortunes of the Titans as recounted in *Prometheus Bound* (and continued, as we shall see, in *Prometheus Unbound*) are due to changes in the circumstances of the power struggle among the gods, so, too, we may look to similarly altered circumstances to effect, or at least to make possible, the resolution of Prometheus' long struggle with the ruler of the gods.

These preliminary indications do, perhaps, give us something to begin with, as we approach the fragmentary tradition on the other plays of the trilogy, just as the audience had some expectations to begin with as they watched the rest of the trilogy (as seems reasonably certain) unfold before their eyes. One thing the contradictions and paradoxes of *Prometheus Bound* make clear: Aeschylus must have intended that, at this stage, the manner of the resolution, of the ultimate reconciliation of Prometheus with Zeus, should be kept thoroughly veiled, that it should not simply be implicit in what has already been shown. This suggests that the subsequent action will show totally new circumstances (as well, perhaps, as new interventions), and favours our view that the evolution concerned was political in nature.

2 Components of the trilogy

The following discussion of the lost plays of the Prometheus trilogy is not intended as a new or original contribution to the many problems involved. It is intended rather as an indication to the reader of what little is known or may be reasonably conjectured about those plays, together with some discussion of a few theoretical reconstructions of the theme of the trilogy as a whole. Uncertainties begin with the actual identification and possible sequence of the lost plays themselves. Here we may set down first of all the majority view (in my opinion the most probable one) and what little evidence supports it, before indicating a few of the alternative arguments to which the various uncertainties have given rise.

Prometheus Bound (*Prometheus Desmotês* or *Prometheus Vinctus*, as it is often called), *Prometheus Unbound* (*Prometheus Luomenos*), and *Prometheus the Firebearer* (*Prometheus Purphoros*), all appearing in the ancient catalogue of Aeschylean plays, are accepted by a majority of Aeschylean scholars as forming a connected trilogy which we may, for convenience, call Aeschylus' *Prometheia*. Common-sense arguments for also accepting this particular sequence of the plays have been indicated in an earlier chapter: that 'the *Un*bound' must follow 'the Bound' and that the name of the third play probably refers in some way to Prometheus' title as 'Firebearer' in the torch festival in his honour at Athens.[1] The third play is thus taken to deal with a time after he had been restored to Zeus' favour and was honoured among men as the bestower of fire. The view that the *Purphoros* was the first play of the trilogy and that the title referred to Prometheus' original theft of fire

---

1 See Thomson's edition of *Prometheus Bound*, pp 33–4, for ancient references to the torch festival in honour of Prometheus and to Prometheus as 'the firebearer' (*purphoros*).

has been refuted on the grounds that, if that were the case, the theft would hardly have been recounted, as if it were fresh information, in the *Desmotês*.[2] To these more general indications about the sequence of the three plays, we may add also the evidence of the three scholia to the *Prometheus Bound*: schol. *PV* 511, which speaks of the release of Prometheus 'in the following play,' schol. *PV* 522, which speaks of the following play as the one in which Prometheus revealed his secret, and schol. *PV* 94, from which it would appear that the *Purphoros* followed the other two plays since we are here told that in the *Purphoros* Prometheus' servitude was said to have lasted thirty thousand years. This, at any rate, seems the most likely (as well as the prevailing) interpretation of schol. *PV* 94, although advocates of the *Purphoros* as the first play in the trilogy have argued otherwise.[3]

Furthermore, supporters of the *Purphoros* as the first and not the third play argue that insufficient mythological material remains for a further play after the freeing of Prometheus and his reconciliation with Zeus have been accomplished, presumably in the *Luomenos*. Thus Pohlenz, quoted with approval by Fitton-Brown, describes 'the ob-

2 So Westphal *Prolegomena zu Aischylos' Tragoedien* pp 207 ff refuted Welcker's view of the *Purphoros* in *Die Aischylos' Trilogie Prometheus* pp 7 ff. On these and many other views of 'the Prometheus trilogy,' see Stoessl *Die Trilogie des Aischylos* pp 122–4; Lloyd-Jones 'Zeus in Aeschylus' pp 55 ff.

3 Pohlenz *Griechische Tragödie*[2], *Erläuterungen*, 40, followed by Fitton-Brown '*Prometheia*' pp 51–2, argues that in the scholiast's statement 'for in the *Purphoros* he [Aeschylus] says that he [αὐτόν = Prometheus] was bound [δεδέσθαι] for 30,000 years,' the perfect tense of the infinitive refers merely to a time before Aeschylus ('the speaker') and not to a time anterior to the actual dramatic context of the information. This is, of course, possible, but in order to claim that the scholiast's statement could also have been derived from a play of which the dramatic date *preceded* the binding, defenders of the *Purphoros* as the first play must argue that the original source of the scholiast's statement was in the form of a prophecy. Pohlenz cleverly points to a passage in which Hyginus (*astr.* 2.6) does in fact use a perfect infinitive in precisely this way for an action which we know from fr 199 of the *Luomenos* actually was a part of a prophecy about Herakles' future wanderings. Thus Pohlenz has demonstrated the *possibility* that the source of the statement in schol. *PV* 94 was also originally in the form of a prophecy. Defenders of this view must then manufacture reasons for such a prophecy in the first play which is, in fact, contradicted in the 'second' play (at *PV* 774, where Prometheus says that his bondage will last for thirteen generations). Fitton-Brown argues 'Zeus imposed a sentence [in the first play] which he later found it inexpedient to carry out in full.' This strikes me as special pleading, particularly since not only schol. *PV* 94 but also two other sources (Hygin. *astr.* 2.15, Hygin. *fab.* 54, which do not however, cite the *Purphoros* as their source) all mention Prometheus' 30,000 years' bondage simply as a fact without any suggestion of unfulfilled prophecy or unfulfilled sentence. (This test is not applicable to the example Pohlenz cites, since *that* prophecy, about Herakles' wanderings, actually did become a fact.)

vious phases' of the struggle between Prometheus and Zeus as 'transgression, punishment, reconciliation.'[4] Nevertheless, proponents of a 'first-place *Purphoros*' are just as hard put to reconstruct their play (without repeating the detailed treatment of the past given in *Prometheus Bound*) as are defenders of a 'last-place *Purphoros*' to reconstruct theirs. Moreover, 'conflict,' 'resolution of conflict,' and 'fruits of conflict' will appeal to many readers of Aeschylus (and particularly of the *Oresteia*) as perhaps a more likely sequence than Pohlenz's somewhat arbitrary 'obvious phases.'

Nevertheless, some uncertainty still remains about the very existence of *Prometheus Purphoros* as a play (whether first or third) in our trilogy. Only one alleged line from it (fr 208, Nauck) is quoted, without context, from antiquity, and there is only one additional ancient reference to the play (schol. *PV* 94) apart from its appearance in the catalogue of Aeschylean plays. Uncertainty is increased by the fact that, while lacking information about the performance of the plays in Aeschylus' 'Prometheus trilogy,' we do have two additional ancient references to 'Prometheus plays' of Aeschylus. One is the mention of a satyr play, simply called *Prometheus*, in the information appended to the Alexandrian *Hypothesis* for Aeschylus' *Persae*; the other is a reference by Pollux (10.64) to a *Prometheus Purkaeus* (*Prometheus the Fire-Kindler*) by Aeschylus, from which Pollux quotes a single verse. (The latter reference is supplemented by another passage in Pollux (9.156) where the word *purkaeus* also occurs in connection with Aeschylus' *Prometheus*.)[5] Hence there is at least a possibility that the *Purkaeus* is a misnomer for the *Purphoros* and that this play may have been the satyr play belonging to that other tetralogy. Thus some critics, pointing to this somewhat shaky tradition on the *Prometheus Purphoros*, have used the familiar argument about the lack of mythological residue (after the first two plays) to cast doubt on the existence of *any* third Prometheus play following *Prometheus Bound* and *Prometheus Unbound*. Theories based on this aspersion have led on the one hand to the improbable supposition of an Aeschylean dilogy (a species otherwise unknown in Greek tragic composition),[6] and on the other to the more reasonable suggestion that an aged Aeschylus left his trilogy incomplete after the

4 Pohlenz *Gr. Tr.*[2] p 77, quoted by Fitton-Brown '*Prometheia*' p 56.

5 Two other brief fragments (206, 207, Nauck), besides the one identified by Pollux (205N), have been attributed with near certainty to *Prom. Purkaeus* by modern editors; to these we may now probably add papyrus fr 278 (Lloyd-Jones); see below, n 10.

6 See Hermann 'De Compositione Tetralogiarum Tragicarum' 306–16; cf also Focke 'Aischylos' *Prometheus*' 263–70.

composition of the first two plays.[7] Another, in some ways more radical, replacement of the traditional belief in a *Prometheia* trilogy is Lloyd-Jones' conjecture that the third play of our trilogy might have been *The Women of Aetna*. Lloyd-Jones' reconstruction of this play (following up a suggestion of Eduard Fraenkel) connects the myth of Prometheus in Plato's *Protagoras* 320D ff with an unassigned Aeschylus papyrus fragment (fr 282, Lloyd-Jones) in which *Dikê* (Justice) is sent by Zeus to those whom he wishes to benefit.[8] The promise to send *Dikê* among men, Lloyd-Jones suggests, might have been part of Zeus' settlement in the *Luomenos*, with its fulfilment taking place in Sicily, once the home of the lawless Cyclopes and Lastrygones, in *The Women of Aetna*. However, granting the numerous Sicilian connections (in the text and possibly in the production) of the first two plays of the trilogy, it is difficult to imagine as its climax a play which would appear to dispense so completely with the Titanic rebel-martyr himself. It might be mentioned too that Lloyd-Jones' speculation also runs counter to the late date now generally (though not universally) accepted for the *Prometheus Bound*, since *The Women of Aetna* was probably composed in honour of Aetna's founding in 476 BC.[9]

The nature of the evidence and the extent of the controversy reviewed will suffice to indicate that we cannot be certain about *Prometheus Purphoros* (either about its existence or about its place in the trilogy). On balance, however, the probabilities still seem to favour the traditional view stated at the beginning of this section. The evidence concerning *Prometheus Purphoros*, though slight, is not negligible. The one fragment quoted as from this play in antiquity ('both being silent where it is right to be silent and speaking timely [or 'appropriate']

7 See Dodds *The Ancient Concept of Progress* pp 37–40, who here follows up a suggestion by D.S. Robertson *Proc. Camb. Philol. Soc.* (1938) 9 ff, concerning the alleged incompleteness of *Prometheus Bound* at the time of Aeschylus' death.

8 See Lloyd-Jones *The Justice of Zeus* pp 100 ff, and for text, translation, and discussion of the unassigned papyrus fragment, see Lloyd-Jones' appendix to vol II², pp 576–81 of the Loeb edition of Aeschylus. (The occurrence of the form ὅτιη in line 9 of the fragment may, however, suggest that the fragment comes from a satyr play (a point to which Lloyd-Jones gives more weight in his comments on the fragment than in his speculative argument in *The Justice of Zeus*), since the word is found only at Euripides *Cyclops* 643.) For the conjecture of Fraenkel referred to by Lloyd-Jones, see *Eranos* 52 (1964) 61 ff.

9 See *Vit. Aesch.* 9; cf Diod. xi.9.1. It should be noted, however, that these 'difficulties' apply specifically to the speculation that *The Women of Aetna* was the third play of 'the *Prometheus* trilogy,' not to Lloyd-Jones' suggestion (made, admittedly, in connection with that speculation) about the kind of compensatory settlement which Zeus may have made with Prometheus and man at the end of the trilogy. Cf below, n 24.

things,' 208N) is reasonably 'Aeschylean' in expression and sentiment and congenial with sentiments expressed by Prometheus earlier in *Prometheus Bound*.[10] Both this fragment and the evidence of schol. *PV* 94 provide some argument against identifying *Prometheus Purphoros* of the ancient catalogue of Aeschylean plays with the Prometheus satyr play also attributed to Aeschylus. We have seen, too, that at least a *prima facie* case can be made (from the evidence of schol. *PV* 94 and from other considerations) for the *Purphoros* being the third play in our trilogy.

The argument that there is insufficient material left for another play after the *Luomenos* is hard to refute (since one cannot compose an Aeschylean play) but is not completely convincing. How can one say how much mythological plot material is actually necessary for an Aeschylean tragedy, particularly for the final play of a trilogy? If Aeschylus' *Eumenides* had vanished except for the title, how much could we have guessed of its actual content, simply from our knowledge of the various mythical traditions? If all that we knew of Aeschylus' *Supplices* was that the fifty daughters of Danaus won sanctuary at Athens, might we not have complained that *that* was rather thin plot material for a whole tragedy? We will leave till later in this chapter various reconstructions which have been suggested for our trilogy. Of the specific content of the *Prometheus Purphoros* we will, obviously, have little to say. However, the view that it dealt with the *results* (representing some kind of advance over the previous impasse) of the Zeus-Prometheus reconciliation seems the most acceptable general hypothesis. In this connection the most probable reference of the epithet *Purphoros* in the final play is to the celebration of Prometheus (as he was known to have been celebrated in the torch festival at Athens) as the bringer of fire to men.

3 The fragments and other ancient evidence[11]

The scene of the *Prometheus Unbound* is once again a distant mountain crag (whether we call it the Caucasus, as in the ancient evidence, or the

---

10 Cf *PV* 377–80, 522–5; for utterances very similar to that of fr 208, above, cf Aesch. *Sept.* 619 and *Choeph.* 582. Terghazi would also attribute papyrus fr 278 (Lloyd-Jones) to the *Purphoros*, but this probably belongs to the satyr play as most scholars, following Fraenkel's assignment, believe: see Lloyd-Jones ad loc., for references and discussion.

11 Except where otherwise noted, the fragment numbers cited in this section are those of Nauck *Tragicorum Graecorum Fragmenta*, which are also used in Murray's editions of Aeschylus (1938 and 1955 OCT) and, in brackets, in vol II of the Loeb edition of

same Scythian crag as in the first play, matters little)[12] where Prometheus is again bound after a sojourn of many years in Tartaros. In three anapaestic fragments (190–2) from the beginning of the parodos, the Chorus (who we learn later are Titans, fr 193, line 1) tell Prometheus they have come to view his sufferings and say a little of their journey there. In a twenty-eight-line quotation by Cicero (fr 193), which most scholars take to be a direct translation from the *Prometheus Unbound*,[13]

Aeschylus. The best and fullest presentation in translation, not only of the actual fragments but of other ancient evidence bearing on the content of the trilogy, is to be found in the appendix to Scully and Herington's translation of the *Prometheus Bound*, pp 99–110. Herington provides his own numbering with a reference to Mette's numbering (H.J. Mette *Die Fragmente der Tragoedien des Aischylos* (Berlin 1959)) where relevant.

12 The situation of the second play in the Caucasus, whereas the first play was set in the mountains of Scythia, is puzzling, and some editors (eg Sikes and Willson, xxviii–ix, following F.D. Allen *AJP* xiii (1892) 51 ff), believe that the tradition of a Caucasian setting is due to careless translation by Cicero (see fr 193 'saxa … Caucasi,' in the last line of the quotation). But the Caucasian setting reappears in other ancient references to the part of Prometheus' experiences with which the *Luomenos* is concerned; cf, for example, Strabo iv. 83. Probably the explanation is that, for the Romans at any rate, Scythia was a vague geographical location (as indeed it *was*, since the Scythians were a nomad people): for them, the 'lofty-cliffed rocks … in the Scythian wastes' mentioned in the opening lines of the *Prometheus Bound* could well have equalled 'the Caucasus,' though the Aeschylean Prometheus, in prophesying Io's wanderings, sets 'the Caucasus itself, highest of mountains' (*PV* 719) at some distance from *his* lofty crag in Scythia. The alternative (as Sikes and Willson observe) is to believe that Aeschylus wished (for reasons unknown) to change the scene of the second play to the Caucasus and simply ignored the difficulties involved in the transference. (For arguments that the *Caucasian* setting is the original, pre-Aeschylean (pre-Greek, even) setting, see West *Theogony* pp 314–15 and references there given.)

13 The question whether Cicero is here (at *Tusc.* ii. 10.23–5) translating a passage of Aeschylus' *Prometheus Luomenos* directly or whether he is quoting a passage of Accius' *Prometheus* based on Aeschylus' *Luomenos* has long been debated. Cicero quotes the passage as from Aeschylus, but doubt has arisen on two scores: under the same Aeschylean rubric, Cicero has just previously quoted a passage which we know to be from Accius; moreover Nonius, a compiler and grammarian of the fourth century AD, quotes vv 14–15 of the Ciceronian quotation as from Accius. Majority opinion favours direct Ciceronian translation of Aeschylus: see especially M. Pohlenz in his Teubner edition of Cicero *Tusc. Disp.* (Stuttgart 1957); Fraenkel 'De novo Acii fragmenta,' and Murray (OCT, ad loc.), and most recently Jocelyn 'Greek Poetry in Cicero' (who doubts the existence of a *Prometheus* by Accius). Fraenkel's chief argument is that it was Cicero's normal practice to omit names of Roman poets quoted while citing names of Greek poets quoted, and adds that Nonius' error arose from misinterpreting the Ciceronian passage in question; Pohlenz' argument is that Cicero himself, a little later (at *Tusc.* ii. 10.26), makes the claim of having ornamented Latin discourse by translating many things from the Greeks.

Among scholars favouring Accius' authorship of the quotation in question, see (in we have part of an address by Prometheus to the Chorus of Titans, bemoaning his sufferings, both his enchainment on the mountain and the visitations of the eagle of Zeus who gnaws at his liver (every third day the eagle returns; between times, his liver grows in afresh). In this passage, also, Prometheus bemoans his inability to die and the long centuries of his sufferings.

The next five fragments (194–9) are apparently addressed by Prometheus to Herakles (who, along with Gê, Mother Earth, is wrongly listed in the ancient catalogue of characters as appearing in *Prometheus Bound*). In the first of these, Prometheus appears to be recounting some of his services to man (the gift of horses, asses, and bulls, to relieve men of toil), as in *Prometheus Bound*. In the next three fragments, Prometheus gives prophetic advice to Herakles about the latter's northern travels, including his visits to the hospitable Gabians and 'the well-ordered Scythians.' In the last of this group of fragments (fr 199) Prometheus, in giving Herakles directions about his western journey to the Hesperides (see Strabo iv.83, who provides fr 199), prophesies the difficulties which Herakles will experience (and overcome, with the help of Zeus) when he meets the army of Ligurians. (A supplementary account in Hyginus, also referring to, though not quoting, *Prometheus Unbound*,[14] gives the circumstances of this encounter: Herakles' passage through the territory of the Ligurians with the cattle wrested from Geryon.)

addition to those cited by Fraenkel in refutation) Stoessl *Die Trilogie des Aischylos* pp 131 ff, who argues, not very convincingly, that the passage is based (by Accius) on *PV* 1021 ff and that, moreover, its content is unsuited to the *Luomenos* because it repeats in places (eg, vv. 5–8) information already given in *Prometheus Bound*.

To the arguments favouring direct Ciceronian translation of Aeschylus here, one might add the further point (for which I am indebted to Professor Elaine Fantham) that the Latin verses provide several instances of unusual words which occur elsewhere in Cicero but not in the fragments of Accius (preserved chiefly by Nonius' quotation of Accius' rare words and forms), viz, *religare* (v 2), *horrisonus* (v 3), *dilaniare* (v 12), *clangor* (v 14), *inflatus* (v 16), *glomerare* (v 25). Of these, *horrisonus* (cf Cic. *Aratea* 13; Lucr. 5. 109), *dilaniare* (cf Cic. *Pro Milone* 33; Lucr. 3 539) and *clangor* (cf Cic. *Carmina*, fr 15, also of an eagle) occur first in Cicero or in Cicero and/or Lucretius. Most interesting in the context of the present discussion is the use of *clangor; clangere* occurs in Ennius and Accius but Accius has *crepitu clangente* (not *clangore*) at *Phiniadae* fr 571 K1.

14 The summary in Hyginus (*Poet. Astr.* ii.6−199aN) adds the interesting aetiological myth, comparable to *PV* 354–72, of the constellation of the kneeling Herakles, which Zeus created to commemorate the moment when his son was brought to his knees in his struggle with the Ligurians.

The next two fragments, though brief, are more central to the action of the play:

May Apollo direct my arrow aright! (fr 200)
This beloved son of a father hateful to me! (fr 201)

Plutarch, the authority for both these fragments, makes their context fairly clear. He tells us (*Mor.* 757E) that the first is spoken by Aeschylus' Herakles 'when he raises his bow against the bird' (the eagle of Zeus assailing Prometheus), and that the second is addressed by Aeschylus' Prometheus to Herakles when saved by him (*Pomp.* 1.1).

Three other pieces of ancient evidence (not all included in all the collections of evidence on the *Prometheus Unbound*)[15] should also be considered in pondering the possible ending of the play. Athenaeus (15. 674D = 202N) tells us 'that in the *Prometheus Unbound* Aeschylus says [men] wear the garland on their heads in honour of Prometheus in requital for [ἀντίποινα] his bondage.' In an earlier passage in Athenaeus (15. 672F: not included in Nauck's collection as there is no explicit reference to Aeschylus), we read that Prometheus consented to pay 'voluntary but painless compensation' to Zeus after Zeus released him from his chains. Hyginus (*Poet. Astr.* 2.15) cites the tradition that Prometheus wore the garland triumphantly since he had sinned but escaped from his punishment and adds that it is for this reason that men wear garlands in victories.

(An additional recently published piece of evidence concerning the garland of Prometheus has been discussed by Herington in his excellent treatment of the fragmentary information on the trilogy. This is an Apulian red-figured vase-painting of the fourth century BC in which, in addition to the figures of the fettered Prometheus, Herakles with the slain eagle, Apollo, and other, anonymous figures, the seated figure of Athena is seen holding a garland.)[16]

---

15 The first of these passages appears in Nauck's collection (fr 202: it is reproduced in Murray's OCT editions but not in the Loeb edition) and in Mette's collection (=M334); the second is not in Nauck but is in Mette (M334, again); the third in neither of these collections. All three appear in Scully and Herington's translated collection (=frr 15, 16, 17 in the order here discussed).
16 See Scully and Herington *The Prometheus Bound* appendix pp 100–1; for the publication of the vase-painting see Trendall and Webster *Illustrations of Greek Drama* p 61 and discussion *ad loc.*

4 The evidence considered

Still proceeding from the known to the unknown, we may now note a few obvious points about the content of the *Prometheus Unbound* in relation to the preceding play. One is the important development that the Titans, the former enemies of Zeus, have been freed. This is not an innovation, or at any rate not a complete innovation, on the part of Aeschylus, for an earlier passage in Pindar tells us of Kronos, the lord of the Titanic order of gods, ruling in the Islands of the Blessed, and another Pindaric passage states that Zeus freed the Titans.[17] Thus a major change has taken place, not necessarily in 'the nature of Zeus' (as some have argued) but at least in the power structure and in the political relations of the gods. Zeus is sufficiently firmly established in his rule that he can permit the coexistence (outside of Tartaros) of his former rivals for power; Prometheus, for his part, now addresses the Titans (against whom he had once conspired with Zeus) as sympathetic visitors in the role which once the sympathetic Okeanids had fulfilled. Secondly, the long quotation by Cicero shows us (if we can take the passage as representing at least the content of a speech from the lost *Prometheus Unbound*) a marked change in the morale of Prometheus. He repeats the account of his cruel impalement by Hephaistos at Zeus' bidding,[18] but it is the new tortures from the eagle of Zeus together with his utter hopelessness and helplessness (both stressed by the Chorus in the preceding play) which now cause him to long for death. In the preceding play, Prometheus has touched several times on his immortality: twice defiantly, as a source of invincibility against Zeus' punishment (*PV* 933 and 1050–3); once at least with resignation – though the release of death is not available, he hopes to find an end of woes in Zeus' fall from power (see *PV* 752–6). Now no such consola-

17 See Pindar *Ol.* II. 68–78 (date, c 476 BC) and *Pyth.* IV. 291–2, (date, c 462 BC), respectively. It is interesting that Pindar, in the latter passage, compares Zeus' freeing of the Titans to 'the changing of sails as, with the passage of time, the wind abates.' This certainly suggests (in a case not very dissimilar to the ultimate reconciliation with Prometheus) a change of policy, with changed circumstances, rather than a change in nature, on the part of Zeus.

18 As we have seen (above, n 13), this element of repetition has led Stoessl to suspect some kind of conflation between material belonging to the first and second plays. But this conclusion hardly seems necessary in a complaint to a different set of visitors, even if they may be presumed to know something of Prometheus' punishment already. So also, in the next fragment (194), Prometheus repeats one of his services to men (the provision of beasts of burden) in terms similar to *PV* 462 ff, but here Stoessl (*Die Trilogie des Aischylos* p 144) only remarks on the similarity as one of the many correspondences which he notes between the two plays.

tions are mentioned and it is 'by the will of Zeus,' not because of what is laid down independently of Zeus, that Prometheus is kept from the death he longs for (fr 193, lines 23–4).

Of the fragments concerning Prometheus' account of the travels of Herakles (frr 109–12) enough remains for us to observe the obvious parallel which such passages must have provided to those dealing with Io's wanderings in the first play. Three of the four passages are clearly prophetic, but we cannot tell whether the same technique of inter-weaving past and future adventures as in the case of Io was followed in the case of Herakles as well. Other correspondences and contrasts have also been suggested between the mythical material involving Io, Atlas, and Typho in the first play and the travels and adventures of Herakles retailed (or presumably retailed) in the second play, though some of these comparisons depend on 'Heraklean material' not actual-ly in the extant tradition on the *Prometheus Unbound*.[19] It is tempting, too, to see the adventures of Herakles the civilizer, and son of Zeus, as providing a more optimistic impression of the world and Zeus' govern-ance of it than do the sufferings of Io and Prometheus, but without knowledge of Aeschylus' actual treatment of the myth such inference must remain conjectural.[20] Again, in two of the four fragments of the play which are concerned with Herakles' wanderings, Herakles meets 'the most just and hospitable Gabians' (fr 196) and 'the well-ordered Scythians' (fr 198), but this contrast with some of the monsters that Io encounters may be due to the accident of survival: if Herakles' encounter with the man-hating Amazons, who treated Io well (*PV* 723–8), had been preserved, something of this imbalance would no doubt have been reduced. On this point, all we can say with some assurance is this: just as Herakles' wanderings in the northern and

19 Note especially George Thomson's comparison (*Prometheus Bound* introduction pp 26–7) of the allegedly Aeschylean descriptions of erupting Aetna at Strabo vi. 1.6 with the volcanic description of *PV* 351–72. If Thomson is right in believing this description as well as Strabo's brief quotation of Aeschylus (= fr 402, 'unassigned' by Nauck) to be drawn from the *Luomenos*, the ascription lends support to Lloyd-Jones' conjecture about *The Women of Aetna* as the third play of the trilogy (cf above, p 103 and n 8).

20 Cf George Thomson, ibid 37: 'Heracles under his father's guidance carried on the work of Prometheus, being the purifier of the earth.' However, Thomson's extension of such reconstructions into the third play (ibid 36–7) leads to considerably more subjective musings about the marriage of Herakles and Hebê as providing a lawful culmination to a thrice repeated mating theme in the trilogy. J.A.K. Thomson 'The Religious Background of the *Prometheus Vinctus*' allots a still more important role to Herakles in the trilogy as a whole: that of 'the young King,' the 'embodiment of *Nikê*' (Victory), who, instead of deposing the old King (as in the previous divine over-throws) is seated in glory, after his victories, by his father's side.

western extremes of the known world (as we can tell from the fragments preserved) balance Io's eastern and southern journeys, so too
we may expect other significant correspondences, contrasts, and ana-
logies to have appeared between Herakles' and Io's adventures and
Prometheus' respective comments on them. But in what, precisely,
these consisted, we cannot tell.

Fragments 200 and 201 (together with their contextual information
from Plutarch) provide us, albeit in somewhat murky fashion, with
some evidence concerning the fulfilment, in the second play, of Prometheus' prophecies about his liberation at vv 770–4 and 871–4 of
Prometheus Bound. The reference to the 'famous bowman' at 872 has
identified the liberator as Herakles and anticipates the use to which
Herakles is about to put the bow in fr 200. The precise dramatic context
of the second of these fragments (201) is, however, ambiguous, and
our choice between the two possibilities is crucial to our view of the
resolution of the play. 'This beloved son of a hated father': Plutarch
tells us (in a different work from that containing the preceding fragment) that Prometheus calls Herakles this 'when saved by him.' Now,
as we have seen, two passages in *Prometheus Bound* state clearly (before
there has been any mention of the eagle) that Herakles will free Prome-
theus from his bonds (770–2) and 'from these present woes' ($\pi\acute{o}\nu\omega\nu\ \acute{\epsilon}\kappa$
$\tau\hat{\omega}\nu\delta$, 872). In view of this and of the unqualified expression 'saved'
($\sigma\omega\theta\epsilon\acute{\iota}s$) used by Plutarch, the more immediately probable meaning of
the context 'when saved by Herakles' would appear to be 'when saved
from his bondage.' This context to a fragment implying continued enmity
between Prometheus and Zeus also appears to provide vindication of
that puzzling passage (*PV* 771–2) in which Prometheus tacitly accepts
Io's ingenuous implication that the one who frees Prometheus will do
so 'with Zeus unwilling' ($\acute{\alpha}\kappa o\nu\tau o s\ \Delta\iota\acute{o}s$, 771). According to this view of
the context of fr 201, then, any real reconciliation between Prometheus
and Zeus must take place *after* Prometheus has been freed.

This sequence of events is, however, difficult (though not quite
impossible) to reconcile with Prometheus' earlier prophecies at *PV*
172–7 and 187–92. There Zeus' expected agreement to the freeing and
compensation of Prometheus as the price of his own safety *might*,
perhaps, be regarded as an enforced and 'unwilling willingness,' but in
that case the validification of the descriptions 'mild of mood' (188) and
'eagerly coming into friendship's bonds' (191–2) would have to be
postponed until *after* the freeing of Prometheus and the saving of Zeus
had been completed. Yet the prophetic passages concerned give no
indication of such a separation of these events.

There is, however, another possible interpretation of Plutarch's contextual gloss. 'When saved by Herakles' could refer simply to Herakles' rescue of Prometheus from the eagle. In this case the deal between Prometheus and Zeus and the reconciliation between them could well occur *between* the shooting of the eagle (without the still-'hated' Zeus' orders) and the freeing of Prometheus from his bonds (which would still be done by Herakles) at Zeus' instruction. This interpretation would allow the reconciliation and mutual bonding (σπεύδων σπεύδοντι, 192) to take place, 'as advertised' in Prometheus' early prophetic passages, in conjunction with the saving of Zeus from his fatal mating and the freeing and compensation of Prometheus. This view of the sequence of events becomes almost compelling when we find that it tallies precisely with an account of the resolution of this mythical struggle given by Probus (a Roman scholar of the first century AD), though without any reference to Aeschylus:

> ... This vulture [as Probus calls the eagle sent by Zeus to devour Prometheus' vitals] Hercules slew, yet feared to free Prometheus lest he should offend his father. But later Prometheus warned Jove away from a mating, prophesying that from it there would be born one who was stronger than the gods themselves. Because of this good office, Jove freed him. Yet that he might not be without punishment [*ne tamen impunitus esset*], he gave him a garland and a ring to wear so that by [lit., 'in'] the ring the memory of the stone or iron [ie, of his enchainment to the rock] might be present and that in the garland the form of the chains might remain. (Probus, on Vergil *Ecl.* 6.42)

The only difficulties facing this second view of the context of fr 201 are Plutarch's unqualified expression σωθείς ('saved') and Prometheus' apparent acquiescence in Io's 'with Zeus unwilling' phrase (771–2). However, the latter difficulty depends merely on an argument from (Prometheus') silence, and even that silence can, perhaps, be explained by the fact that the eagle complication had not yet even been introduced at this point in *Prometheus Bound*: a correction of Io's half-truth at this point would be a gratuitous and confusing scruple not to be expected in what Io herself describes a moment later as a 'prophecy no longer clear to understand' (775). As for the slight imprecision of Plutarch's expression, 'when saved by him,' we should remember that Plutarch's *own* context for his quotation of the tag from Aeschylus' *Prometheus Luomenos* (he is comparing the feelings of the Roman people for Pompey – also a beloved son of a hated father – with Prometheus' feelings for Herakles) is hardly one in which the distinction with which *we* are interested would be of much concern.

On balance, then, the second view of the context of fr 201 seems the more probable, and we may tentatively conclude that Prometheus' revelation of the secret and the reconciliation of Prometheus and Zeus took place between the shooting of the eagle and the actual liberation of Prometheus from his bondage.[21] One further interesting feature of Probus' account (which has been helpful in reaching this conclusion) is that here too we find reference to 'the garland of Prometheus' which, as we have seen, did apparently appear in Aeschylus' version (see fr 202 = Athenaeus xv. 674D). In Probus, the garland and the ring are clearly regarded as token *punishment* of Prometheus, a reminder that Prometheus is still to be regarded as an offender, albeit one now restored to favour.

Concerning the actual delivery of the secret to Zeus and the final bargaining which may have preceded it, we have no further information in the fragments. Two independent pieces of information do, however, afford one possible clue. In our discussion of the mythical tradition, we have seen that according to Pindar (*Isthmian* viii.27 ff, where there is no question of Prometheus being privy to the matter), Themis herself warns Zeus and Poseidon of the danger of mating with Thetis. In *Prometheus Bound*, Themis and Gaia are described (209–10) as one and the same goddess, and Gaia (or Gê, as she is also called) must, as we have seen, have been a character in either the second or third play of the trilogy. This combination of circumstances, together with the fact that Prometheus owes his secret knowledge to Gaia, makes it reasonable to guess (as many commentators have done) that Gaia is in some way an intermediary between the two antagonists in the revelation of Prometheus' secret to Zeus.

One further condition of Prometheus' liberation as foretold by Hermes in the first play (*PV* 1026–9) has still to be fulfilled. This is the condition of the substitution: one of the gods is to appear as a 'successor to his labours' ($\delta\iota\acute{a}\delta o\chi o\varsigma$ ... $\pi\acute{o}\nu\omega\nu$) and is to be willing 'to go to

---

21 Unterberger *Der Gefesselte Prometheus des Aischylos* p 137 also raises this question but decides that the sequence ('revelation of the secret': 'freeing of Prometheus') no longer matters, since Prometheus' rebellion has now become objectless and Zeus is now ready to free Prometheus as he has his brother Titans. This sounds plausible, but I cannot quite accept it; too much has been made by Prometheus, in the earlier part of the first play, of the crucial importance of his knowledge of the secret for his own liberation and reconciliation with Zeus. Cf also Gagarin *Aeschylean Drama* p 135, who also warns us against forgetting 'that it is Prometheus – the rebel who is eventually saved by his knowledge – who must have been Aeschylus' primary interest.'

sunless Hades and the murky depths around Tartaros.' Though we have no ancient reference to the lost plays of the *Prometheus* trilogy in this connection, two passages in Apollodorus (II. 5.4 and, in less detail, II. 5.11) relate a legend in which this condition is actually fulfilled. Herakles had accidentally and fatally wounded the centaur Chiron, who wished to die but, being immortal, could not. Prometheus (or, according to the second passage, Herakles) offered Zeus Chiron in his place; Chiron then gave Herakles his immortality and so died.[22] There seems little doubt that this was the fulfilment in the Aeschylean trilogy of the anticipation provided in the first play. If our suggestion that the reconciliation might have occurred between the shooting of the eagle and the loosing of the bonds be sound, this arrangement with Chiron, to fulfil Zeus' conditions, would also have taken place during this interval.

That some form of reconciliation between Prometheus and Zeus took place (presumably at the end of the second play) cannot reasonably be doubted. Apart from any interpretative inferences of our own, which we may draw from other trilogies of Aeschylus or from what has preceded in this one, is there any evidence concerning the submission of one god to another in such a reconciliation? Prometheus has said (*PV* 175–7) that he will insist on both freedom from his bondage and compensation for his outrageous suffering as his price for saving Zeus. We know that he was freed, but we know too that formal replacement of a prisoner (Chiron) was exacted by Zeus. (It is significant that the first anticipation of this occurs in Hermes', not in Prometheus' prophetic statements.) The epithet *Purphoros* ('Firebearer') in the title of the (presumed) third play certainly suggests (from what we know of the cult significance of Prometheus *Purphoros* at Athens) that Prometheus was restored to honours perhaps higher than he had enjoyed before.[23]

22 For this explanation of the Apollodorus passages in connection with the *Prometheus* trilogy, see Robertson 'Prometheus and Chiron.' Lloyd-Jones, on the other hand (*The Justice of Zeus* p 97; cf also Grossmann *Promethie und Orestie* p 63, n 84), thinks that Apollodorus means simply 'that Chiron satisfied the condition laid down by Zeus by giving up his immortality so that Prometheus could be released.' But if one reads the two Apollodorus passages in conjunction, one finds that the first (in II. 5. 4), which is primarily concerned with *Chiron's* plight, emphasizes the exchange of immortality (Chiron's) for mortality (Herakles' – the only mortal of the three), so that Chiron may die, while the second passage (in II. 5. 11), which is primarily concerned with *Prometheus'* problem, emphasizes the exchange of Chiron for Prometheus. In both passages, Chiron dies, which is what he wants, but in the second it is clear that he has voluntarily become Zeus' victim in place of Prometheus.

23 See the evidence adduced by George Thomson, introduction 33–4, concerning the significance of the epithet *Purphoros* ('Fire-*Bearer*') in connection with Prometheus

Was there in this case too any equivalent compensation in Zeus' favour? Here the several references to the 'garland of Prometheus' (clearly attached to *Prometheus Unbound* by Athenaeus) are all-important. There is, to be sure, some ambiguity attaching to the significance of this garland. In the passage in which Athenaeus actually mentions *Prometheus Unbound* (15.674D-fr 202), we hear of it as worn by men 'in Prometheus' honour, in requital for his sufferings.' But from the earlier passage in Athenaeus (15.672F) it is quite clear that the garland was *originally* the symbol of submission, 'voluntary but painless compensation' to Zeus on Prometheus' part. (This is also clearly the case in the passage quoted earlier from Probus, on Vergil *Ecl.* 6. 42, though, as I have noted, there is no reference to Aeschylus' play in that passage.) Hyginus, on the other hand, (*Poet. Astr.* 2.15) emphasizes only the (secondary and later) honorific aspect of the garland as worn by both Prometheus and men when victorious. Indeed, the suggestion that Prometheus' triumph consists in having transgressed and got away with it seems to pervert the original significance of the garland entirely.

We may conclude then, simply on the evidence, that honour was preserved on both sides and even that for every necessary (and substantial!) concession to Prometheus, in return for services rendered, a compensatory symbol of submission (all-important in divine as in human politics) was rendered to Zeus.

5 Theoretical reconstructions of the trilogy

From the foregoing discussion of the fragmentary evidence concerning the Prometheus trilogy, it will be clear that any attempt at a systematic reconstruction of it must be quite theoretical in nature. (Lloyd-Jones' speculations, already discussed, concern mainly the third play of the trilogy and are different in kind from the theories based mainly on

(especially his references to Soph. *O. C.* 54–6 and schol. ad loc.) and concerning the torch festival called the *Prometheia* (Harpocration, *s. v.* λαμπάς). Any doubt concerning Harpocration as a late author (second century AD?) for reliable information about fifth-century BC festivals may be allayed in this instance by the corroboration supplied by fifth-century references to Prometheus as 'torch-bearer' in a ceremonial sense. (As has been mentioned earlier, above, chapter 2, n 7, belief in the inauguration of the Prometheia as the denouement of the trilogy renders its initial production at Sicily considerably less likely, unless one argues that the trilogy might have been *composed* with Athenian production in mind.)

Promethean material now to be considered.)[24] Most of these systematic reconstructions depend on 'elaborations' of the fragments by means of information from mythical or dramatic material drawn from other sources or on some form of patterning and amplification of the fragments on the basis of our knowledge of *Prometheus Bound*. Two examples (the reconstructions of George Thomson and J.A.K. Thomson, respectively) we have already considered briefly in connection with our discussion of the fragments themselves.[25] Another more detailed 'prospectus' for our trilogy is to be found in Friedrich Solmsen's imaginative if somewhat subjective exposition in accordance with the pattern which he believes all Aeschylean trilogies to have followed. This recurrent pattern supposes an Aeschylean extension and development of the Hesiodic sequence of divine overthrows with, in this case, 'The third thrower,' Zeus, gaining ultimate victory and an advance in wisdom through his own struggles and suffering.[26] A less imaginative and yet, in the end, equally 'theoretical' reconstruction is that of F. Stoessl.[27] This commentator begins (reasonably enough) by drawing inferences about the action of the second play from various prophetic passages in the first. (Thus, for example, from *PV* 167 ff we conclude that the second play will develop the stipulated threat to Zeus' power, while *PV* 257–8 indicate that the freedom of Prometheus will continue to depend on the will of Zeus.) However, even this procedure is fraught with pitfalls which Stoessl does not always see. Thus, while he rightly infers from Prometheus' prophecies at *PV* 940 ff a drastic change of circumstances in the second play, when Zeus' rule will be threatened, he tends to blame Zeus' imminent danger entirely on his intransigence in not freeing Prometheus and not to heed the signs, in the closing scenes of *Prometheus Bound*, of an increasing intransigence on the part of Prometheus as well. It is precisely on such points as these that the silences of the trilogy must make us hesitate before basing a reconstruction of the second play too confidently on an

---

24 For Lloyd-Jones' conjecture concerning *The Women of Aetna* and the conclusion of our trilogy, see above, p 103, and nn 8–9 of this chapter. As we have observed, the view that man must be taken into account (possibly, as Lloyd-Jones suggests, by Zeus' gift of justice to man) in the final settlement between Prometheus and Zeus need not depend exclusively on this conjecture. Cf Lloyd-Jones' agreement with Unterberger on this general consideration about Zeus' relations with man by the end of the trilogy in his review of her study (above, n 21) *CR* 20 (1970) 241–2.

25 See above, p 109 and n 20 of the present chapter.

26 Cf Solmsen *Hesiod and Aeschylus* part II, chapter 2, esp pp 146–77.

27 Stoessl *Die Trilogie des Aischylos* pp 125 ff.

interpretation of the first. However, it is in the second part of Stoessl's reconstruction that its most theoretical and subjective aspects appear. Here the critic insists on a structural relation between the first and second play of our trilogy, which he bases in part on an alleged counterpoise between each scene of the *Agamemnon* and *Choephori*, in part on his reconstruction of 'the Danaid trilogy' of Aeschylus, in part on his own special requirement of the *Prometheus Unbound*, namely that it should reverse, in each successive scene, the pattern of *Prometheus Bound*.[28] Both assumptions involved are, in my opinion, gratuitous; however, they result in some highly ingenious, if somewhat conjectural, recomposition of the lost *Luomenos* on the part of the critic.

One further reconstruction (among many others) of the missing plays of the *Prometheia* requires, since it involves a fresh interpretation of certain aspects of the whole trilogy, more detailed consideration here. Professor C.J. Herington, in the first part of his study of the problem,[29] sets it down as his major thesis that the traditional 'four elements' of nature (earth, air, fire, and water) play an integral part in the structure and meaning of each play and of the trilogy as a whole. In Prometheus' opening invocation (*PV* 88–90), Herington finds the four elements clearly indicated, with *aither* representing 'the pure upper atmosphere, which is a form of fire.' In the cataclysm at the end of the play, we find the elements in confusion (see *PV* 1082–8; cf 1043 ff), while Prometheus makes his final appeal, this time to but two of the elements, *Earth* and *Aither*.[30]

Herington believes that it can be shown that 'the elements ... marched in majestic sequence through the entire trilogy ...'[31] To complement the known intervention of Ocean in the first play and the probable intervention of Earth (along with the known Chorus of her Titan sons) in the second play, he argues for the intervention of *Aither*, in some form, in the third play, *Prometheus the Firebearer*. These interventions are also regarded as marking a progression from failure (on the part of Ocean) to partial and then finally complete success in the resolution of the conflict between Prometheus and Zeus over Prometheus' gift of fire to man.

Herington's scheme, though structurally neat and intellectually satisfying, finds little real support either in the expectations set up in

28 Ibid 129 ff.
29 C.J. Herington 'A Study in the *Prometheia*. Part I: The Elements in the Trilogy.'
30 Ibid pp 180–2.
31 Ibid p 182. For the discussion summarized in this paragraph, see pp 182–5 and, for guesses concerning the form of the final successful intervention, p 189.

Prometheus Bound or in the fragmentary evidence of the lost plays. In the first place, it is questionable whether the elements as invoked by Prometheus at the beginning and end of *Prometheus Bound* will quite bear the degree of dramatic personification with which Herington invests them.[32] Even in the case of Ocean, who *does* appear, it is hard to connect his arrival very closely with Prometheus' rhetorical though moving appeal to 'springs of rivers and unnumbered smiles of the waves of the sea ...', particularly as Prometheus' own reactions to Ocean's appearance (first of scornful surprise, 298, 330–1, then of dismissal) do little to encourage that connection. In the case of Earth, how successfully her 'universally accepted' intervention in the second play can be related to Prometheus' aforementioned appeals to the forces of Nature we can only guess, since we have no information at all on Earth's role in that play. But it is in the dramatic personification of Aither which Herington creates for the intervention in the third play that his ingenious theory runs into its greatest difficulties.

Ouranos, the only pre-Olympian cosmic deity not yet employed, is Herington's choice for this role.[33] To effect the necessary identification, Herington seeks to blur the distinction (admitted by this critic and well supported by usage) between *ouranos* as the vault of the heavens and *aither* as 'the fiery or airy stuff' of which it is made. In the case of non-scientific, poetic usages, where both terms are used in a somewhat vague locative sense (eg, for the location of the stars, *Ag*.6, *PV* 1049–50; the place of origin of divine laws, *O.T.* 866–7, or of blessings, *Eum.* 905), Herington has some success in this attempt. But the Empedoclean fragments which Herington cites (and which are essential to the 'scientific' influence he asserts) do not really substantiate his insistence on the interchangeability of *ouranos* and *aither* and certainly not in the sense of ethereal *fire*, which is vital to his argument. In only one fragment (Empedocles B22, line 2) of the four cited in this connection

32 Herington himself draws attention (ibid p 181, n 4; p 183, n 11) to other examples in Greek literature of appeals to Earth and *Ouranos* and particularly to Sun who is traditionally invoked as all-watcher, though remarking (p 183, n 11) on the unparalleled invocation to Earth and *Aither* together at *PV* 1091–3. That the invocation of the elements detected behind Prometheus' words at 88 ff is somehow different in significance from his invocation of the sun in the same passage is hard to accept, despite 'the clear syntactical separation of the sun from Prometheus' other witnesses' which Herington remarks (p 181, n 4). On the conventional nature of invocations to the elements, cf above, chapter 3, n 5, especially the reference to Barrett on *Hipp.* 601 (Barrett's list of 'elemental invocations' in tragedy includes one to *aither*, at Euripides' *Ion* 1445).
33 Herington 'The Elements in the Trilogy' pp 185–8.

(B22, B71, B98, B109) is *ouranos* mentioned, along with the other three elements, where (apart from metrical considerations) we might expect to find *aither*, and in *none* of these fragments is either *ouranos* or *aither* used to indicate the fiery element which, in each case, is represented by another entity.

The second part of Herington's reconstructive theorizing about the *Prometheia* consists of his development of an earlier, rather neglected suggestion that the final scenes of Aristophanes' *Birds* may parody elements in our trilogy and shed light on the two lost plays.[34] In *The Birds* (1494–1552), Prometheus, presented as the champion of men (1545) and the enemy of the gods (1547), advises Peisthetairos about a peace treaty by which he may get the best of Zeus and the other gods. The key elements in the proposed treaty terms are that Zeus should give back the sceptre to the Birds and should allow Peisthetairos to marry his (Zeus') girl, Basileia, who looks after not only the thunderbolts but also the virtues of good counsel ($\epsilon\dot{v}\beta ov\lambda\acute{\iota}\alpha$), lawfulness ($\epsilon\dot{v}\nu o\mu\acute{\iota}\alpha$), and self-control ($\sigma o\varphi\rho o\sigma\acute{v}\nu\eta$) (1534–40). The plan is successful, for the Birds hold the trump card in that they can, if peace is not made, cut off the gods from men's savoury offerings to them; Herakles and Poseidon are the two representatives of the Olympians, and the glutton demigod manages to prevail over Poseidon's suspicions (1605) that he (Herakles) wishes to deprive his father Zeus of his kingdom. The peace is completed and Peisthetairos returns in triumph, 'bringing ineffable blessings to the race of birds, blazing like a star or like the sun and shaking the very thunderbolt of Zeus.'[35]

The various items in these scenes which Herington notes as relatable, in one way or another, to known features of Aeschylus' *Prometheia* do tend to support the hypothesis that this trilogy provided the material for Aristophanes' parody of divine mythology. Such elements are the emphasis on Zeus' sceptre (compare *PV* 168–71, 761), the motif of the marriage fatal to Zeus, the appearance of Poseidon and Herakles, the hint of a filial plot against Zeus (Herington does not mention this), and, of course the whole idea of bringing the *tyrannical* ruler of the gods to terms by means of some special hold which his weaker adversary has over him. Parody will, of course, inevitably twist and manipulate features of the original, sometimes to suit the new situation, sometimes for comic effect, sometimes for both together.

34 Herington 'A Study in the *Prometheia*. Part II: *Birds* and *Prometheia*' esp pp 238 ff. (The suggestion which Herington develops is that of W.H. van de Sande Bakhuyzen *De Parodia in Comoediis Aristophanis* (Utrecht 1877) 89–101.)
35 Herington '*Birds* and *Prometheia*,' pp 239 ff; cf Aristophanes *Birds* 1706–1730.

Thus 'the marriage fatal to Zeus' now becomes (if the parody theory is sound) *Peisthetairos'* marriage (paradoxically, Zeus' continuing power depends on his *keeping* Basileia, which he fails to do). Herington would extend this sort of conversion into the more hypothetical features of the original trilogy as well:

> ... we would suggest that Aristophanes completed his play by borrowing the Aeschylean triumph, but substituting the comic hero for the original Prometheus, and further making him ... not merely the representative of Zeus but the successor of Zeus.[36]

How far does this parody hypothesis take us in the reconstruction of Aeschylus' trilogy and particularly of its finale? We must remember, first of all, that it *is* a hypothesis (however reasonable) and cannot be used as evidence about the lost plays; moreover, in view of the conversion element in parody, we can still only reconstruct, in places where we lack the original, possible or probable elements suitable to the conversion which we have. Secondly, the theory, even if sound, does not provide us with much of the content of the mysterious final play.

On the credit side, however, Herington's hypothesis does supply some support (not evidence) for certain reasonable guesses which we have already mentioned about the trilogy's development. Chief among these are the idea of the reconciliation between Zeus and Prometheus as involving some kind of practical, quasi-political deal, including perhaps some new civilizing gift to man (here Prometheus' securing of the civic virtues for the Birds' new state, 1539–40, is remarkably suggestive) and the belief that, as the grand finale, Prometheus himself is allowed to appear as *purphoros*, now officially bringing fire to man, just as in the parody Peisthetairos appears carrying the fire-bearing (*purphoros*, Birds 1749) thunderbolt of Zeus. It is, of course, part of the conversion, necessary to the new situation, that the Aristophanic Prometheus, let alone Peisthetairos, is still Zeus' enemy while by the finale of the *Prometheia* Prometheus and Zeus will have (as Prometheus has prophesied at the beginning of the *Prometheus Bound*) with mutual eagerness returned to friendship with one another (cf *PV* 191–2).

36 Herington '*Birds* and *Prometheia*,' p 242.

CHAPTER SIX

The Zeus problem
in *Prometheus Bound* and
the trilogy

The off-stage characterization of Zeus in *Prometheus Bound* and the
difficulties which many critics have found in harmonizing it both with
the eventual reconciliation of Zeus and Prometheus and with widely
held views on the Aeschylean conception of Zeus have for many years
been the subject most debated in connection with this play. There
already exist several bibliographical surveys listing various views and
positions which have been adopted by scholars on this problem.[1]
Hence it will suffice to indicate here the main lines of the discussion
and to limit detailed comment to one or two studies which have sought
to break through the critical deadlock by reassessing certain assumptions on which much of the argument has been based.

In general, earlier studies of the play have tended to side emphatically with Prometheus or with Zeus. Of these, the majority have dwelt
on the harshness and injustice of Zeus and have then sought to miti-
gate what has seemed to them an un-Aeschylean conception by improv-
ing the picture, in various ways, in reconstructions of lost plays of the
trilogy. Passing over the more extreme examples of 'Zeus-improvers'
and of 'Zeus-defenders'[2] we may note a few of the more eloquent and
sustained arguments for an evolving Zeus in the *Prometheus* trilogy.

1 See, among several summaries of scholarly opinion on this matter, Séchan *Le Mythe de
Prométhée* chapter 4, pp 49 ff; Lloyd-Jones 'Zeus in Aeschylus' pp 55–6; Burns 'The
Meaning of the *Prometheus Vinctus*.' (Burns provides an extensive bibliographical
survey; however, his categorical arrangement of the various positions taken on the
problems of the play occasionally obscures real differences of opinion among scholars
assigned to one or another of his 'groups.')
2 Among early examples of 'Zeus-improvers,' who regard the Zeus of the first play as
particularly in need of reform, see Case 'On *Prometheus Desmotes*, Lines 980–81,' and
the citation of nineteenth-century German scholars (eg Dissen and Caesar) there

L. Séchan, for example, suggests the *gradual* development of a more just and benevolent Zeus, the first sign of which he finds in the liberation of the Titans, now regarded as apologists for Zeus.[3] In support of the idea of an evolving divine nature, Séchan offers the comparisons of gods who grow (in mythology) from infants to adults, and of gods who have evolved from nature gods to divine personalities. Neither of these comparisons, however, really fits the present situation. The anthropomorphic conception of an infant god growing to maturity does not involve the sort of change from harsh tyrant to just and benevolent god which Séchan envisages for the Prometheus trilogy. On the other hand, the change from nature god to divine personality involves not the continuous development of a single divine being, affected by changing experiences, but the reflection of different conceptions of the gods in different periods of ancient civilization.

George Thomson combines his view of the amelioration of Zeus with his generally optimistic reconstruction of the trilogy, which we have already discussed.[4] As evidence of the new benevolence of Zeus, Thomson points (as does Séchan) to the freeing of the Titans and to Zeus' kindly purpose in sending Herakles to improve men's lot. It should be observed, however, that Zeus' intentions in this matter, if indeed they are involved at all, are in no way clear from the fragments. As we shall see from more balanced studies of Zeus in *Prometheus Bound*, Thomson's view of the vindictiveness of Zeus in the first play pays insufficient heed to the necessities of his newly won position and to the usual treatment afforded divine rebels by victorious gods. (Consider, for example, Prometheus' own complicity in the punishment of his fellow Titans, *PV* 219–21.) Moreover, the idea that Zeus must be taught moderation, that he cannot be a law unto himself,[5] is applicable more to human tyrants than to divine ones. (Where in Aeschylus is Zeus presented as wielding less *power* than in *Prometheus Bound*?) Finally, Thomson's summation:

– And the divine feud [between Zeus and Prometheus] was finally resolved

given; Todd 'The Character of Zeus in Aeschylus' *Prometheus Bound.*' (Scholars cited in the following three notes also tend to exaggerate the villainy of Zeus in *Prometheus Bound* in their arguments for 'evolutionary' theories in this trilogy.) Inevitably, there has also been a corresponding group of 'Zeus-defenders' in connection with our play. See, for example, the introductions to the editions of Wecklein (tr F.D. Allen) pp 7–13 and of Sikes and Willson xxiv ff.

3 Séchan *Le Mythe de Prométhée* pp 49–57.
4 Thomson, in the introduction to his edition, sections IV and V. Cf above, chapter 5, pp 109, 113 and nn 20, 23.
5 Cf Thomson section II, pp 1–12.

> by Athena, who completed her father's purpose by her patronage of the city
> which stands at the summit of human civilization –[6]

however splendid as a dramatic and cultural climax to the Prometheus
theme as seen by this critic, has, of course, no support whatever in the
fragmentary evidence concerning the lost parts of the trilogy.

Several other studies which share this evolutionary view of Zeus in
the *Prometheus* trilogy find in this alleged presentation the reflection
of the Greeks' own evolving ideas, though they differ somewhat in
their account of the factors involved. A general comment of Wilamowitz', to the effect that Aeschylus expounded through the inner development of divine individuals (*Personen*) what was in reality the
development of concepts of God (*Gottesbegriffs*) in the mind of the
people, gives an early expression of this approach.[7] It is given full
development in Solmsen's view of the evolution of Zeus in the
Prometheia.[8] Solmsen explains the Zeus of *Prometheus Bound* as Aeschylus' view of the Zeus of Hesiod's *Theogony*, a work which the dramatist
regarded as true of the initial features of Zeus' reign and of 'the spirit in
which Zeus had won and consolidated his reign.' Pointing to the great
progress in moral sensibility since the time of Hesiod, Solmsen heartily
supports the assumption, which he finds is shared by several critics,
'that the moral ideas which are absent in *Prometheus Bound* must have
been introduced in the sequel.'

Solmsen's attempt to distinguish the Zeus of *Prometheus Bound* as
'Hesiodic' and so quite different from Aeschylus' own conception has
been rightly challenged by G. Grossmann, who points out that Zeus'
'injustice' to Prometheus and man, as well as the element of blame
attaching to Zeus over Io's sufferings, actually begins with the Aeschylean treatment;[9] certainly we must agree, at least, that the Zeus of
Prometheus Bound is harsher than the Hesiodic Zeus. Grossmann,
however, tends to find the reflection of the mid-fifth-century *Zeitgeist*
more in the political than in the theological and moral implications of
Prometheus Bound. Thus *he* rather exaggerates the contrast between the
Zeus of Hesiod and the despotic Zeus of *Prometheus Bound* (there is,

---

6 Ibid section v, p 37.
7 Wilamowitz *Griechische Tragödien* II p 46, quoted with approval by Solmsen *Hesiod and Aeschylus* p 151.
8 Solmsen *Hesiod and Aeschylus* pp 124–57; for the specific points cited from Solmsen's discussion in the present paragraph, see pp 148 and 147, in that order, and Solmsen's references ad loc.
9 Grossmann *Promethie und Orestie* pp 71–3.

after all, nothing 'democratic' about the Zeus of Hesiod!) in the interest of the contemporary political application which he alleges. The Zeus of *Prometheus Bound*, he finds, agrees 'not with archaic myth but with contemporary civic conditions, the despot being the precise opposite of the ideal citizen-statesman.'[10] Grossmann and Solmsen share, however, the unwarranted assumption that, since it was a fifth-century conviction that *human* rulers required *sophrosyne* (moderation, self-discipline) to survive, Aeschylus must have applied this lesson to Zeus himself in the lost plays of the trilogy. Grossmann's emphasis, it is true, lies more exclusively on the necessity for the political change in Zeus, in accordance with fifth-century Greek political ideas;[11] Solmsen merely includes the political in his view of the gradual moral purification of Greek ideas of the gods: he even applies to Zeus' putative experience in the *Prometheia* Aeschylus' own ordinance, 'wisdom cometh by suffering,' which was applied to men at *Agamemnon* 176 ff.[12] Once again we may ask (as in our discussion of Thomson's similar views) whether we are entitled to apply Zeus' law for his subjects to the ruler of gods and men himself. Power may be limited by power, as we saw in the 'divine overthrows' of the *Theogony* and in the Aeschylean Prometheus' own account of the Titanomachy; it may even be forced to come to terms by real threats. But that Zeus' power should be responsive to the same ethical code as applies to man seems a contradiction in terms, since the imposition of that code depends on the chastisement of Zeus, the harsh *charis* which comes from those who sit aloft in power (*Agamemnon* 182–3).

We may well find reasons (as many scholars have)[13] for rejecting the idea that an individual god (and particularly the ruler of the gods) could be represented by Aeschylus as undergoing a specific change of the kind that Solmsen and others describe. What of the other and, on the face of it, more reasonable view of Wilamowitz (and applied to Zeus in the *Prometheia* by Solmsen) that developing gods merely reflect the changing views of men? Once again, as I implied in my discussion of Séchan, such a view seems useful only when we are explaining different conceptions of Zeus in different periods: it may explain, for example, the difference between the Zeus of Hesiod and the Zeus of Aeschylus or (possibly, though less probably) the different impression of Zeus given at the beginning and the end of a poet's career. But how

10 Ibid p 73.
11 Ibid p 78.
12 Solmsen *Hesiod and Aeschylus* p 164
13 See below, pp 124 ff and nn ad loc. in the present chapter.

this idea can be used to explain away the alleged change in Zeus (without, according to one critic, involving the evolution of Zeus) in the first and last plays of the same continuous trilogy is very hard to see.[14]

Many scholars who find the Zeus of *Prometheus Bound* incompatible with their idea of Zeus in Aeschylus have also resisted as inconsistent with Greek ideas of the gods the idea of an evolving Zeus who 'learns by suffering' or whose nature in some way changes through his experiences. Both these alleged difficulties were stressed by W. Schmid, whose solution to the problem was ultimately to deny Aeschylean authorship to *Prometheus Bound* and who questioned its authenticity on many counts: this extreme view, which has had and still has its supporters, should not perhaps be considered (at least not as a solution to the Zeus problem) unless all else fails.[15]

L.R. Farnell, who agrees with both Schmid's points about Zeus (that he is 'un-Aeschylean' in *Prometheus Bound* and that his character reformation would be conceptually unacceptable to the Greeks), adopts an uncompromising and (so far as I know) unique position with regard

14　Professor Herington tells us in 'Aeschylus: The Last Phase' p 400 that he has replaced the concept of 'an evolving Zeus' with that of 'an evolving Aeschylus.' This explanation may be acceptable when applied to the different representations of Zeus which Herington finds (ibid pp 387–403, passim) in different (early and late) Aeschylean productions, viz, the 'primitive' Zeus of the earlier plays, including *Persae* and *Septem*, contrasted with Zeus πανεργέτης, Zeus παναίτιος, of the *Suppliants* trilogy, the *Oresteia*, and (hypothetically) the end of the *Prometheia* (cf ibid pp 398–9 and, for the larger context of this distinction, pp 387–97). But Herington makes just as much of the difference between 'the archaic power-god' of the first play of the *Prometheus* trilogy and the reformed Zeus, Zeus the 'healer of the cleavage' (ibid p 398), of the final play. Since the new Zeus (Zeus under 'a new aspect') has come about (as Herington argues subsequently; see below) as the result of his experiences in the trilogy, it is difficult to see how this critic has in any way abandoned the idea of 'an evolving Zeus.' Indeed, that he has not done so becomes even clearer from his recent introduction to the play: see Scully and Herington *Aeschylus: Prometheus Bound* pp 17–18.

15　See Schmid *Untersuchungen zum Gefesselten Prometheus* pp 281 ff and *Geschichte der Gr. Lit.* I[3] pp 281 ff. Cf Albin Lesky, *Greek Tragedy*[2] tr H.A. Frankfort (London 1967) pp 88–9, who admits to considerable doubt about the Aeschylean authorship of the play; cf also Taplin 'The Title of *Prometheus Desmotes*,' who shares Lesky's doubts. (The question of the authorship of *Prometheus Bound* is not settled yet and perhaps never will be. It has been reopened recently by the major work by Mark Griffith *The Authenticity of Prometheus Bound*. However, the strongest arguments against authenticity are not those concerning the depiction of Zeus and his rule in this play. See below, appendix, pp 141 ff, where various arguments for and against Aeschylean authorship of our play are reviewed.)

to the problem.[16] He argues that the Zeus of *Prometheus Bound* and of
the trilogy must simply be accepted as an egregious exception, explicable only as 'the aberration of genius' carried away by a poetic desire to
celebrate the potter's god, even at the expense of the 'righteous and
benevolent' Zeus depicted elsewhere in Aeschylus and Greek literature. There is a refreshing honesty about Farnell's refusal to exploit the
silence of the missing plays by inventing easy explanations; nevertheless, he does little to explain the paradox with which his own view of
Zeus and Prometheus, individually, must leave him. He appears to
regard the work as primarily a celebration of Prometheus, to whom he
will allow no fault to be attributed; yet he admits that Prometheus must
give up the secret before his release without, as far as Farnell can
envisage, any apology or change of attitude on Zeus' part.[17]

On the other hand, H.D.F. Kitto's criticism of Farnell's and (in the
matter of the evolutionary view of Zeus) Schmid's position, shows a
like intransigence in another direction.[18] While Farnell insists on the
independence of the Prometheus trilogy from other views of Zeus,
even in Aeschylus, as a sort of poetic licence on Aeschylus' part, Kitto
insists just as vigorously on the autonomy of the poet in presenting an
evolving Zeus, whether or not this presentation agrees with prevailing
Greek ideas on the gods. For Kitto, 'the kernel of the trilogy' lies in 'the
slow coalition of power and intelligence ... typified in the reconciliation
of Prometheus and Zeus.'[19] If this view offends historians of Greek
religion, Kitto is not concerned: 'The *Prometheus* is a play and if you
treat it as a document in comparative religion it will not work.' The
statement has a certain appeal, as have all championings of 'literary'
over more pedantic arguments. But the question concerns not so much
'the primacy of literary criticism' (Kitto's phrase) as the necessity of
envisaging, from what the poet tells us in the first play, this radical
transformation of Zeus in the reconciliation or compromise (or both)
which we know must take place.

The objection to the evolutionary view of the treatment of Zeus in
the *Prometheus* trilogy has received much authoritative support; one
feels that defence of it in terms of the autonomy of the poet can (like
denials of the authenticity of *Prometheus Bound* which are based on the
Zeus problem) be entertained only if less drastic explanations of the
matter prove untenable. Recent discussions of the trilogy have tended

16 Farnell 'The Paradox of the *PV*.'
17 Ibid pp 47–8.
18 Kitto 'The *Prometheus*' esp *ad fin*. (Cf above, chapter 3 n 15.)
19 Ibid p 19; the following two quotations are from pp 19 and 20.

to abandon the evolutionary theory (though there have been some notable exceptions)[20] in favour of the explanation that the poet has chosen to show different aspects of Zeus in accordance with the different themes and varying dramatic contexts in which that ubiquitous but always off-stage (and so constantly elusive) force is deployed. This subtler approach has, on the whole, proved more satisfactory, although it, too, has been subjected to certain inconsistencies and over-ingenious elaborations. In Herington's comments on Zeus in the trilogy, for example, we have seen that the 'new aspect' of Zeus allegedly appearing in the third play amounts really to a new conception of the god whose metamorphosis (in this instance at least) seemed to have been caused by his experiences throughout the course of the trilogy.[21] On the other hand, in Leon Golden's more elaborate description of the different aspects of Zeus in Aeschylus,[22] to which we must now turn, some may find those aspects too incompatible for accommodation within a single divine figure.

Golden posits what at first appear to be 'two Zeuses' in Aeschylus: the Zeus of the *Suppliants* who, as the fair and just protector of the innocent, he calls 'the Zeus of the *Polis*' and the Zeus of the *Prometheus Bound* whom he calls 'the Zeus of Nature,' in that he symbolizes the uncontrolled destructive powers in the world. In the *Prometheia*, it is alleged, the gap between the two is bridged by the necessity of Zeus' yielding (in order to maintain his rule) to Prometheus, who is described as the symbol of man's cultural and intellectual achievement. Thus man, the embodiment of Promethean intelligence and knowledge, is said to affect (at least indirectly) the outcome of the struggle between 'the just Zeus' and 'the savage Zeus.'

Intellectually, there is a certain neatness to Golden's thesis, but there are many difficulties in the way of ready acceptance. In the first place, it is a large assumption to state that Aeschylus' Zeus *must* be derived from his daily experiences of life (might not traditional myth have affected it as well?) and that, therefore, Aeschylus' Zeus stands (somewhat vaguely) for all the ultimate forces in society and nature (a question-begging description which dispenses too easily with the awkward contradictions between the two Zeuses). Secondly, even if we

20 See, for example, Yu 'New Gods and the Older Order' esp pp 19–21; Wartelle 'La Pensée théologique d'Eschyle' esp 568, 573–4, 577, and Grossmann *Promethie und Orestie* (cf above, pp 122–3 and nn 10 and 11).
21 Thus the 'evolutionary theory' about Zeus in the trilogy returns through the back door, as it were. Cf above, n 14.
22 Golden *In Praise of Prometheus* pp 107–12.

recognize this as a theoretical possibility, it is hard to imagine a theatre audience, familiar with the Zeus of traditional mythology, readily accepting the embodiment of these two opposed abstractions in a single god. Thirdly, there is no real basis for describing the Zeus of *Prometheus Bound* as the 'Zeus of Nature' simply because he punishes Prometheus by a natural cataclysm; moreover, as we have seen, Zeus is not *merely* 'savage, cruel and arbitrary'[23] in *Prometheus Bound*: he has accepted Promethean guile to achieve his present status and even the Chorus admit that his plans for the universe involve a certain *harmonia* (*PV* 551), a word implying some kind of orderly government. Finally, it is never made clear just how 'the Zeus of the *Polis*' and 'the Zeus of Nature' do come together in the one god at the end of the *Prometheia*.

Golden sets up his two Zeus polarities which he believes to be resolved at the end of the *Prometheia* by reference only to *The Suppliants* and *Prometheus Bound*. The Zeus of *Agamemnon* (and of the *Oresteia* in general) he appears to regard as the Zeus of the happy resolution, the amalgam of the two Zeuses, which, he hypothesizes, comes at the end of the *Prometheia*.[24] Here again Golden seems to me to overestimate the role of man and of Prometheus, whom he regards as a symbol of human intelligence, particularly when he says in connection with the founding of the Areopagus in *Eumenides*:

> It is a solution, also, that is in harmony with the action of the *Prometheus Bound* where it is predicted that Zeus, who symbolizes the totality of power in the universe, must eventually yield to Prometheus who represents the forces of human intellect and civilization. The symbolism of that play indicates that man, the recipient of Prometheus' civilizing gifts, can use them to influence the way in which the protective and destructive forces represented by Zeus affect his life.[25]

But, as we have seen in our study of *Prometheus Bound*, Prometheus does not, in fact, complete the civilization of man. In the solemn catalogue of the arts which Prometheus bestows there is no mention of the civic arts by which the *polis* will be made possible.

In this welter of conflicting views and ever subtler refinements of the

23 Ibid p 108.
24 Cf ibid p 113: 'The conception of Zeus which we have observed in our analysis of the *Suppliants* and the *Prometheus Bound* is given its most profound and clearest formulation in the *Agamemnon*.' Golden goes on to speak of the theology of the *Agamemnon* as 'the climactic statement of the Aeschylean view of Zeus' and as 'a harmonizing line of evidence' which supports his foregoing conclusions about the *Prometheia*.
25 Ibid p 125.

problem of Zeus in *Prometheus Bound* and its sequel, the studies of Hugh Lloyd-Jones and of Karl Reinhardt have been valuable in very different ways.[26] Lloyd-Jones' refutation, up to a point a convincing one, of the alleged incompatibility of the 'Zeus-of-the-*Prometheus*' with Zeus elsewhere in Aeschylus, would allow us to look for a basis of reconciliation between Prometheus and Zeus, at the end of the trilogy, which need not involve a conversion of Zeus in accordance with some *a priori* conception of what he ought to become. Reinhardt's observations, on the other hand, will be found most useful in providing a philosophic frame of meaning to the practical solution of the Zeus-Prometheus problem to which Lloyd-Jones' argument points the way.

Against the argument for the evolution of Zeus' nature in the sequel to *Prometheus Bound*, Lloyd-Jones repeats the arguments advanced by Schmid, Farnell, and Reinhardt to the effect that there is no evidence elsewhere in Greek literature to support such a conception. The alleged transformation of the Furies in Aeschylus' *Eumenides*, which is most frequently cited as an exception in this matter, Lloyd-Jones dismisses (with Farnell) as a change in their immediate design of avenging upon Athens the acquittal of Orestes, rather than a change in their essential nature. The Erinyes, he argues, simply 'do a deal' with Athena, and in consequence their attitude changes. Thus the Furies do not give up their former prerogatives: '... nowhere does the text say that the Erinyes are handing over their functions to the Areopagus. They nowhere promise to give up their present pursuits.'[27] But surely, in simple fact, the action of the play tells us this: if the Furies do not say they are allowing the curtailment of their functions, it is because they actually do so, in turning over to Athena the business of applying justice to Orestes (*Eum.* 431–5), then in accepting the Areopagus (which certainly curtails their activity), and finally, after persuasion and bribery, in acquiescing benevolently in the judgment of acquittal for Orestes. If they did not at first regard this acquittal as a curtailment

26 Lloyd-Jones 'Zeus in Aeschylus'; cf also his *The Justice of Zeus* 95–103; Reinhardt *Aischylos als Regisseur und Theolog* pp 58 ff, 64 ff, esp pp 68–75.

27 Lloyd-Jones 'Zeus in Aeschylus' pp 64–7; cf pp 56–7. Similar arguments have been advanced recently by Gagarin *Aeschylean Drama* pp 71–5, though Gagarin is more concerned with arguing that no change from the Furies' idea of justice is involved in the founding of the Areopagus; indeed, this institution is regarded by Gagarin as 'an instrument for assisting the Furies in their role' (p 74). These are debatable points (one might begin by referring to Athena's gentle rebuke to the Furies' view of justice and the concessions which follow, *Eum.* 430 ff) but the central point at issue is somewhat different from that of our discussion here.

of their powers, of what *they* had intended to do to Orestes, why do they make such a fuss about it from vv 778 to 879?[28]

Now, it is true, as Lloyd-Jones says, that the Erinyes 'do a deal' and (as M. Gagarin has also argued recently) that what they abandon specifically in response to Athena's bribes and threats is their design of avenging upon Athens the acquittal of Orestes. However, I would argue that in their previous restraint (involving, as I have indicated with regard to vv 431–45, the curtailment of their prerogatives) and in the form which their final acquiescence takes (this goes far beyond the immediate Orestes situation: showering blessings, they become benevolent as well as disciplinary guardians of the state), the Erinyes do, in effect, change their nature – for in the case of these gods their activities determine in a very special way their nature. It is true also that in their reconciliation with Athena, some of their old awesome functions are retained (see vv 927–37), despite the continuing limitation involved by the functioning of the Areopagus. To these functions, new prerogatives and functions (895, 901–15, 956 ff, 990 ff), many of them benign, are added; it is part of Aeschylus' skill and subtle feeling for the original nature of the Erinyes that, so far as possible, he lets this new benignity appear as the other side of the coin of their avenging of unnatural crimes. (See, for example, vv 956 ff, 976 ff.)

In all this discussion of the Erinyes as treated in *Eumenides*, we must be careful to decide what can be said that is of relevance to the problem of Zeus in *Prometheus Bound* and its sequel. The discussion has shown, I think, that Greek gods can change, at least in Aeschylus. But here two points of importance must also be noted. The first is Reinhardt's observation, in *his* rebuttal of the idea of an evolutionary presentation of Zeus in the *Prometheus* trilogy, that the Erinyes in Aeschylus do not evolve or develop but simply *change* from curse to blessing when influenced by a third element, the spirit of Athena.[29] Thus they present no substantial parallel for the kind of $\pi\acute{\alpha}\theta\epsilon\iota\ \mu\acute{\alpha}\theta\circ\varsigma$ development which, as we have seen, some critics have envisioned for the Zeus of the *Prometheus* trilogy. Secondly, the Erinyes are in some ways a special case, deities whose reality seems to reside almost exclusively in their social function, so that any dramatic representation of a change in (at least) the methods of retributive justice must involve a change in these

28 'O you younger gods, you have ridden down the ancient laws and snatched them from my hands' (*Eum.* 778–9, repeated at 808–9); 'That I should suffer these things … !' (*Eum.* 837 and 870).

29 Reinhardt *Aischylos als Regisseur und Theolog* pp 71–2.

primordial divine personalities. While the changed aspect of the Furies at the end of Aeschylus' *Eumenides* may give some limited support to the idea of a Zeus at the end of the *Prometheus* trilogy very different from the Zeus of the beginning, we cannot apply the analogy too closely.

What, then, of the view that the Zeus of *Prometheus Bound* must change, whatever the traditional Greek view of their gods, because he is so 'un-Aeschylean' and because such a god could never become reconciled with Prometheus, champion of men? Lloyd-Jones tackles the first part of this problem by assailing arguments for the advance in ethical thought, the theological refinement amounting almost to a Zeus religion, which many commentators find in the other plays of Aeschylus. Here I think (in company with several other critics)[30] that Lloyd-Jones overstates his case. However, he does succeed in isolating the question most relevant to our problem: namely, are the differences in dramatic context sufficient (without recourse to other explanations) to explain the differences between the off-stage tyrant of *Prometheus Bound* and the Zeus of the other passages which he examines?

In the case of *The Suppliants* (the play which, for practical dramatic reasons, celebrates Zeus beyond all others) Lloyd-Jones examines particularly those passages which stress Zeus' power and alleged defence of justice among men. The impression of an all-powerful Zeus which we obtain from *Suppl.* 86–103, 590–9, 816, 1048–9 (as also from *Sept.* 255, *Ag.* 1485, *Eum.* 918) is not, in his view, contradicted by the major limitation of Zeus' power which we find in *Prometheus Bound*, namely, that Zeus cannot escape fate. 'Zeus' omnipotence,' Lloyd-Jones reminds us, 'is limited and so is different from the kind of omnipotence that is familiar to modern thinking.' (One might also argue that once Zeus has survived the 'fatal' limitation of the marriage threat, there seems no need to speak elsewhere of Fate's limitation of Zeus.)[31]

With regard to the *Suppliants'* passages dealing with Zeus and Justice (eg, *Suppl.* 143, 403, 307; cf also *Choeph.* 948 and the various passages in the *Septem* where Zeus and Justice are alleged to be on the

30 Cf, among others, Golden *In Praise of Prometheus* pp 114–26; Hammond 'Personal Freedom and its Limitations in the *Oresteia*'; Lesky 'Decision and Responsibility in the Tragedy of Aeschylus.'
31 The other limitation of Zeus' power in the *Prometheus Bound* which Lloyd-Jones mentions (p 66) is his inability to kill Prometheus. Here one readily agrees with the critic that this 'limitation' would hardly contradict the Greeks' idea of Zeus' omnipotence; immortality was an essential part of their conception of the gods, and one would hardly expect one of Zeus' attributes to contradict their belief about the gods in general.

side of the defenders), Lloyd-Jones argues convincingly that the ethical aspect of Zeus need be no more advanced than in such Hesiodic passages as *Erga* 252 ff, 274 ff. What advances there may seem to be, can, I think, be regarded more as a matter of degree and emphasis, and here the dramatic context, particularly in the case of the Suppliant Maidens' pleas, can account for a good deal of that increased emphasis.

The situation is somewhat different with regard to passages concerning Zeus and justice (and other ethical values) in the *Oresteia*. With regard to the so-called 'Hymn to Zeus,' *Ag.* 176–82, and with regard to Athena's founding of the Areopagus in the *Eumenides* (to take but two of the more obvious examples), a case can be, and has been, made for a rather more elaborate conception of the justice of Zeus than Lloyd-Jones will allow.[32] But even if we accept Zeus' concern for justice among men, and for its evolution through tragic suffering in the *Oresteia*, we may still ask ourselves how closely this impression of Zeus need be applied, while still avoiding inconsistency, to Zeus in the very different circumstances of *Prometheus Bound*. Lloyd-Jones expresses both aspects of the question with characteristic bluntness:

> The gods by their laws encourage righteousness among men. [This may be said to encompass the justice of Zeus in the other extant plays of Aeschylus, even if it be more advanced than Lloyd-Jones allows.] But they themselves are not obliged to obey those laws ...

and:

> There is no reason why a god ... should not be portrayed ... as acting ruthlessly, particularly since in this instance [ie, in *Prometheus Bound*] Zeus was defending his own supremacy against a challenge ... Prometheus is a personal enemy, who has defied Zeus' authority; why should Zeus show him mercy, any more than he showed mercy to any other of his defeated rivals?[33]

Now there is no doubt that the statement at the end of the first quotation does describe what we see in *Prometheus Bound*: Zeus *is*

32 This is, of course, a major critical question with a bibliography (including a further article of Lloyd-Jones, 'The Guilt of Agamemnon') far too extensive for full reference here. See, in addition to the articles referred to above (n 30), Dodds 'Morals and Politics in the *Oresteia*' (esp p 31, where Dodds specifically relates Zeus' lesson of πάθει μάθος to 'those Athenians at the end of the third play σωφρονοῦντες ἐν χρόνῳ ...'); Lebeck *The Oresteia* pp 25–8.
33 'Zeus in Aeschylus,' p 66.

governing according to no fixed pattern (ἀθέτως, 150), by his own private laws (ἰδίοις νόμοις, 403), as the Chorus say. Furthermore, I believe (though not all readers will agree) that the second quotation provides a reasonable explanation (though not necessarily justification) of Zeus' extreme harshness to Prometheus. Doing good to one's (political) friends and evil, extreme evil, to one's (political) enemies is quite consistent with the climate of the preceding divine power struggles, in which Prometheus himself has played his part on the same terms. (Indeed, at least a part of Prometheus' indignation with Zeus is that he is not, after all that he has done for Zeus, being treated as a *friend*, whereas for Zeus, Prometheus' challenge to his authority over the issue of mankind has changed Prometheus' status to that of enemy.) Thus Lloyd-Jones' account of the matter shows us a Zeus in *Prometheus Bound* who is at least credible and not in open contradiction with the Zeus of the other extant plays of Aeschylus, since the 'new' characteristics which Zeus shows here are ones which would not be occasioned by the circumstances of the other plays. But what Lloyd-Jones does not, perhaps, consider sufficiently is whether the Zeus revealed in these unusual circumstances is presented as acceptable or whether, unlike all other presentations of him in extant Aeschylus, he is shown in such an unsympathetic light that a change of attitude on Zeus' part (not only to Prometheus but also to his whole rule over gods and men) must clearly take place before Prometheus (or even the poet and the audience) can come to terms with him. Here it seems to me that the indications which the poet gives the audience are unmistakable. First, the cruel and arbitrary nature of Zeus' tyranny (witness the pejorative terms applied to it by Hephaistos and by the Chorus and the harsh characterizations of the minions Kratos and Hermes) are clearly presented in the most unsympathetic light. Secondly, there is the sympathetic presentation of Prometheus both as the rational element which Zeus needed to establish his new rule and as the philanthropic element without which man is doomed. In any reconciliation between Zeus and Prometheus, these Promethean qualities must again be exploited: they may not require a change in Zeus' nature, but they will assuredly require a change in his manner of ruling and his attitude toward his subjects.

Nevertheless, though we may look forward to some such ideal conclusion of the trilogy, the indications are that the changes necessary for that solution to take place were presented, dramatically, in fairly practical political terms. Ultimately, the reconciliation and the new order of things (for gods and men) which may have issued from it may have

transcended these practical political manoeuvres, but it seems probable that (as in the case of the brilliant transformation scene at the end
of the *Eumenides*) a certain element of political bargaining was an
essential means to that achievement. (Emphasis on this element, even
if too exclusive, is, perhaps, the most useful feature of Lloyd-Jones'
hard-headed treatment of the thematic development of both these
trilogies.) Since I have argued throughout this study for the importance
of divine politics as a key to understanding at least the mechanics of
this trilogy (in so far as we can understand it from the limited evidence), I conclude this discussion of the Zeus-problem in the
Prometheia with a brief review of the political indications relevant to it.

   In this connection, no single passage in the extant play of our
trilogy, or in the fragments of the *Prometheus Unbound*, is so helpful to
our guesses about the nature of the Zeus-Prometheus reconciliation as
the long passage (199–241) in which Prometheus tells us of the power
struggle between Zeus and the Titans, of his own role in that struggle
and its results (cf also vv 439–40), and of his fall from favour. From that
passage we have seen that past changes in the government of the
universe and reversals (good and bad) in the fortunes of the gods have
come about by such means as changes in alliances and special prophetic knowledge as to what sort of course would prove victorious. These
passages are also most instructive about what does change the attitudes and policies of the gods toward one another. Before we insist that
a prior change in the nature of Zeus is necessary for any reconciliation
between Prometheus and Zeus, we should ask ourselves whether a
change in the nature of Prometheus was necessary before Prometheus
himself, due to circumstances (Gaia's prophecy and the Titans' repudiation of it), changed his allegiance to side with Zeus. Before we
insist on the impossibility of the Zeus-of-*Prometheus Bound* being reconciled with Prometheus, later in the trilogy, we should remind ourselves
that Prometheus himself had previously helped set up and organize (cf
PV 439–40) the new regime of Zeus which he so execrates in *Prometheus
Bound*.[34] Yet no one would argue that this change of attitude on

34 Herington makes this point, introduction pp 14–15. Cf also Podlecki 'Reciprocity in
   the *Prometheus Bound*' (also cited by Herington in this connection), who makes the
   important point that the various unpleasant characteristics attributed to Zeus are also
   attributed to Prometheus, in one passage or another, and not always by unsympathetic witnesses. Herington wonders whether Zeus and Prometheus might eventually
   be brought together by the mutual attraction of the good qualities in both their
   characters. I think it more likely that necessity, the politics of survival (or, in Prometheus' case, of liberation), as Prometheus' own prophecies have suggested, dictated
   the reconciliation.

Prometheus' part involves a change in his nature. Now it is true that other hints about Zeus' activities subsequent in time to the action of *Prometheus Bound* do indicate substantial changes in his treatment of a wide variety of his subjects. There is the gentle delivery of Io, prophesied by Prometheus himself (*PV* 848 ff), and the apparent release of the Titans (*Luomenos*, frr 190–3); even the beneficent Labours of Herakles, though we cannot be sure of Zeus' role here, may be thought of as carrying on Prometheus' own civilizing mission for mankind. All of this, it may be argued, augurs well for Zeus' future reconciliation with Prometheus. Nevertheless, as Lloyd-Jones has pointed out, Zeus has not reformed sufficiently to release Prometheus except for the specific reason of self-preservation, and all the indications of the first play are that, as far as his treatment of allies and adversaries is concerned, political circumstances rather than changes in temperament dictate its vagaries. Thus Prometheus speaks of his own mistreatment as due to a tyrant's typical mistrust of friends (224–5) and warns Okeanos of the danger of trying to soften the tyrant's heart except 'at the right moment' in the future (379–80). So, too, we have interpreted in political terms the constant references in *Prometheus Bound* to the *newness* of Zeus' rule which Hephaistos (35) and the Chorus (149–50) give as explanations of its harshness. (That even the gods can change their *ways* (τρόποι) is clear from Okeanos' advice to Prometheus at vv 309–10.) As opposed to various commentators who have taken this as further evidence for the evolutionary view of Zeus in the trilogy,[35] Reinhardt has argued that 'new' and 'young' in connection with Zeus' tyranny refer not to Zeus' age but to the newness of his rule over the 'old' Powers, not to potential growth and maturity on the part of Zeus himself but to the ways of power which new tyrannies show in politics.[36]

That harmony would, in the end, be established between Zeus and Prometheus we have known from Prometheus' first clear prophecies (*PV* 168 ff, 187 ff) before passionate defiance, occasioned by Io's visit, obscured his vision and prolonged his agony.[37] That Prometheus'

35 See, for example, Todd 'The Character of Zeus' pp 62–3; Thomson introduction, p 11, among the many 'evolutionists' who so interpret the references to the newness of Zeus' rule in the *Prometheus Bound*.

36 Reinhardt *Aischylos* p 69. (The references in the play to the *newness* of Zeus' rule, of his ways, and of his fellow Olympians are to be found at vv 96, 149, 309–10, 389, 403, 439, 942, 955, 960.)

37 Cf Grossmann *Promethie und Orestie* p 74, who makes much of 'trilogy anticipations' of this kind in Aeschylus and compares *Suppl.* 1034 as a possible anticipation of resolution or reconciliation of another kind later in that trilogy.

expression εἰς ἀρθμὸν ... καὶ φιλότητα (*PV* 191: 'to cordial bonds and general amity'; the words have a formal ring) looks to a political reconciliation is also clear, since it is only in political terms that Prometheus deals with Zeus at all. And what little we can glean of the *conditions* of reconciliation (the substitute prisoner, Chiron; Prometheus' wearing of the garland chain) has also indicated a political compromise in which the status of the ruling god has been maintained.

The most spectacular effects of the reconciliation on the trilogy's action are (if we accept the sketchy impression suggested of the third play) the triumphant return of Prometheus as official firebearer to men, with Zeus' blessing and, possibly, the establishment of the torch race in his honour. Can we go further and suggest some contribution to Zeus and his rule by Prometheus with his special quality? The union of Promethean knowledge with Zeus' power has long been a favourite conception of those critics arguing for the transformation, or at least the moral regeneration, of Zeus at the end of the trilogy. Reinhardt is one of the few critics who have retained something of this without espousing the theory of an evolving Zeus. Reinhardt views the struggle with which the trilogy is concerned as beginning with a 'falling asunder' (*Entzweiung*) or separation in the essence of the divine, in which each part is then driven to an extreme: the complete separation of 'the Power element' (= 'the Olympian element') from 'Spirit and Resistance' (*Geist und Widerstand* = 'the Titanic element') results in the increasing cruelty of the Olympian element toward men and earth.[38] Though Reinhardt polarizes Olympian omnipotence (*Allmacht*) and powerless Titanic knowledge or awareness (*Bewusstein*) as two divine elements in opposition (each implying and completing the other; neither able to oust the other), their coming together in the reconciliation of Prometheus and Zeus does not, for Reinhardt, imply a development in the nature of Zeus. We have seen that for Reinhardt the polarization is itself a feature of the original separation in the divine essence; earlier, Reinhardt has reminded us that the 'fixed' gods of Hesiod are foreign to the Aeschylean conception and that 'a higher and secret order lies hidden behind the divine order which is pushed into

38 Reinhardt *Aischylos* p 74. For the completion of this sequence of thought, including an indication of how the opposition described is reflected in man's condition, see pp 74–5. Note Reinhardt's powerful description of Prometheus in this connection: 'To the question, "What is Prometheus?" I would answer, "An *aition* [ie, an essential 'cause'] of the relation between man and god, a cause, to be sure, of Aeschylean proportions"' (p 75). For a simpler treatment of the Knowledge vs Force view of the Prometheus-Zeus struggle, but one which treats the theme in political rather than in theological terms, see also David Grene '*Prometheus Bound*.'

visibility.'[39] Thus the reconciliation of Zeus with Prometheus (here representing 'powerless Titanic knowledge') would appear to mean that the cruel persecuting aspect of Zeus, brought into play in the struggle with the adversary, would now cease to exist (or at least cease to be manifest) and that the original divine order comprising both power and knowledge would operate instead.

Subtle and profound though Reinhardt's exposition is, one feels that it expresses insights too individual and, at the same time, too dependent on modern philosophic ideas to stand as an explanation of Aeschylus' own meanings.[40] However, this difficulty applies more to the expression than to the core of Reinhardt's interpretation. That core, if I have read it right, insists that Prometheus, in his reconciliation with Zeus, brings nothing to Zeus which was not, in some sense, there already. Other critics to whom we have referred have also suggested that Zeus appears in different aspects in different plays.[41] Though one may quarrel with the details of their exposition, that much is certainly true. It is here that Lloyd-Jones' reminder that the Zeus of this play is in a situation very different from elsewhere in the extant plays is particularly relevant: here, Zeus' insistence (elsewhere so prominent) on justice *among men* is irrelevant to the theme and plot; here, too, the trilogy begins, at least, with the political morality of divine power struggles largely inherited from the mythological tradition.

It is for this reason that one prefers to envision the actual reconciliation between Zeus and Prometheus in a practical and political light, just as our earlier study of Aeschylus' treatment, in *Prometheus Bound*, of earlier struggles among the gods has encouraged us to do. Long before, prophetic knowledge from Gaia and Promethean intelligence in the form of guile have helped Zeus in his victory over the Titans and in the establishment of his new regime. Now Prometheus' prophetic knowledge, again from Gaia, again makes Prometheus a necessary ally. Changed circumstances, for both antagonists, and the resultant changing attitudes at last make reconciliation possible, and Prometheus, as he has prophesied, is able to extract his freedom and new honours (including, perhaps, 'official' recognition of his gift of fire to

39 Reinhardt *Aischylos* p 70: 'Eine höhere und geheime Ordnung wird verdeckt von einer in die Sichtbarkeit gerückten.'
40 Colleagues better versed in these matters than I have commented on the overtones of German idealist philosophy in the form of Reinhardt's exposition.
41 Most recent critics who have at least formally eschewed the idea of an 'evolutionary Zeus' in this trilogy (eg, Reinhardt, Golden, Herington, Lloyd-Jones) have at least this much in common, though, as we have seen, their respective interpretations and, in places, reconstructions, differ greatly.

men) as the price of his secret knowledge. (Other blessings for men, analogous with the gifts which the 'converted' Erinyes bestow in the *Eumenides*, must remain still more conjectural.) Gaia had prophesied, before the battle with the Titans, that not by force but by intelligence would the new master rule. The same prophecy, it would appear, applies in the new circumstances. Once more Promethean intelligence is allied (presumably to the benefit of mankind) with Olympian power, and Zeus will continue to reign supreme.

APPENDIXES

BIBLIOGRAPHY

Some views on the authenticity
of *Prometheus Bound*

Preliminary comments

The question of the authenticity of *Prometheus Bound* has been the subject of many studies, several of them of book-length. It is not my intention in this appendix to reproduce the detailed research, statistics, and arguments of these specialized studies; such a procedure would be neither feasible (within the scope of this study) nor practical, for the material is readily available, and Aeschylean scholars will, in any case, wish to consult it at first hand for themselves. All that is intended here is to provide the non-specialist readers of the play with some knowledge of the controversy and of the main difficulties which have led certain scholars to doubt the Aeschylean authorship of *Prometheus Bound*; to indicate ways in which at least some of those difficulties have been, or may be, met (whether successfully or not, the reader must judge); and to give an indication, for what it is worth, of my own tentative opinion on the matter.

Two recent books, C.J. Herington's *The Author of the 'Prometheus Bound'* (Austin 1970) and Mark Griffith's *The Authenticity of Prometheus Bound* (Cambridge 1977) have, between them, reviewed all the major preceding arguments as well as providing much fresh material and argumentation of their own. The differing conclusions of these studies, the former accepting (at least as reasonably probable), the latter rejecting the play's Aeschylean authorship, serve as a preliminary indication of the uncertainty (never, perhaps, to be resolved) which continues to bedevil the matter even, or perhaps particularly, for specialists in Aeschylean tragedy. Among earlier studies, the student will want to have some familiarity with the influential work of Wilhelm Schmid, particularly his *Untersuchungen zum Gefesselten Prometheus* (Stuttgart 1929), which, though not the first to cast doubt on the authenticity of our play, first drew general attention to the question by the vehemence of its wide-ranging arguments against the play's Aeschylean authorship. Schmid's work has been much discussed in many articles and reviews; Jean Coman's *L'Authenticité du Prométhée enchaîné* (Bucarest 1943), the only book-length study, until the present decade, attempting to deal with most of Schmid's arguments, though useful on several literary and dramatic points, lacks, in some respects, the scholarly assurance of the major contributions to this debate.

There have, of course, been numerous technical studies as well (concerning metre, vocabulary, style, etc.) either devoted specifically to our problem or having important bearings on it. However, as far as the general reader is concerned, the most important points in such work have all surfaced in one or another of the books just mentioned. And of these there can be no doubt that the last of them, Griffith's full and conscientious study, will, whether or not one agrees with his conclusions, provide for some time to come the most important source-book for material (primary and secondary) and for careful discussion of all aspects of the problem. It is one of the strengths of Griffith's book that, while it takes careful account of previous research, it provides its own re-examination of many aspects of the problem (or else refines previous research in various significant ways), making good use of various lexicographical, stylistic, and metrical studies of Greek tragedy published since the earlier onslaught of Schmid on the authenticity of *Prometheus Bound*.

In some respects, recurrent scholarly doubts during the past century concerning the authenticity of all or parts of *Prometheus Bound* have gone full cycle. They began with observation of metrical anomalies, picked up impetus from close study of the play's vocabulary and other linguistic and stylistic arguments, subsequently became enmeshed in frontal attacks (most notably those of Wilhelm Schmid) based initially (though by no means exclusively) on the play's allegedly un-Aeschylean themes and thought, and have recently been revived by Griffith's study, whose strongest arguments stem from refinements and extensions of the more technical and less subjective part of the examination.[1] In view of this sequence, it may be useful to begin our

1 In addition to the works already referred to above, bibliographical summaries of the controversy on the authenticity will be found in Schmid *Untersuchungen* pp 1–5 and in Coman *L'Authenticité* pp 5–8, esp p 7 nn 1–6; cf also Griffith *Authenticity* chapter 1, for a good general survey of the problem and of several recent studies shedding

discussion with the most celebrated part of Schmid's attack and to consider separately the more technical arguments (by no means neglected by Schmid) in their most recent formulation. For there can be little doubt that the mainspring or first cause of Schmid's work lay in his belief that the depiction of Prometheus as a noble champion of men against the tyrant Zeus must be a product of fifth-century αὐθαδία rejecting authority and tradition, rather than of Aeschylus, whom Schmid regarded as consistently pious toward Zeus.[2] Schmid finds the play's re-creation of the mythical tradition (the new presentation of the Zeus-Prometheus confrontation; the wide-ranging significance now given to the gift of fire; Prometheus' possession of a secret giving him power over Zeus) to be one which we would expect not of Aeschylus but of the new humanism exemplified in the first stasimon of Sophocles' *Antigone*. Schmid does, indeed, regard our play (along with the *Antigone* passage) as an historical source of great significance: our oldest evidence of the existence of 'the sophistic' and its radical spirit about the time of the mid-fifth century. Both here and elsewhere[3] Schmid states his conviction that Aeschylus remained quite untouched by the new problems and intellectual concerns of the Sophists. Accordingly, Schmid ascribes *Prometheus Bound* to an unknown but accomplished poet of the mid-fifth century, who modelled himself on Aeschylus but dared to give expression to this '*altsophistischen Lebenschaung*' so alien to him (conclusions which, in the matter of ascription and approximate date, do not differ substantially from those of Griffith's recent study).[4]

Schmid specifically rejects[5] two possible 'ways out,' suggested by Welcker and his followers, which would enable us to see this presentation of the Zeus-Prometheus struggle as by Aeschylus, though atypical. The view that Aeschylus was merely dramatizing 'the folk-tradition' in *Prometheus Bound* Schmid is surely right in rejecting: there is no evidence of such a folk-tradition along these lines, and all the indica-

additional light on it (see n 14 to p 3, and Griffith's bibliography). Of earlier, 'pre-Schmid' studies on the question, that of F. Niedzballa, *De copia verborum et elocutione Promethei Vincti* (diss. Breslau 1913), is one of those most frequently cited.

2 See, for example, Schmid *Untersuchungen* pp 91–107 passim.

3 Cf also Schmid *Geschichte der griechischen Literatur* I. 3, pp 281 ff.

4 Schmid *Untersuchungen* p 96; cf also Schmid *Geschichte* p 281. Cf Griffith *Authenticity* pp 253–4. (With regard to the date, Griffith adds, after mentioning 'echoes' of *Prometheus Bound* in Aeschylus *Eum.*, Sophocles *Aj.*, *Ant.*, and *O.T.*, that 'any attempt to be more specific in dating the play before or after, say, 440 B.C. would be presumptuous ...')

5 Schmid *Untersuchungen* pp 89–91.

tions are, as we have seen, that the poet is breaking new ground with
this daring recreation of the Prometheus myth. The other, fairly standard, view, that Zeus develops in the trilogy, Schmid counters by the
(somewhat slim) evidence against the possibility of Greek gods developing provided in a line from Callimachus:

ἀλλ ἔτι παιδνὸς ἐὼν ἐφράσσατο πάντα τέλεια
(... but even as a child, you [Zeus] already knew-and-devised all things to
their completion) (Hy. 1, 57)

We have already debated this question at some length in an earlier
chapter[6] where we concluded that whether (as seemed likely, at least
in the case of the Erinyes) or not Aeschylus could have conceived of the
possibility of a real change or development in the gods, a change of
attitude on the part of Zeus (and perhaps of Prometheus) in view of the
changed political circumstances seemed all that was necessary for the
solution of the quarrel with Prometheus. This line of argument
(tempering, as it were, the sentimental view of a necessarily benevolent
Aeschylean Zeus with considerations of Realpolitik) also goes a long
way toward explaining the harsh impression of Zeus in the first play
(as we take it to be) of the trilogy.[7]

For his more general conclusion concerning the sophistic nature of
the theme and thought of Prometheus Bound (and so, in his view, of its
non-Aeschylean authorship), Schmid has prepared the way with an
impressive and interesting list of 'words in the sophistic sphere.'[8]
Something of his prejudice against such material as unworthy of Aeschylean tragedy (as he would have it) appears in his insistence on the
'poetic inferiority,' the 'lack of poetic fantasy' implicit in such terminol-
ogy, an anticipation, in one detail, of Schmid's thunderous (and somewhat ranting!) peroration to this part of his argument against the
authenticity of the Prometheus Bound.

Herington, the chief contemporary defender of the authenticity of
our play, readily accepts Schmid's case for sophistic/rhetorical
influence and, indeed, adds further significantly sophistic expressions

6 See above, chapter 6.
7 Schmid, abandoning Prometheus Vinctus as un-Aeschylean, fastens on Prometheus
  Luomenos as providing the appropriately merciful (gnadenreichen) god of the Zeus-
  Prometheus conflict and then proceeds to reconstruct the Luomenos in a manner
  favourable to this interpretation. See Geschichte pp 285–6; Untersuchungen pp 97 ff,
  Méautis L'Authenticité et la Date du Prométhée Enchaîné p 8 excoriates (rightly, in my
  view) Schmid's attempt to separate the two plays.
8 Schmid Untersuchungen pp 75 ff. Cf also Griffith Authenticity pp 217 ff.

to Schmid's list.[9] But it is, of course, part of Herington's fundamental view of the Aeschylean corpus that *Prometheus Bound* (and its trilogy) shares with the '*Suppliants* trilogy' and the *Oresteia* both the involvement of the gods in human feuds ('the cosmic split,' as he describes this new Aeschylean preoccupation) and the intrusion of contemporary philosophic speculation.[10] One does not have to go the whole way with Herington's argument for this 'last phase' of Aeschylus' work[11] to grant him, particularly in the case of the '*Prometheia*' and the *Oresteia*, at least hints of the similarities he finds so striking. However, though the new idea of 'the cosmic split,' as Herington defines it, may itself be a reflection of the new sophistic way of looking at the universe and at man's affairs, we do not find nearly as marked sophistic overtones in the *Oresteia* and *The Suppliants* as in *Prometheus Bound*. As for specific expressions or conceptions reflecting contemporary sophistic or scientific thought in *The Suppliants* and *Oresteia* (to match Schmid's list for *Prometheus Bound*), one can point to only a few; of these (apart from the repeated occurrence of the words εὑρίσκω, μανθάνω, νόσος in all three works, especially *Oresteia* and *Prometheus Bound*), perhaps the most significant are the idea of the father as the exclusive parent which we find in *Eumenides* (658 ff), and which some scholars regard as reflecting certain fifth-century medical opinions, and the emphasis on πειθώ as a substitute for βία, which, as Herington points out, is 'central to the *Eumenides* (e.g., 5, 970 ff.),' as well as prominent in *Prometheus Bound* (as Schmid has observed), and which 'perhaps can be observed already in *Suppliants* 621–24.'[12]

We have already discussed the possible influence of earlier sophistic thought, and its forerunners, on *Prometheus Bound*, in connection with Prometheus' two great speeches on his founding of the arts.[13] There it was suggested that Aeschylus himself could have been familiar with the kind of evolutionary ideas on civilization (blending the mythologi-

9 Herington *Author* pp 94–6.
10 See ibid pp 96–7 and references there given to Herington, 'Aeschylus: The Last Phase' pp 388–90 (esp 390), 396–7; 'Aeschylus in Sicily.'
11 Cf the qualifications expressed concerning this point in the generally sympathetic review of Herington's *Author* by T.C.W. Stinton, in *Phoenix* 28 (1974) 261–2.
12 For this recurrence of the words εὑρίσκω, μανθάνω and νόσος (often in a metaphorical sense), see Herington's table 2, *Author* p 32. On *Eum.* 658 ff ('father as exclusive parent') cf ibid 94 and references there given. For Herington's argument against Schmid on βία/ πειθώ in Aeschylus, see ibid p 95; cf again Stinton's review (above, n 11) p 262 for further observations of the importance of πειθώ in Aeschylus and indeed in Greek tragedy generally.
13 Cf above, chapter 4.

cal and the secular) which we may attribute to Xenophanes, Anaxagoras, and Protagoras. This possibility, together with the indications which Herington has given of at least hints of the same kind of advanced and progressive thinking in the *Oresteia* and possibly in the '*Suppliants* trilogy,' leads us to the tentative conclusion that such sophistic traits as do appear in *Prometheus Bound* need not, in themselves, prevent us from regarding it as the work of Aeschylus. But the fact that there are considerably more of these indications in the thought, vocabulary, and rhetorical expressions[14] of this play than in any other extant play of Aeschylus (including those of Herington's 'final phase') must remain a source of puzzlement if not outright disquietude.

Structure and dramatic style

Prometheus Bound undoubtedly offers several features of tragic composition (when we consider the structure of the play as a whole and the relations and various functions of its constituent parts) which are markedly different from what we find in the other extant plays of Aeschylus. Only slightly less atypical are features affecting the internal economy of the play, the handling of stichomythia and of other kinds of dialogue exchange, the kinds of observations allowed to the Chorus-leader, the use of lyrical and anapaestic passages by actors, and the like. Finally, certain rhetorical devices not found elsewhere in Aeschylus appear in the long speeches of Prometheus, though this feature may perhaps be more readily explained by the peculiarities of the dramatic situation.

Perhaps the most anomalous feature in the composition of *Prometheus Bound* (considered as an Aeschylean play) is the relatively minor part played (both quantitively and otherwise) by the Chorus. Griffith notes that the choral lyrics and anapaests in our play compose only thirteen per cent of the total number of lines, whereas the average for the other five extant Aeschylean plays is forty-two per cent. Here it is not the number of odes but the low number of strophic pairs per ode (less than three throughout, with the possible exception of three in the

14 On the rhetorical expressions of *Prometheus Bound* as allegedly more artificial and
   sophistic than those in other Aeschylean plays, see Griffith *Authenticity* pp 201–14,
   esp pp 207 ff (Cf below p 161.) At the end of this discussion, Griffith admits (p 221)
   that Aeschylean familiarity with sophistic ideas is 'quite possible' but qualifies this
   assurance with the comment that we would not expect such strong sophistic
   influence before 450 BC.

first stasimon) which is 'un-Aeschylean,' though in keeping with Sophoclean and Euripidean practice.[15] However, the very proportions of this disparity, together with the fact that the Chorus clearly fulfils few of the functions normally associated with the Aeschylean Chorus (eg, *inter alia*, that of expanding or generalizing on the theme by means of mythological parallels or excursions into the mythological background of the dramatic situation) lead one to look for other explanations than that of non-Aeschylean authorship: surely an imitator of Aeschylus (as the alleged unknown author of the play must be, in many other respects) would himself be unlikely to depart so far from Aeschylean practice unless there were good reasons suggested either by the dramatic situation or by the circumstances of the dramatic production. And such explanations would apply as well (or almost as well) to a play composed by Aeschylus himself.

Two possible explanations of this general kind are, perhaps, worth considering. First and foremost is the fact that Prometheus himself, present on-stage throughout the whole of the action,[16] is, in the dramatic circumstances as we have described them in earlier chapters, the only possible spokesman for the past and for its significant application to present circumstances. Thus a large area which might otherwise have provided much material for choral odes is automatically taken over by the protagonist. So, too, in the matter of mythical paradigms, object lessons, or cautionary tales by which one or another character in the play might have been warned or advised by choral song: what little of this there is in *Prometheus Bound* is again, for the most part, expressed by Prometheus himself, eg, in his warnings to Ocean embodied in his accounts of the sufferings of Atlas and Typho at Zeus' hands. Indeed the very idea of these minor godlets, the Okeanids of the Chorus, providing either background knowledge or extensive mythical paradigms to the god who claims such complete knowledge of the past and future as Prometheus is itself anomalous. No, the role

---

15 See Griffith *Authenticity* pp 123 and 127, tables 5 and 6, for the statistical comparisons summarized above.

16 Cf Coman *L'Authenticité* pp 66 ff, who stresses this point in expounding the different role of the Chorus in *Prometheus Bound* from that of most other extant Aeschylean plays. Note also Coman's useful summary of various scholarly criticisms, beginning with Westphal's in 1869, of the Chorus in this play as un-Aeschylean. One of the most detailed of these, covering content and form as well as 'rhythmic structure,' is to be found in Kranz *Stasimon* pp 226 ff (discussed by Coman pp 72–9). Coman's own description of the *Prometheus* Chorus (pp 66–71), and his defence of it as Aeschylean, has some general similarity with that suggested above. He adds, however, some dubious comparisons with the Chorus in *Septem* and *Eum*.

which we have seen the Chorus fulfilling in this play is rather that of a
gentle audience helping to draw Prometheus out by their sympathy,
providing just the right element of mild rebuke to show up the more
egregious quality of Prometheus' noble defiance of Zeus and (like the
actual audience whom perhaps they help direct in this) remaining
staunchly loyal to their friend at the crisis (see vv 1063–70), as Prometheus himself remains the loyal champion of men. In all this the role of
the Chorus of *Prometheus Bound* may well remind us of one of the
functions of the Sophoclean Chorus (it is interesting to note that the
choral lyrics in Sophocles' *Electra* take up only eleven per cent of the
play, in contrast to twenty-two and a half per cent in *Antigone*). This is
not to say, of course, that the poet of *Prometheus Bound* is imitating
Sophocles; rather, the dramatic situation of the play happens to dictate this relatively minor (and, for Aeschylus, unusually minor) role for
the Chorus. But what the Chorus have to do in our play they do
admirably, in manner and (if we may, in small part, anticipate another
objection) in metres well-suited to their role.

Another (and possibly complementary) explanation of the limited
role and (according to some) lyrical weakness of the Chorus in
Prometheus Bound has been suggested by Focke: if the play was produced in Sicily, Aeschylus could well have been faced with a lack of
trained *choreutae* and so reduced and simplified the activity demanded
of the Chorus.[17] We should bear in mind both these considerations
when pondering 'un-Aeschylean' metrical features of the *Prometheus'*
choral odes.

While the Chorus of *Prometheus Bound* sing less than we might
normally expect in Aeschylus, the solo singing by the actors (Prometheus at vv 114–19 and Io at vv 566–608) is, as Herington has re-
marked, unique in extant Aeschylus.[18] We have already discussed
these passages in our detailed analysis of the play.[19] Many critics seem
prepared (justifiably in my view) to accept these lyric outbursts as
explicable, even in Aeschylean drama, by the particular dramatic exigencies of the moment, and the same explanation surely accounts for
the unique metrical structure (iambics alternating with anapaests, with

---

17 See Focke 'Aischylos' *Prometheus*' p 297. Focke believes that, for the same reasons, the
    Chorus may have been kept in the chariot (and so have been unavailable for dancing)
    until v 397.

18 Herington *Author* p 92.

19 See above, chapter 3, p 36 and n 7; p 57 and n 36. (The peculiar metrical structure
    of Prometheus' opening soliloquy, mentioned below, has also been discussed in this
    part of chapter 3.)

one lyric outburst) which we have observed in Prometheus' opening soliloquy (88–127). Griffith, however, remains unconvinced. Despite his admission that Aeschylus was capable of a 'bold experiment' such as the *kommos* of *Cheophori*, he insists on the 'un-Aeschylean' quality of these metrical alternations and lyric passages outside of *kommoi* or *epirrhemata*.[20]

This must suffice as a summary treatment of the structural anomalies which have been noted in the sung lines of Chorus and actors. Certain formal peculiarities of the stichomythic passages, to which we now turn, are in some ways more striking and will require more detailed comment.

As we approach the more minute details of structural devices, we shall have to take greater care about what we may call typically Aeschylean or, perhaps more important in this examination, un-Aeschylean. Most scholars involved with the authenticity problem of *Prometheus Bound* give at least token recognition to the obvious difficulty that we have only six other plays of Aeschylus out of a total of at least eighty on which to base our comparisons and contrasts; yet even the best of these scholars sometimes fail, in making individual judgments on various structural, stylistic, and metrical details, to pay sufficient heed to the limitations implied by this recognition. This fault seems, indeed, to be an occupational hazard of this kind of investigation. Once the authenticity of a play, or even a passage in a play, is being put to the test, anomalies and atypical usages appear in every other line: a frequency which is the more amazing when often the suspect play is said to be the work of a skilful imitator of the poet to whom the play or passage has hitherto been so trustingly assigned.[21]

Let us consider briefly the kind of generalization (and its limitations) which we seem justified in making about Aeschylean stichomythic patterns. Griffith comments, on the basis of his own observations and of those of two major studies of tragic stichomythia which he cites, 'Strictness and formalism in stichomythia are characteristics of Aeschylus above all.'[22] This observation is then applied so closely as a criterion

20 See Griffith *Authenticity* pp 108–110 (on Prometheus' soliloquy) and pp 119–20 (on Io's and, incidentally, on Prometheus' monody).
21 Cf Schmid *Untersuchungen* p 96, where the author of *Prometheus Bound* is described as an accomplished poet who modelled himself on Aeschylus. (The by now classic parody of too-eager authenticity-doubters is, of course, Douglas Young's celebrated 'Miltonic Light on Professor Denys Page's Homeric Theory.' Griffith cites this cautionary tale but does not always heed it.)
22 Griffith *Authenticity* p 136. (The ensuing criticism of Griffith on stichomythia in *Prometheus Bound* is based on his discussion pp 136–42.)

of Aeschylean practice that the asymmetrical transitions from two to
one line stichomythia (at *PV* 377 ff and 964 ff) are taken as un-
Aeschylean signs; then (by a sort of guilt by association) even *PV*
40–81, where the 'uncharacteristic' (on the basis of six other plays!) 2:1
arrangement at least follows a strict consistency, also come under
suspicion.

Now what seems reasonable to assert, on the limited evidence, is
that in stichomythic and other conversational passages Aeschylus
shows a liking (more marked than in the other tragedians) for formal
patterns and arrangements, *and that these patterns are often closely related
to the sense or the emotions expressed in the passage.* Sometimes this concern
for sense and context along with form causes breaks in the more
regular forms (eg, 1:1, 2:2); indeed, to put the matter the other way
around, one might say that the very irregularity itself gives formal
emphasis to some heightening of emotion or rapidly changing circumstance. Griffith himself provides examples of this, though he does
not explain the disruption in quite these terms, at *Choeph.* 892 ff (where
'the stage is full of movement, violent action is being threatened') and
Choeph. 766 ff ('where the Chorus abandons the single-line pattern to
give vital instructions'). The context, then, is allowed to excuse these
otherwise un-Aeschylean aberrations. Is it not possible, then, to look
to the context of *PV* 377 ff and *PV* 964 ff (in these cases to the emotional
development of the exchanges between Prometheus and Ocean, and
Prometheus and Hermes, respectively) to explain the irregularities in
stichomythic pattern to which Griffith takes exception?

In the case of 377 ff, there would appear to be excellent dramatic
reason for the interruption of two-line sequence by a single line utterance (383) and then for the eventual transition to a 1:1 sequence
(386–92). The passage occurs at the end of the scene involving Ocean's
abortive intervention 'in Prometheus' own best interests.' Ocean has
made his main appeal in a formal *rhesis* (307–29); after an exchange of
precisely five lines each (in which each expresses hints of irritation,
well controlled, with the other), Prometheus proceeds to give his
answer – and his warning to Ocean – in another set speech (340–76), a
much longer one because Prometheus has much more to say which is
relevant to the theme and the dramatic situation. At the end of the
speech, his irritation with Ocean again gleams through, particularly at
vv 373–4. In the final exchange between the two, Prometheus' replies
become increasingly sharp and he breaks into a single-line riposte to
deliver his first really insulting remark (383: 'Excessive zeal and empty-
headed folly!') in reply to Ocean's inquiry as to the probable penalties

of his own enthusiastic daring on Prometheus' behalf. Ocean keeps his temper with his gently ironic comment (again a 'two-liner') about preferring to remain ill with this illness, that of seeming a fool when he is actually wise. However, when Prometheus, in another 'one-liner,' takes the credit for *this* particular form of trouble for himself, Ocean, in a curt (at long last) single-line rejoinder, accepts Prometheus' increasingly broad hints that he should take himself off. All hope of an *entente cordiale* abandoned, the passage ends in a series of unfriendly (especially on Prometheus' part) single-line exchanges.

All in all, the Ocean scene (so often the subject of complaint by the detractors of this play)[23] seems to me a little gem dramatizing misplaced intervention properly rebuked. Moreover, the arrangement of speeches and dialogue in it surely illustrate admirably Aeschylus' liking for formal patterns adapted to the dramatic progression of the scene.

A somewhat similar process seems discernible (though less clearly) in the other asymmetrical interruption of two-line alternations at 964 ff. The context is the altercation between Hermes and Prometheus. Again the passage of stichomythia is preceded by a speech from Prometheus' interlocutor stating what he requires of the rebel god and a longer one from Prometheus, embodying his refusal. This time, however, both speeches are shorter and disagreement is replaced by open hostility. As in the former scene, the quarrel develops in the stichomythia but far more sharply, for the preceding speeches have already included an exchange of insults. As in the earlier scene, the distichs which open the dialogue exchange embody the more measured and controlled thrusts and counter-thrusts; the break into a one-line utterance indicates an increasing curtness and irritation on the part of one of the speakers; then this single-line curtness is eventually picked up by the other speaker and the quarrelsome dialogue moves into its last phase of an unbroken sequence of single-line utterances (977–86) until Prometheus' passionately defiant speech (987–97) dispels all possibility of Hermes' fulfilling his mission.

However, the discernment of this stichomythic pattern is somewhat complicated by at least one major textual uncertainty. Vv 968–70 are all assigned to Prometheus in the manuscripts. This so grossly breaks both the pattern and sense of the dialogue that few modern editors and commentators hesitate in rejecting this ascription by their editorial

23 Cf, for example, Schmid *Untersuchungen* p 7; Stoessl *Die Trilogie des Aischylos* pp 118 and 124.

predecessors of antiquity.[24] We may safely ascribe vv 968–9 to Hermes; next, Reisig's conjecture that one of Prometheus' two-line responses has dropped out before v 271 seems eminently reasonable; it has been accepted in Murray's Oxford text, and as Page notes, in quoting it in his apparatus, 970 by itself 'non intellegitur'; moreover, it has the distinct advantage of preserving a distich response for Prometheus, which is formally repeated in his next two responses at vv 972–3 and 975–6. According to this arrangement, then, it is Hermes in this case who first breaks into terse one-line sarcasms, initially at v 971 ('You seem to luxuriate in your present troubles') and again at v 974 ('Then d'you blame me as well, in some way, for your woes?') to which Prometheus, in each case, replies with more expansive, generalizing, two-line comments. Then, like Ocean in the earlier altercation, Prometheus too (after Hermes' next one-liner at 977) breaks into the same terse form of rejoinder and the 1:1 pattern is established till the end of this sequence of exchanges.

We have examined Griffith's two most 'irregular' examples of stichomythia in *Prometheus Bound*; since the breaks in regularity enhance rather than destroy the pattern employed by relating it closely to the dramatic development it seems unfair to call such passages 'un-Aeschylean' for these irregularities. Therefore, it seems all the more odd to 'view the technique of 40–81 with suspicion' because there too we find the uncharacteristic 2:1 arrangement, albeit in much more regular, sustained form. Indeed the very regularity of the pattern in this passage (2:1 for forty-two lines) would seem to mark it as 'Aeschylean': at any rate it exhibits a more sustained regularity or 'symmetrical structure' than do the other 'rare occasions,' cited by Griffith, where Aeschylus abandons the strict 1:1 or 2:2 arrangement.[25] (It seems, in any case, excessive to cite such instances as 'rare' for Aeschylus, when we have only six other extant plays for comparison.) And it seems probable that at *PV* 40–81 the break with the more usual 1:1 or 2:2 stichomythic divisions may also be related to the dramatic impact and sense of the lines. It is the dominant and aggressive Kratos who,

---

24 Among modern editors, Mazon in the Budé edition is a regrettable exception here. For the well-supported view that 'the attribution of a speech to such-and-such an interlocutor rests on no tradition that reaches back to the author,' see M.L. West *Textual Criticism and Editorial Technique* p 55, cited by O. Taplin *Proc. C. Philol. Soc.* ns 23 (1977) 121, and references there given. (*Change* of speaker presumably does go back to the author, but the sign for it, a bare *paragraphos*, is very vulnerable to corruption.)

25 Viz, *Pers.* 787 ff; *Choeph.* 479 ff; *Eum.* 582 ff, cited by Griffith p 137.

throughout, speaks two lines to the more sympathetic but more submissive Hephaistos' one.

Two other more regular passages of dialogue in *Prometheus Bound*
merit a brief glance in connection with the point I have been seeking to
make. The first (609–34) comprises the first exchange between Prometheus and Io, followed by a supplementary request (relating to the
preceding dialogue) by the Chorus-leader. The structure of the passage
is as follows:

> *Four verses* from Prometheus (609–12), promising Io to tell her everything
> she wishes to know.
> *Two verses* from Io (613–14) asking about the offence for which Prometheus
> is being punished.
> *Seven verses* (615–21) of 1:1 stichomythia between Prometheus and Io con-
> cerning Io's first question.
> *Two verses* from Io (622–3) asking about the time limit to her own woes.
> *Seven verses* (624–30) of 1:1 stichomythia between Prometheus and Io con-
> cerning Io's second question.
> *Four verses* from the Chorus-leader (631–4) requesting a modification in the
> agenda just agreed upon by Prometheus and Io.

Nothing could be more patterned, more formally precise than this
dramatic section. If Aeschylus is concerned with careful formal patterns in stichomythia, this passage is surely Aeschylean. Yet all that
Griffith thinks worth commenting on in the passage is 'the interruption
of one-line stichomythia by a two-line utterance at 622' which he finds
'remarkable': that and an implicit agreement with Jens that such an
interruption is 'un-Aeschylean.'

Finally, let us look at *PV* 757–82, a stichomythic passage which has
drawn little attention among testers of the authenticity of the play since
it is a model of Aeschylean regularity of the 1:1 variety until its concluding distich at vv 780–1. This is the second dialogue between Io and
Prometheus. The Titan has concluded the first part of Io's future
wanderings (till she reaches Asia); Io has bewailed her lot and spoken
longingly of death; Prometheus has 'consoled' her by comparing his
own worse lot, who cannot die, for whom 'there is no end of pains laid
down until Zeus fall from power' (755–6). Now, in the stichomythic
passage, the first twelve verses (757–68) are concerned with Io's questions and Prometheus' answers on Zeus' ('probable') fall; the second
twelve (769–80) with the related releases of Zeus (from his future

danger), and of Prometheus and Io (from their woes) – save that the twelfth verse (780) leads into a couplet in which Io is given the choice as to whether she will hear more of her own coming woes or of Prometheus' liberator. Thus this passage shows, though in a much more regular pattern, a concern for the significant arrangement of lines in relation to content similar to that we have observed in the dialogue of the Prologue (36–81) and, in a somewhat more subtle manner, in the other two passages (377 ff and 864 ff) which we have examined.

This discussion of the formal aspects of five passages of stichomythia in *Prometheus Bound* seems to me to vindicate rather than cast doubt upon their Aeschylean authorship; there is, at any rate, nothing which we may call un-Aeschylean about them. What leads Griffith to view four of these five passages with suspicion, to one degree or another, is their departure from the strict 1:1 or 2:2 arrangement. But we have far too few extant plays of Aeschylus to regard this procedure as rare or exceptional. All that we can say from the limited evidence available is that Aeschylus shows liking for pattern, for symmetrical structures, in his stichomythic passages; that when he abandons the more obvious forms of this patterning (the 1:1 or the 2:2 arrangement) he tends to replace them by other more elaborate forms (as at *Pers.* 787 ff; *Cho.* 479 ff; *Eum.* 582 ff, compare *PV* 40–81); and that slightly more irregular breaks in such patterns (as at *Cho.* 766 ff and *Cho.* 892 ff; compare *PV* 377 ff and 964 ff) are made in response to some requirement of the dramatic action. And indeed the latter device, far from showing an un-Aeschylean disregard for formal patterns in stichomythia, often exploits their use, for the dramatic effects achieved (as at *PV* 377 ff, 964 ff) by breaks in or departures from the regular patterns clearly depend on the prior establishment of these patterns. Perhaps the most (and it is hardly the worst) which can be said about *Prometheus Bound* in this regard is that while it continues to exhibit typical Aeschylean formalism in its handling of stichomythia, it shows some advance in the technique (already observable in the *Oresteia*) in adapting formal patterns to the dramatic requirements of the scene. It is also true, of course (as Herington and others have observed)[26] that the patterns of this play's line arrangements generally (including the extensive use of quatrains for the iambic utterance of the Chorus-leader) exhibit a 'meticulous formalism' unparalleled in Greek tragedy. But by Griffith's own admission, the tendency toward strict formalism in patterns of

26 Cf Herington *Author* p 32 and references there given.

iambic dialogue is certainly more marked in Aeschylus than in Sophocles or Euripides. Hence it does not seem really improbable that in the last of the few Aeschylean plays extant (and in a play in which the 'static' dramatic situation lends itself to formal and rhetorical composition generally) we should find the poet developing to a high degree the structural formalism already associated with his work.

Vocabulary

Study of word occurrence and usage as a test of the authenticity of *Prometheus Bound* (or of any other play), though given considerable weight by Schmidt and Niedzballa, is, particularly in its grosser applications, a notoriously inadequate tool. For one thing, the particular subject matter of the play must always be a highly determining factor in much of its word usage. For another, the consideration which so greatly restricts the usefulness of many authenticity tests applied to our play, namely the small number of other Aeschylean plays available for comparison, is particularly relevant here. Finally, the elements of chance, context, and metrical convenience in the required context are all factors which may affect the choice of one or another of nearly synonymous words.

Certainly, Griffith's word studies of *Prometheus Bound* attempt to meet, by a sequence of increasingly subtle refinements, all the drawbacks to this procedure: if the vocabulary test is to be used at all in testing our play's authenticity, then Griffith's statistics (and particularly his criteria for 'significant' words) provide a far better basis for judgment than do any of his predecessors. Griffith conscientiously describes his criteria for 'significant *Eigenwörter*' (Schmid's term for words occurring in *Prometheus Bound* and in no other Aeschylean play) and applies these criteria consistently. Nevertheless, the complex and yet inevitably arbitrary nature of Griffith's criteria for determining the number of 'significant' *Eigenwörter* reveals the near-impossibility of this task as much as it does the conscientious effort of this researcher. For example, only repeated *Eigenwörter* are to be considered so as to avoid (but only to a degree!) the element of chance usage, and of these only those repeated outside an area of one hundred lines of each other so as to make allowance (again, to some degree) for an author's tendency to repeat an unusual word once he has used it.[27] And inevitably the

27 Griffith *Authenticity* pp 162–3.

most contrived of Griffith's conscientious criteria is the one which
would seek to remove the contextual difficulty:

> ... if the peculiar sense of an *Eigenwort* is such that, in my view, not more
> than one of the other six plays provides a context in which that word could
> be thought at all likely to occur, then I do not count that word as
> 'significant.'[28]

Here the tell-tale refinement, 'not more than one,' indicates the arbitrary or contrived nature of the criterion. On the one hand the scholar
does not want to be accused of including as 'significant' *Eigenwörter*
words whose use the peculiar context and subject matter of *Prometheus
Bound* may have dictated; on the other hand, he does not want to give
away too much, to lean over backwards in his scrupulosity and so omit
from his 'significant' list words which might conceivably have occurred
elsewhere in the extent Aeschylean corpus, even if they do rather fit
the *Prometheus'* context. And so he hits upon the very human, but
logically somewhat puzzling, compromise of requiring that 'more than
one' of the other extant Aeschylean plays should provide such a
possible (though unused) context for repeated *Eigenwörter*, if they are
to be judged significant. Here, too, the recurrent problem of the very
limited number of Aeschylean plays available for control purposes
obviously complicates the issue further. If twelve other plays were
extant, would 'more than two' of these twelve plays have been required to provide the requisite context; if nine, 'more than one and a
half,' and so on?

   Difficulties of other kinds show up in other aspects of Schmid's and
Griffith's comparative statistics. *Agamemnon* provides 703 single occurrences of *Eigenwörter* to *Prometheus'* 554; 63 double occurrences to
Prometheus' 47; 12 triple occurrences to *Prometheus'* 18. 'Here again,'
Griffith comments, '*Prom.* stands out most strikingly.' Clearly, Griffith
(like Schmid) is here taking precise note of the fact that *Agamemnon* is
over half as long again as *Prometheus*; yet who is to say precisely how
many lines of a play are needed for 'significant *Eigenwörter*' (which, as
Griffith allows, turn out to be 'insignificant' words)[30] to appear? Or *just
how much* significance, in the context of determining characteristic
usage, Aeschylean and un-Aeschylean, is to be attached to single as

28 Ibid p 163
29 See Griffith ibid p 158, for this revision of Schmid's table of repeated *Eigenwörter*; cf
    Schmid *Untersuchungen* p 45.
30 Griffith *Authenticity* p 164.

opposed to double, double as opposed to triple occurrences of *Eigenwörter* in any given play?[31] Possibly computer analysis might be able to answer such questions (though I doubt it); certainly no such answers are forthcoming so far in the authenticity debate. When Griffith comes to compare the *Eigenwörter* and repeated *Eigenwörter*, as defined by his own more refined criteria, in *Prometheus Bound* with those in other Aeschylean plays, he chooses *Persae* and *Septem* for the comparisons, presumably because of their similar length to *Prometheus*. Again, for what the statistics are worth, *Prometheus* comes out highest (and so most suspect?) both in total number of 'significant' *Eigenwörter* and of repeated 'significant' *Eigenwörter*. One would have preferred, however, that this comparison, by Griffith's criteria, had been made between *Prometheus Bound* and *Agamemnon*, in view both of the late date of *Agamemnon* and of the large number of *Eigenwörter* which it exhibits.

Let us approach the problem in another way. Let us, for the moment, allow both the arguments and the conclusions drawn from them that *Prometheus Bound* is an egregious case in the Aeschylean usage of *Eigenwörter*. Is the play which, in Schmid's raw list of numbers of *Eigenwörter* per play, in proportion to length of play,[32] comes next to *Prometheus Bound*, ie, *Agamemnon*, to be regarded as the next most un-Aeschylean in this matter? Or, to turn to Griffith's comparisons of occurrences of *Eigenwörter* (now more closely defined) in *Persae*, *Septem*, and *Prometheus*, is *Persae* to be regarded as less Aeschylean in this respect than *Septem*, because it offends more in this respect than *Septem*, though admittedly not as badly as *Prometheus*? Or does the offence, in the occurrences of *Eigenwörter*, lie merely in being *egregious* (at either extreme) in this respect ('odd play out,' as it were)? If so, we must regard the *Eumenides* as rather un-Aeschylean in its usage here; this play's number of *Eigenwörter* in relation to length is, at 31.4 per cent (according to Schmid's table), well below the average for Aeschylus, whether we include *Prometheus* or not. Indeed, the discrepancy between *Eumenides* and both *Persae* and *Agamemnon* in this matter is greater than the discrepancy between *Prometheus* and *Agamemnon*.

These random shafts will not be confused by the reader with a scientific rebuttal of the arguments from *Eigenwörter*, whether by Schmid or by Griffith. (In the interest of simplification, they have

31 Schmid *Untersuchungen* pp 45–6 finds two occurrences of *Eigenwörter* in an Aeschylean play common but three or more increasingly rare, except in *Prometheus* which has 21 triple occurrences, 7 quadruples, and 2 septuples.
32 Ibid pp 43–4, reproduced by Griffith *Authenticity* p 157.

ignored among other things Griffith's interesting comparisons, in this
matter, of Sophocles' *Ajax* with three Aeschylean plays.) They may,
however, suffice to warn the reader to be hesitant about the use of this
criterion for judging the authenticity of our play and about accepting
both Schmid's and Griffith's conclusions that their respective statistical
studies of this matter point unmistakably to an un-Aeschylean feature
of *Prometheus Bound*.[33]

Other aspects of *Prometheus Bound*'s vocabulary which have been
studied in this connection include types of words employed and usage
of particles. With regard to the former, Griffith's careful study (which
considers principally compounded adjectives, adverbs, and neuter
nouns with *-ma* suffix) shows that our play fits well with Aeschylean
usage.[34] This will come as no surprise even to the more casual reader of
Prometheus Bound (and of Aristophanes' *Frogs*), since he will already
have found at least some reassurance concerning the questioned authenticity of the play in the familiar features of the grand or elevated
tragic style reflected in these usages.

The use of particles in *Prometheus Bound*, and its significance for our
problem, is a more complex matter. Here, Herington's study and
conclusions[35] are recommended to the general reader to whom the
present summary is addressed. Herington admits the considerably
greater and, in particular, *wider* use of particles in *Prometheus Bound*
over that of the other six plays (six particles, for example, are used from
one to six times in *Prometheus* and not in any other extant Aeschylean
play, while nine additional particles are used more often in *Prometheus*
than in any of the others). However, before regarding these statistics as
providing serious doubt about *Prometheus'* authenticity, one should
heed both Herington's reminder concerning the versatility shown in
Greek particle usage in general (the 'eccentric content and tone' of our
play leading us to expect 'a correspondingly eccentric choice and
deployment of particles')[36] and his observation, statistically sup-

33 Griffith ibid p 172; Schmid pp 43–50, passim.
34 See Griffith *Authenticity* pp 148–57; his conclusions are to be found at pp 156–7.
    (*Griffith* does not, of course, go so far as to suggest that this compatability indicates
    Aeschylean authorship: 'We have merely seen,' he comments, 'that the author of
    Prom., like Aeschylus, in his desire for elevated and grandiose diction uses the words
    most effective for that purpose.')
35 Herington *Author* pp 63–75.
36 See ibid p 72 (for the next comment cited, ibid p 74). To Herington's general observa-
    tion we might add that the protagonist of our play is bound and cannot gesture: this
    may have led to some increase in those verbal gestures, particles. Griffith, on the
    other hand, rejects, for the most part (*Authenticity* pp 175–6), Herington's explanation

ported, that (apart from the idiosyncratic usages) *Prometheus Bound*
seems often to extend (sometimes to a surprising degree, it is true)
tendencies in particle usage noted in the later plays of Aeschylus.

Syntax and style

In this brief summary, we must restrict ourselves to comment on a few
of the syntactical and stylistic features of *Prometheus Bound* which have
been singled out as sufficiently egregious to arouse suspicion.
Griffith's section on 'Syntax and Phraseology' appears, at first reading,
to make several impressive points against the Aeschylean authorship.
On closer examination, however, not all the evidence is quite as damn-
ing as it initially appears to be. His treatment of πρίν in *Prometheus
Bound* and in Aeschylus is a case in point.

Griffith reminds us that 'the growing frequency of constructions
other than the infinitive after πρίν is a traceable historical process,'[37] and
then makes much of the fact that πρίν ἄν + subjunctive occurs six times
in *Prometheus*, while 'the only possible parallel in Aeschylus is fr. 327.'
However, the 'possible parallel' is, in this case, an almost certain one:
Porson's correction of Eustathius at Aesch. fr 327 is generally and
reasonably accepted: πρίν ἄν in the first verse of the fragment leads us
to expect the subjunctive rather than the infinitive (χρᾶναι) given by
Eustathius. More significant still is the point that none of the other
examples of πρίν in Aeschylus (apart from *Prometheus*), with one possible exception, occurs in a context where πρίν ἄν + subjunctive might
be used;[38] all of the *Prometheus'* examples of πρίν ἄν + subjunctive, on
the other hand, occur in a truly prophetic context (which is far more

here, and, from his own more detailed comparison of *Prometheus'* particle usage with
that of the other Aeschylean and some Sophoclean and Euripidean plays, comments:
'The message is clear ... *Prom.* fits squarely with Euripides, almost with Sophocles
who, of the three, uses particles most freely, rather than with Aeschylus.'
37 Griffith ibid p 191, citing J. Sturm *Geschichtliche Entwicklung der constructionen mit prin*
(Würzburg 1882) 20, as his authority.
38 Of the three Aeschylean occurrences (apart from *Prometheus*) of πρίν + infinitive after
a negative main verb, only *Ag.* 1067 provides an example where πρίν means 'until' in
a clause referring to future time. Even here, in the context (Cassandra's refusal 'to
accept the bit,' and the consequences of this refusal, are compared to what happens to
horses who take that risk), the clause is not clearly and purely prophetic as in the cases
of the 'πρίν ἄν + subjunctive' prophecies in *Prometheus Bound*. Of the other Aeschylean examples of πρίν + infinitive after a negative, the one at *Sept.* 1054 is a historical
not a prophetic clause, while the one at *Suppl.* 772 is part of a generalization and is
again not a prophetic (i.e., future-looking) clause ('The debarkation of an army is not
wont to be successful before [or 'until'] the ship is well secured').

recurrent in *Prometheus* than in any other play of Aeschylus) after a
negatived principal statement. Thus, unless there is anything remarkable about the use in the mid-fifth century of πρίν ἄν + subjunctive
after a negative, when πρίν means 'until' and looks toward the future,
I cannot see why this construction should be regarded as 'un-
Aeschylean.' This leaves us with but one usage of πρίν in *Prometheus* (at
v 481) which might be called slightly unusual: πρίν and the indicative
with the sense of 'until,' (after a negative idea carried over from an
earlier main clause) in a purely historical context; at *Septem* 1054,
Aeschylus uses πρίν and infinitive in a similarly historical context
where πρίν means 'until' after a negative main verb (implied).
Griffith's comment on *PV* 481, that this 'indicative example indicates
that *Prom.* may simply be more advanced than Aeschylus,' is surely an
overstatement.

Two other syntactical and stylistic oddities which have been much
discussed in *Prometheus Bound* are the high proportion of resultative
perfects (ie, the use of the perfect to describe the present state of a
person or thing, which may be the object of the verb, as the result of an
earlier action) and the similarly high proportion of enjambement (the
device of running one iambic trimeter into the next, without the usual
verse-end pause, by means of some lead-in word or group of words).

Previous research on resultative perfects has been well summarized
by Herington.[39] The usage gradually increased throughout the fifth
century; there are more examples in Sophocles and Euripides than in
Aeschylus (with or without *Prometheus*) and far more in Aristophanes,
though perhaps the latter is not a fair comparison. However, the usage
is not downright un-Aeschylean (there are some six other examples,
apart from *Prometheus'* five) and is, moreover, hard to distinguish
precisely; hence we can hardly use it as an argument against authenticity. Even as an argument for the late date of the play, it is less strong
than other arguments: why are there so few examples of resultative
perfects in *Oresteia*?

Enjambement of the type described above (a favourite Sophoclean
device) occurs at least eighteen times in *Prometheus Bound* (according to
Yorke's reckoning; Griffith, adopting slightly more liberal criteria for
the phenomenon, works this up to twenty-four) as compared with
eight occurrences elsewhere in Aeschylus, of which seven are in
Oresteia. Yorke regards these statistics merely as an argument for the
late date of the play, while for Herington the comparative figures
exemplify further *Prometheus Bound*'s extension of stylistic tendencies

39 Herington *Author* pp 41–4.

already observable in the later plays.[40] To this point we might add that a play with so many prophetic, didactic, and expository speeches (well over half the examples occur in such passages) might be expected to have several more closely connected lines, and in any case, despite the statistics, the iambics of *Prometheus Bound* rarely achieve a Sophoclean fluidity.

Other more minor stylistic anomalies which have been alleged against *Prometheus Bound* may be found in Griffith's study. More interesting than these, however, are Griffith's own observations of certain features of the play's rhetorical technique, eg, the devices, more artificial than in other Aeschylean plays, used to mark 'ring composition' and the play's distinctive use of 'signpost formulae' to mark parts of a long speech.[41] Griffith hesitates between calling 'this self-conscious desire for order and symmetry' 'archaic' or 'sophistic' and remarks that elsewhere Aeschylus does not display such concern for these artificial divisions of speeches. Once again Griffith does not, perhaps, take sufficient account of the dramatic circumstances of *Prometheus Bound*, which require an unusually large amount of expository, prophetic, and didactic speech-making of its central figure. It is not surprising, then, that more formal stylistic devices for breaking up these expositions (in which we have already admitted certain sophistic overtones) should make their appearance.[42] The question is not so much whether such devices appear in the other extant plays (which do not really require them); it is rather whether we are prepared to accept as Aeschylean a play with the central figure and the thematic material

40 See Yorke 'Trisyllabic Feet in the Dialogue of Aeschylus' and 'The Date of the *Prometheus Vinctus*,' both cited by Herington *Author* pp 46–7; Herington's own conclusions are on pp 48–9. Griffith *Authenticity* p 96, cf 192, rejects Yorke's and Herington's explanations and insists on the un-Aeschylean nature of this technique.
41 Griffith ibid pp 207–14.
42 Stinton, review in *Phoenix* 28 (1974) 259, has complained with some justice that stylistic discussions of *Prometheus Bound*, up to and including Herington's (and the criticism might be extended to Griffith as well), have concerned themselves too exclusively with 'countable details' while it is the more pervasive aspects of the play's style (he cites 'sapheneia and imagery' as two examples of what he has in mind) which raise greater doubts about its authenticity among perceptive readers. This is not the place to embark on this more wide-ranging study (and in any case Mr Stinton is the scholar most eminently qualified for its elucidation); however, if an explanation of these more wide-ranging stylistic differences should be possible, I feel that it can only be possible in terms of subject matter and theme and dramatic structure. If (to take but one brief example) the poet of *Prometheus Bound* had not, for sound dramatic reasons, given the 'treatment of the past' to Prometheus but had given it to the Chorus instead (as in *Agamemnon*) then the imagery of great stretches of the play might well have been much richer and more 'Aeschylean.'

of *Prometheus Bound*. And as we have already suggested, there are insufficient reasons for the rejection of Aeschylean authorship on these grounds.

Metrical anomalies

This is too complex a topic for detailed consideration in this summary. Scholars capable of distinguishing the more worrying features (as far as acceptance of authenticity goes) among the many anomalous and, in some cases, unique metrical phenomena of *Prometheus Bound* will, in any case, wish to consult the original research studies on the subject. With regard to the lyric metres, Griffith provides the first systematic study of these in relation to the lyric metres of the other extant plays of Aeschylus and of Greek tragedy generally, and this feature of his book will probably remain one of his major contributions to the authenticity study. His similar comparative study of recitative anapaests is also of importance. In the study of iambic trimeters in *Prometheus Bound*, and in the relevant comparisons, Griffith has made considerable use of earlier work. In this section, then, I shall content myself with selecting, mainly from Griffith's chapters, what appear to be the most egregious features of *Prometheus Bound*'s metrical usage.[43]

Concerning recitative anapaests, among the most disturbing features which Griffith notes from his statistics on *Prometheus Bound* are the differences from other Aeschylean plays in the choices among possible types of metra and in the length of anapaestic runs without paroemiac. The first of these differences is, of course, a matter of degree rather than of an absolutely 'un-Aeschylean feature': all extant plays of Aeschylus naturally show some divergency from each other in choices of various possible anapaestic metra, but the *Prometheus* is more divergent than any other, especially in the high proportion of spondaic metra and the correspondingly low proportion of purely anapaestic metra. The second difference may perhaps be explained by the fact that most of the anapaestic runs concerned in the *Prometheus* are chanted by actors, not by the Chorus. (Compare, for example, the relatively low percentage of paroemiacs in Clytemnestra's anapaestic runs in *Agamemnon*.)

In the use of iambic trimeters, three points (in addition to the matter

43 See Griffith *Authenticity* chapters, 3, 4, 5, for discussion of lyric metres, recitative anapaests, and iambic metres, respectively, in *Prometheus Bound*; cf also, particularly in the case of the iambic metres, Griffith's bibliographical references there given. (In my own brief comments, below, I am indebted to Mr T.C.W. Stinton for the observations on anapaestic 'runs' in *Prometheus Bound* and in *Agamemnon* and for the suggestion of possible Pindaric influence in the use of the dactylo-epitrite metre.)

of 'Sophoclean *enjambements*' already discussed) may be noted: the frequency of resolution, the number of 'first foot anapaests,' and the high proportion of interlinear ('non-stop') hiatus. The number of resolutions per 100 iambic lines in *Prometheus Bound* is 4.8, a number which it shares with *Agamemnon* and the lowest of the extant plays. By this criterion alone, then, *Prometheus* would appear merely to be a later Aeschylean play, since the extant corpus shows a small but fairly steady decrease in resolutions from *Persae* (11.0) onwards. Among these resolutions the unusually high number of 'first foot anapaests' (twelve, excluding one proper name) has often been noted; the average for an Aeschylean play is 2.4 and the highest occurrence elsewhere in extant Aeschylus is five in *Agamemnon*. However, the location and context of several of the *Prometheus'* first foot anapaests should perhaps be noted: as Stinton has pointed out, three of them come in the description of Aetna, 'where Aeschylus is drawing either on Pindar or their common epic source.'[44] No less than five others (plus one 'proper name,' first foot anapaest) all occur in Prometheus' prophecies to Io:[45] three of these involve striking topographical features, which have to be included somehow in the iambic lines; a fourth gives a characteristic feature ($\mu o\nu \acute{o}\delta o\nu \tau \epsilon\varsigma$, 796) of the daughters of Phorcys; while the fifth ($\acute{\epsilon}\pi\alpha\varphi\hat{\omega}\nu$, 849), has almost the status of a 'proper name anapaest,' since it is the participle giving the explanation of the proper name Ἔπαφος (851). These considerations do, I think, reduce the exceptional element in the number of first foot anapaests in the play.

No such argument can, however, reduce the oddity of the very large number of lines exhibiting interlinear 'non-stop' hiatus in *Prometheus Bound*.[46] The statistics establish fairly clearly that the Greek tragedians accepted interlinear hiatus but attempted, to a considerable degree, to limit it to instances in which there is some pause in sense after the initial line. No such attempt can be observed in the examples of hiatus in *Prometheus Bound*, in which out of 130 instances of interlinear hiatus 52 are of the 'non-stop' variety. To my mind *Prometheus* is so exceptional in this matter that the phenomenon suggests lack of revision (understandable, perhaps, in the last play of an ageing poet) rather than un-Aeschylean authorship; for why should a poet who has imitated

44 Stinton *Phoenix* p 261; cf *PV* 368 and Pindar *Pyth*. 1.21f.
45 I am indebted to Dr Martin Cropp for this and the following observation.
46 This matter has been well summarized in the discussion and tables supplied by Herington *Author* pp 37–40. Note also his references to E. Harrison 'Interlinear Hiatus in Greek Tragic Trimeters' *CR* 55 (1941) 22–5, and *CR* 57 (1943) 61–3, where this eccentricity of *Prometheus Bound* was first observed. Cf also Griffith *Authenticity* pp 100–1, who regards this feature of the play as one more count against its Aeschylean authorship, and Stinton 'Interlinear Hiatus in Trimeters.'

Aeschylus successfully in many respects show such disregard for this fairly prominent aspect of Aeschylean trimeters and (as far as we can tell) of tragic trimeters in general?[47]

With regard to the lyric metres of *Prometheus Bound* and their various departures from what we know of Aeschylean practice, we must content ourselves here with mention of the more remarkable features among the many discussed in Griffith's study. A few preliminary observations should, however, be made with regard to the use of this kind of evidence in pondering the question of authenticity. Even more than in the case of stylistic features, the small number of Aeschylean plays available for comparison is a decidedly limiting factor in deciding what is, or is not, 'Aeschylean' in the use of lyric metres. Thus the employment in our play of a metre which does not appear elsewhere in extant Aeschylus (though appearing elsewhere in tragedy) should indeed be noted but need not in itself be taken as a sign of un-Aeschylean authorship. Secondly, even the absence from our play of lyric metres which seem (from the limited number of extant plays) to be particularly favoured by Aeschylus may also be accepted with some degree of composure by the defenders of *Prometheus Bound*'s authenticity: not only may the poet have had his reasons for excluding that metre in a particular play or production but also the metre in question may not have appeared quite as universally favoured elsewhere by the poet if all his plays were extant.

Examples of the first type of anomaly (for Aeschylean lyric usage) occur in the opening stanzas of the second and third *stasima* of *Prometheus Bound* (526–35 = 536–44; 887–93 = 894–900) which encircle the long Io episode. These are in the dactylo-epitrite metre, which does not occur elsewhere in Aeschylus; it does appear quite frequently in Sophocles and Euripides, though often in less pure a form than in the present instances. (Examples of dactylo-epitrite also abound in Pindar, to whom Aeschylus may be indebted here as, possibly, elsewhere in the play, eg, as we have noted, in the description of the fall of Typho, *PV* 351–72; compare Pindar, *Pythian* 1. 15–28.) An example of the second type of anomaly (the 'negative' one) in the choral odes of *Prometheus Bound* is the lack of any strophic iambic odes, which are sometimes regarded as the most characteristic feature of Aeschylean lyrics. (There are, to be sure, some purely iambic stanzas not in strophic responsion in *Prometheus Bound*, though these fall far below the average number for an Aeschylean play.) This lack may, however,

47 If find it difficult to agree with Griffith, on the very limited evidence which he cites from the fragments, that 'Interlinear hiatus seems not uncommon among the minor tragedians …' (ibid n 86 to p 101).

be simply a part of the restriction of the role of the Chorus generally in this play, for which some explanations have already been suggested.[48] Finally, among the various unusual lyric sequences in *Prometheus*, we should mention the strophic pair (160–7 = 178–185) in the epirrhematic parodos, of which Griffith observes, 'there is no parallel in tragedy for a stanza starting in pure iambics ... and ending in dactyls.'[49] But even supposing this to be as unusual as the lack of *extant* parallels suggest, need we regard Aeschylus as less capable of such an innovation than some unknown imitator?

Less striking than these examples of surprising inclusions or omissions of one or another prevailing stropic rhythm, but perhaps more significant for the authorship question, are the lack of syncopation in the trochaic verses of the first stasimon (415–17 = 420–2), whereas elsewhere in Aeschylus trochaics tend to be syncopated, and the favouring of resolution over syncopation in the lyric iambics, again in contrast to more common Aeschylean practice.[50] However, in the matter of resolution and syncopation in Aeschylean lyric iambics, while it is possible to state the dramatist's preferences and tendencies, Griffith's own 'few' examples of unsyncopated iambic strophes in other Aeschylean plays (and of the proportion of resolutions to metra there found)[51] would seem to forbid our calling even this feature of *Prometheus'* lyric iambics downright un-Aeschylean.

Theme and dramatic conception

Before turning to external evidence relevant to the authenticity problem, we should, perhaps, address ourselves briefly to a question which cannot admittedly be answered with complete objectivity and yet which, in my opinion, should not be completely ignored in these deliberations. Are the theme and the dramatic conception of *Prometheus Bound*, both as contained within the play itself and as implied in the probable trilogic development for which we have argued in chapter 5, of the kind which we could, from our limited knowledge of his work, readily associate with Aeschylus? Griffith rejects such considerations,[52] but is one justified in ignoring possible similarities of

48 Cf above pp 146–8.
49 Griffith *Authenticity* p 37.
50 For the details, see Griffith ibid pp 37–9 and 66 (on trochaics); pp 60, 62–3 (on lyric iambics).
51 Ibid p 35.
52 Ibid p 6: '... any interpretation of the play is liable to be affected by our decisions as to its author and its possible place in the trilogy.' Must we, then, know who composed a play before we can interpret it? This seems to me to place too little confidence in the author of *Prometheus Bound*, whoever he be.

this kind which *Prometheus Bound* may exhibit with the other extant works of Aeschylus, while insisting on the importance of similarities and differences in syntax, style, metre, and the like, even though the latter may often be easier to assess?

We have already touched on aspects of this topic in rebutting (with the help of Herington) Schmid's arguments that the view of Zeus implied in *Prometheus Bound* and other alleged sophistic elements in the play marked it as un-Aeschylean.[53] To the larger, more general formulations of the question, I believe that the answer should also be affirmative. The cosmic proportions of the theme, the opposing of different conceptions of the gods (presented dramatically as the opposition of the old versus the new gods), the clear hints of some form of reconciliation between these conflicting elements, the need of long stretches of time and even of space for this solution, and the obvious requirement of trilogic development for its achievement: all these features surely point to the poet of the *Oresteia* (and some of them to the poet of the '*Suppliants* trilogy') as their author. One is tempted to invoke also the well-known thesis-antithesis-resolution pattern which Herington, in common with earlier commentators, associates with the Aeschylean trilogy,[54] in spite of the severe reservations which we have seen that other scholars, insisting on 'the unchanging gods,' have imposed upon it. Allowing for an element of over-simplification in such formulations, one cannot doubt that in the *Oresteia*, Aeschylus does present us with a development, an improvement in the way in which man may expect to achieve justice without perpetuating bloodshed. Nor can we doubt that the responses evoked within the limited perspectives of the first play (eg, recognition of the justice of the death of Agamemnon) are reversed, though not contradicted, by the responses evoked (eg, recognition of the justice of Clytemnestra's death, sympathy for Agamemnon) in the second, and that these responses in terms of individual sympathy are, in a sense, dispensed with in the resolution, which takes place on a higher, more impersonal plane at the end of the *Eumenides*. And even in the '*Suppliants* trilogy,' we can, despite the pitifully slim evidence, assert with confidence that in the course of the trilogy the victors are converted to victims (as in the *Oresteia*) and that by the end of it at least one of the warring couples has been transformed by a potentially fruitful union of love. This degree at least of development and of resolution is clearly discernible in both these trilogies.

53 Cf above pp 142–6, of this appendix; cf also chapter 6.
54 See Herington *Author* pp 78–81, and further references there given.

In the case of the *Prometheus* trilogy, an analogous development and resolution must surely have taken place. Even from the fragments of the *Luomenos* it is clear that there has been a change of circumstances which we had not foreseen in the first play (eg, the freeing of the Titans by Zeus) and a change in the morale, if not in the attitude, of Prometheus, who now wishes he could die (fr 193, 23–4) but who earlier boasted that Zeus could never kill him (*PV* 1053). (One is tempted to speculate that the element of reversal in the *Luomenos* might also, analogously to the change in sympathy in the second play of the *Oresteia*, have involved a change in our attitude to Zeus: something of that kind at least seems hinted at in the dramatically ironic prophecy of Prometheus about Io's gentle deliverance *PV* 848f.) Certainly, too, in the sequel to *Prometheus Bound* there must be a resolution involving a reconciliation of the warring elements: this much is clear from the prophetic utterances in *Prometheus Bound*, from the external evidence which we have already cited, and from the fact that, while Zeus continued to reign, Prometheus enjoys high honour even in fifth-century Athens. (That this reconciliation was celebrated by the establishment in the *Purphoros* of the torch race in honour of Prometheus, paralleling the establishment of the Areopagus in the *Eumenides*, also seems probable, but this is unprovable and not essential to our argument.) In view of these similarities in theme, in dramatic conception, and in overall trilogic structure, it seems perverse to deny an essentially Aeschylean stamp to the poet's treatment of the Prometheus theme, in so far as we can discern it. Indeed, the poet himself seems to help us to this conclusion when he hints (in Prometheus' prophecy, *PV* 848–76, about Io, the Danaids, and his own liberation) at thematic parallels between his own '*Suppliants* trilogy' and this one. Aeschylus was surely a master, for all we know the only master, of the connected trilogy. In view of the arguments just presented, it seems idle to deny him at least a master role in the creation of this one.

External evidence

We come finally to the ancient external evidence concerning the authenticity of *Prometheus Bound*. About this it is possible to say very much or very little: very little, if one restricts oneself to the limited evidence itself, all of which favours Aeschylean authorship; very much, if one wishes to expatiate on our limited knowledge of how the Alexandrians compiled their lists of Greek tragedies and other didascalic information and how they collected and catalogued their own holdings of tragic texts; more still, if one dwells critically, again from very limited knowledge, on the uncertainties of the preceding tradition concerning the titles, productions, and authorship of fifth-century Greek tragedies. It should constantly be borne in mind, however, that arguments (mainly *argumenta ex silentio*) impugning the ancient evidence for the Aeschylean authorship of *Prometheus Bound* can also be applied in the case of many other Greek tragedies whose authorship has been accepted on no stronger external evidence but whose texts have given no occasion to doubt that evidence. Thus, *when we are talking of external ancient evidence only*, it seems unfair to treat that evidence more lightly than we would in the case of any other fifth-century Greek tragedy.

Scholars both for and against the Aeschylean authorship of *Prometheus Bound* admit, as they must, that in antiquity the play was certainly ascribed to Aeschylus and that no doubts about its authenticity were raised at any time in the ancient world. *Prometheus Desmotês* (along with *Prometheus Luomenos* and *Prometheus Purphoros*) appear in the Catalogue preserved in codd. MV. Thus, not only was *Prometheus Bound* in the Alexandrian catalogue of Aeschylean plays but also, as Herington observes,[55] the earlier strata of *Prometheus* scholia in these manuscripts provide evidence of ancient commentaries, which assumed the play to be Aeschylean, by scholars familiar with a far wider range of Aeschylean works than is available to us. Other ancient testimonia (of slightly varying weight) to the Aeschylean authorship of *Prometheus Bound* include three ancient scholia, one to Euripides' *Phoenissae* 208 (in which Euripides is said to have followed Aeschylus (see *PV* 84–41) in his naming of the Ionian Sea), one to Aristophanes *Frogs* 814, and one to Homer's *Iliad* (which quotes *PV* 2 and refers to Aeschylus); a quotation of *PV* 377–80 in Cicero, *Tusculan Disputations* iii. 31.76, where Cicero ascribes the lines to Aeschylus; a reference, in the ancient *Life of Aeschylus* 17, to 'the Prometheus plays of Aeschylus ... in which all the characters were gods.'[56]

Doubts concerning the adequacy of the external evidence for the authenticity of *Prometheus Bound* tend, therefore, to concentrate on the

---

55 Herington *Author* p 18.
56 See Coman *L'Authenticité* pp 9–10; cf also Schmid 'Epikritisches zum Gefesselten Prometheus' *Philologische Wochenschrift* no 7 (1931) 218–23, whom Coman cites here. Unlike Coman, however, Schmid does not regard *testimonia* dating from the Alexandrian period and later as firm evidence of Aeschylean authorship. (I have cited only the more impressive of the ancient *testimonia* listed in Coman's work. The apparent inaccuracy of the comment, quoted above, from the *Life of Aeschylus*, Coman, p 26 n 2, seeks to explain by reminding us of Io's divine parentage on her father's side.)

uncertainty of the tradition of the play between the mid-fifth century and the Alexandrian period two centuries later, and on the knowledge and precision of the Alexandrian scholars originally responsible for the Aeschylean catalogue and for the ascription of Aeschylean texts which have come down to us. Observations concerning the lack of known comments by extant authors upon an Aeschylean *Prometheus* (or, indeed, of any *clear* comment on Prometheus plays at all)[57] before the time of Cicero, may safely be set aside: the same obscurity was the fate of many other Greek tragedies whose authenticity scholars find no reason for doubting.[58] (Moreover, as we have seen, Herington has eloquently argued for the possible parody of the finale of the *Prometheus* trilogy at Aristophanes, *Birds*, 1494–1552,[59] and Aristophanes' liking for Aeschylean parody was second only to his similar enjoyment at Euripides' expense.)

Lack of didascalic information (that is, factual information concerning the author, date, and circumstances of production) in the Alexandrian *Hypothesis* which has come down with *Prometheus Bound* is, likewise, not in itself evidence against the play's authenticity, though such information would, of course, be of considerable assistance in this and related questions concerning the play. The possible Sicilian production of the play may explain the lack of at least some of this didascalic information, but in any case, though we are fortunate in possessing such hypothesis-statements in the case of the other plays of Aeschylus,[60] they are lacking in the case of many extant Greek tragedies, including five of the seven extant Sophoclean plays. Nevertheless, it is on the transmission of such didascalic information in general in the period between the production of the plays and the Alexandrian catalogues and editions that much of the debate about the reliability of the Alexandrian evidence still continues. Griffith asserts, no doubt correctly, that Aristotle's (lost) *Didascaliae* 'seem to have formed the starting-point for most subsequent scholarship on tragedy

---

57 There is one reference to *Prometheus* in Aristotle *Poetics* 1456A3; no author is mentioned, and unfortunately a textual uncertainty renders the comment obscure. Griffith's comment (*Authenticity* n 21 to p 227) that the use of the singular, *Prometheus*, would seem to indicate that he (Aristotle) was only familiar with one Prometheus play, seems gratuitous, particularly in view of the casual manner in which the text of the *Poetics* refers to ancient works.

58 Griffith admits as much (ibid p 8); nevertheless he refers to this 'neglect' again at pp 226–7, particularly by contemporaries such as Aristophanes. But on this latter point, see the reference to Herington in the following note.

59 Herington 'Birds and Prometheia.'

60 In the case of *The Suppliants* this good fortune has only recently been completed with the discovery of *Pap. Oxy.* 2256.3.

and comedy.'[61] The numerous doubts which Griffith expresses concerning the accuracy of Aristotle's record are based on arguments which are, of necessity, indirect and inconclusive.[62] Griffith's main point here is that Aristotle and subsequent compilers of *didascaliae* had no official source for the *titles* of plays produced each year; he presents a most haphazard and varied series of methods by which Aristotle and his successors may actually have come to identify various plays. And given this uncertainty in ascertaining the names of the original productions, the implication is, subsequent uncertainty in the identification of texts and of their authors must follow.

In all of this, Griffith seems to interpret our lack of knowledge always in the most pessimistic way. Because one does not know how productions and subsequently texts of individual plays were identified (and how these identifications were recorded, whether officially or otherwise) need that mean that no such ways of identification existed? Once one chooses to employ the argument from silence destructively, one can become almost nihilistic. For the implications of Griffith's scenario go far beyond the question of the authenticity of *Prometheus Bound*. If the situation was really as chaotic as Griffith suggests, then the Alexandrian catalogues of the works of the ancient tragedians must be quite unreliable, save where other external ancient evidence serves to corroborate them,[63] Callimachus and his colleagues must be mere uncritical compilers, and Aristotle, as the earliest authority on whom they heavily depended, must be a broken reed indeed.

In fact, when Griffith comes to describe what may have gone on in the compilation of the Alexandrian catalogues and in the assignment of tragic texts to specific tragedians, he does little to restore our confidence. Considering the very shaky didascalic tradition on which,

61 Griffith *Authenticity* p 228; cf also his references ad loc. (The following discussion is based on parts of Griffith's section, 'The Tradition,' pp 226–45.)

62 Eg, links are, not unreasonably (though of what *kind* we cannot know), assumed between Aristotle's *Didascaliae*, the official Athenian inscriptions concerning winning performances known as the *Fasti*, and earlier Athenian 'wall-inscriptions' of all tragedies and comedies at least as far back as the 420s. Doubt is then cast on the latter because a Roman inscription of comic playwrights and their production (presumably based, originally, on such Athenian inscriptions) shows gaps in the knowledge, concerning the names of the plays and concerning particular performances. Then, by association, similar doubt is cast on Aristotle's tragic *Didascaliae*.

63 As we shall see, Griffith gives little credit to possible assessment by Alexandrian scholars of internal evidence, eg, of stylistic details and the like, in judging a play's authorship. But this may be because he believes (as he suggests, gratuitously, of Callimachus, *Authenticity* p 244) that they were not particularly interested in problems of authenticity.

it has been suggested, Callimachus had to build and the allegedly uncertain authorship of many of the tragic texts which he had had collected, the picture of the great Alexandrian editor now searching for a play to fit a piece of didascalic information, now assigning anonymous tragedies on hand to poets not previously credited with them, is a frightening one indeed. Here, for example, is Griffith's conjecture as to how the misattribution of *Prometheus Bound* might have arisen:

> The *didaskaliai* may have listed a victory (or even a second or third place) one year for Αἰσχύλος Προμηθεῖ or Προμεθείαι, apart from the fourth play produced with *Persians* in 472; or there may have been no clues at all as to whether Aeschylus had composed other plays on this subject. But neither Sophocles or Euripides was supposed to have composed an entire play on this theme, and, as we have seen, relatively little interest was shown in obtaining the actual works of the other tragedians. Kallimachos found three Prometheus-plays, now known to us as Δεσμώτης, Λυόμενος and Πυρκαεύς, all of which he attributed to Aeschylus. In the absence of any rivals to the position, this attribution was canonized, and remained virtually unchallenged until this very century; Kallimachos' οὗ ἡ ἀρχή would ensure 'correct' attribution among his successors.[64]

(The tendency, suggested above, of Alexandrian, as well as fourth-century, scholars to neglect tragic poets other than the three famous names, supports Griffith in his belief, finally stated at the end of his study,[65] that while we do not know who wrote *Prometheus Bound*, it must have been one of a list of lesser (mostly younger) contemporaries whose other works have disappeared; Euphorion, son of Aeschylus, and Philocles, nephew of Aeschylus, are chosen as the most likely candidates.)

Generally speaking, then, Griffith's treatment of 'the tradition' is not very successful in destroying the strongest argument of the defenders of the authenticity of *Prometheus Bound*, the fact that its Aeschylean authorship was not doubted in antiquity. Two or three specific points in connection with this external evidence should, perhaps, be given more prominence than Griffith allows them. One is the point, well emphasized by Herington,[66] that the Alexandrian scholars were much more concerned about, and alert to the possibilities of, misattribution than Griffith would allow. Another is the unquestioning acceptance of both *Prometheus Bound* and *Prometheus Unbound* as Aes-

64 Ibid p 237.
65 Ibid p 254.
66 Herington *Author* p 18.

chylean by that great Roman Hellenist, Cicero.[67] A third is the encouraging fact that the tradition attributes to Aeschylus all three plays
(*Prometheus Bound*, *Prometheus Unbound*, *Prometheus the Firebearer*)
which we have taken to form the Prometheus trilogy. It has been
argued earlier in this study that *Prometheus Bound* seems to imply, in its
own theme and composition, a trilogy development of the kind of
which we have found Aeschylus capable. Thus, in this aspect of the
argument, the external ancient evidence seems also to afford at least
some slight support.

Concluding comments

We have seen that the Aeschylean authorship of *Prometheus Bound* has
been questioned on many different grounds: its subject matter and
general theme; its use of the Chorus in the overall dramatic structure;
its stylistic and even syntactical anomalies (in comparison with other
extant plays of Aeschylus); its vocabulary (where, however, we found
it next to impossible to determine criteria adequate for the investigation); finally, and perhaps most tellingly, its many metrical peculiarities (again in comparison with the rest of extant Aeschylus) both in the
iambic and the lyric passages.

It would be tedious to summarize again the pros and cons of the
various arguments here involved; however, one or two general
observations may, perhaps, be risked. In the areas listed above, most
of the arguments against authenticity which have been based on obvious or major features of the play (such as the treatment of Zeus; the
alleged sophistic material; the calculated departures, within highly
structured passages, from typical Aeschylean dialogue patterns; the
atypical features of the choral odes; the use of certain artificial rhetorical devices) have, on closer examination, failed to be really convincing;
at least reasonable counter-arguments can, in most of these cases, be
found. On the other hand, certain recurrent minor features of style,
syntax, and metrical practice (such as the use of particles, the relatively
high proportion of resultative perfects and of enjambement, the insouciance with regard to non-stop hiatus, the lack of syncopation in
trochaic verses, and the constant favouring of resolution over syncopation in lyric iambics) are much more difficult to explain away, though

67 See Cic. *Tusc. Disp.* iii.31.76, in which Cicero quotes *Prometheus Bound* 377–8, 379–80,
   translated into Latin, and describes the lines as, respectively, spoken to and by
   'Aeschylus' Prometheus.' Cf also the quotation at *Tusc. Disp.* ii 10.23–5 (fr 191N of
   Prometheus Unbound) which, as we have seen, Cicero also ascribes to Aeschylus.

some attempt to do so has been made in the foregoing discussion. By no means all of these features are specifically un-Aeschylean in themselves (often it is the number of incidences of a grammatical or metrical phenomenon which arouses comment); hence, one hesitates to deny Aeschylean authorship on such grounds alone. Nevertheless, the sheer volume of anomalies (both of this and of the large-scale kind mentioned earlier) which *Prometheus Bound* displays when compared with the other extant Aeschylean plays must continue to worry the conscientious reader.

Against these real difficulties we have set down what most critics would allow to be the strongest arguments for the defence: first, the very limited number of extant Aeschylean plays on which to base claims (particularly with regard to vocabulary, metrical practice, and the choice of lyric metres) as to what is, or is not, Aeschylean; second, the complete acceptance of the play as Aeschylean in antiquity; third, the Aeschylean nature (at least according to our arguments) of the theme and of the overall dramatic conception of this play and of what we can reasonably conjecture from the fragments and the tradition about the trilogy. To these arguments we might now add a fourth: the marked features of Aeschylean style which *Prometheus Bound does* manifest:[68] so much so, in fact, that, as we have seen, even the disbelievers speak of an imitator of Aeschylus as the possible author of our play. This last hypothesis is, perhaps, important for more than the obvious reasons: it reduces some of the force of objections to what *we* think, from our very limited evidence, to be clearly un-Aeschylean features, for would not a clever imitator have been particularly careful to avoid such obvious inconsistencies as unworthy of his model?

If, from the various arguments suggested, the reader, like the present author, should decide that belief in the Aeschylean authorship of *Prometheus Bound* should not, in the present state of the evidence, be abandoned, he must nevertheless admit that real difficulties lie in the way of its certain and unqualified acceptance. Some of these difficulties (the high incidence of non-stop hiatus, for example) may perhaps be explained as owing to inadequate revision of the last play of an ageing Aeschylus; others, perhaps, to circumstances of production of which we have no real knowledge; others still, to possible posthumous revi-

---

68 See, for example, Griffith *Authenticity* pp 148–57, on 'Types of Words' used in *Prometheus Bound*; cf also Herington's ironic description of 'the Prometheus-Master' as 'uncannily like Aeschylus in so many respects' (*Author* pp 107–8; cf ibid chapters 2–3 passim). Even Schmid seems to regard the author of *Prometheus Bound* as, in many respects, imitative of Aeschylean style: cf *Untersuchungen* p 96 and *Geschichte* p 281.

sions or even completions of parts of the play (here, the allegedly
atypical choral lyrics are the most likely objects of such speculation) by
contemporary tragedians, particularly members of the poet's family.[69]

Readers of this summary of the authenticity debate concerning
Prometheus Bound may feel that, in places at least, it represents a
defensive rearguard action against assault troops boasting far superior
equipment. If one has, for many years, read and discussed the play as
an Aeschylean tragedy, complete objectivity in assessing the recent
assaults on that belief is difficult to sustain. Thus, for example, it seems
inevitable that part of one's general impression of what is typical of
Aeschylus (particularly in the matter of themes and dramatic conceptions) is based on the play in question as well as on the other extant
plays. The element of subjectivity may not, it is true, be limited to one
side of the debate, but, for obvious reasons, the defenders of the
traditional and habitual position are more liable to the kind of circular-
ity of judgment, however unintentional, just suggested. Nevertheless,
much of the evidence which has been used against acceptance of the
Aeschylean authorship of *Prometheus Bound* does seem capable of
being interpreted in more than one way. If the more argumentative
(and perhaps inconclusive) parts of this appendix have succeeded in
indicating this, they will have served their purpose.[70]

69 Eg, Euphorion, Aeschylus' son; Philocles, Aeschylus' nephew. Cf Griffith's comment: 'Nor can we rule out the possibility of multiple authorship, with Euphorion or
   another member of the family completing a tragedy or trilogy begun by Aeschylus,
   for production after his death, perhaps even in his name' (*Authenticity* p 254).
70 The reader is also referred to observations on our problem in a recent work of Oliver
   Taplin, *The Stagecraft of Aeschylus* appendix D, 'The Authenticity of *Prometheus Bound*'
   pp 460–9, in which Taplin clearly indicates his doubts about the Aeschylean authorship of the play as we have it. This doubt has already been expressed by Taplin in
   an earlier chapter (chapter 5) in connection with various atypical features in the stage
   presentation of *Prometheus Bound*, some of which will be considered in the following
   appendix ('Notes on the Staging of *Prometheus Bound*'). Apart from his discussion of
   these features, Taplin does not advance any substantive arguments against the
   authenticity which are not presented in Griffith's work (which appeared after Taplin's book was completed). However, since Taplin's appendix is concerned rather
   with attacking 'some of the main arguments on which the generally accepted defence
   of the play rests' (p 240), the reader may find it useful in evaluating the present
   assessment of Griffith's formidable onslaught on the authenticity of *Prometheus
   Bound*.

Notes on the staging of
Prometheus Bound

Very little is known in detail about the staging of Greek tragedy in Aeschylus' time and even with regard to the whole of the fifth century, which saw, in its final quarter, the completion of the first permanent theatre, controversy still rages over the use, and the date of introduction, of various features of stage equipment and machinery. For a full discussion of the history of these controversies, and for the present state of scholarly opinion on them, the reader is referred to a selection of special studies.[1] This appendix will be concerned merely with suggesting to the reader the probable state of the Greek theatre at the end of Aeschylus' career (when we believe *Prometheus Bound* to have been presented) and with discussing a few specific problems about the staging of *Prometheus Bound* in particular. (We have already mentioned the possibility that *Prometheus Bound* was first produced at Sicily,[2] but we shall have to assume that, if that was the case, no major differences in the actual physical staging of tragedies obtained.)

In the earliest tragedies of the City Dionysia at Athens, both actor(s) and Chorus performed, on the same level, in the *orchêstra* or dancing-ground levelled out of the south slope of the Acropolis. Above the

---

1 Among the numerous reference books on various aspects of the ancient Greek theatre, the following will be found most useful for our purposes: Pickard-Cambridge *The Theatre of Dionysus in Athens* chapters 1–3; Arnott *Greek Scenic Conventions*; Taplin *Greek Tragedy in Action* (Berkeley and Los Angeles 1978) chapters 1–2; Taplin *The Stagecraft of Aeschylus*. (See also the various editions of the plays, most of which express the editors' views on controversial matters of staging.) For the 'factual' material summarized and (where indicated) for some of the conclusions relevant to *Prometheus Bound*, the present notes have drawn particularly on these works; reference to them will be made by author's name alone.

2 See above chapter 2, p 24 and n 7; cf below, n 21.

performer between the *orchêstra* and the sacred buildings commanding the hilltop, the audience ranged itself in a rough semi-circle on the slopes. About the beginning of the fifth century BC, an elementary *theatron* was constructed, an earthen auditorium consisting of a rising series of terraces on which wooden planks (*ikria*) were placed for seats. At this early stage, the only other distinction between spectators' and performers' areas was the entry passage (or passages; there may have been one on each side) leading into the circular *orchêstra* on the far side from the spectators. (These were later built up to form the permanent *parodoi* marking the boundary of the spectators' portion of the *theatron*.) Physically, the sacred character of the ancient theatre was already marked by the small altar (*thymelê*) of Dionysus in the centre of the *orchêstra*; to the right and further down the slope from the *orchêstra*, the audience could also see the old temple of Dionysus.

In addition, there was a temporary wooden building or hut (*skênê*), originally set outside of the *orchêstra* circle, on the far side from the audience, which was used as a changing-hut for the Chorus and actors and for the storing of costumes and such makeshift theatrical props as were in use. At a certain point, probably during the career of Aeschylus, this *skênê* was moved to the rear of the *orchêstra*, forming a temporary and movable backdrop to theatrical performances. This *skênê* was to become the ancestor of the permanent stage-building or 'scene' for later tragic productions. At the time of the erection of 'the Periclean Theatre' during the last half of the fifth century, and possibly before, this movable wooden *skênê* was fitted into slots (which are still discernible in the remaining stones) in the permanent masonry of a retaining wall behind the *orchêstra*.

Scholarly opinion is divided as to when, during Aeschylus' career, this wooden structure first came to be used, or regarded, as an actual part of the dramatic setting – a palace or a temple with at least a central door – in the way it was certainly used from the latter part of the fifth century onwards. One recent authority, Oliver Taplin, has argued that we know of no certain need of such a stage building in any of Aeschylus' plays before the *Oresteia* trilogy,[3] Aeschylus' last production (with the probable exception of the *Prometheus* trilogy), in 458 BC. On the other hand, as Taplin cites Bethe as observing, it is quite possible that the wooden *skênê* was also used (before and after the *Oresteia*) as a feature of the theatrical setting, such as the rock of Prometheus in *Prometheus Bound*.

Some mention, at least, should be made of the unending con-

3 See Taplin *Stagecraft* 453 ff.

troversy concerning the existence of a raised stage in the Greek theatre of the fifth century, though the issue, in the terms in which it is currently expressed, is not, perhaps, crucial to our view of the specific problems of the staging of *Prometheus Bound*. Here it will suffice to sketch the main elements in the controversy and the main positions taken with regard to them, and to refer the reader to a representative selection of recent scholarly opinion on the matter.[4]

It is now generally agreed that the high raised stage described by Vitruvius (a Roman architect of the Augustan period) belongs to the post-classical period. Reaction against the traditional (mainly nineteenth-century) acceptance of late evidence (based on Alexandrian and later authorities) for this and other features of the classical Greek theatre caused majority scholarly opinion to veer in the opposite direction and to reject the existence of *any* raised stage before the theatre of Lycurgus in the fourth century. Recently, however, some modification of this view has set in, and several scholars have argued for the use of a low raised stage (about four feet high) throughout fifth-century tragic productions. There is no archaeological evidence for this in Aeschylus' time and practically none in the time of the Periclean theatre: a point which is emphasized by opponents of the raised stage view but met by its defenders with the observation that one could hardly expect such evidence from the days of wooden *skenai*. As Arnott has put it, 'the raised stage problem is a matter not of facts ['of hard evidence' might have been a happier phrase, here] but of interpretation.' Pickard-Cambridge, the most authoritative opponent of any raised stage for fifth-century tragedy, argues that the idea (as well as lacking archaeolo-

---

4 See, for example, Taplin *Stagecraft*, esp pp 441–2, appendix B and appendix C (Taplin *Stagecraft* pp 441–2 regards the idea of a low raised stage for fifth-century tragedy as at least a reasonable hypothesis; he tends to doubt, pp 452–9, the presence of the *skênê* as a background to the action before the production of the *Oresteia*); Pickard-Cambridge *The Theatre of Dionysus* pp 69–74 (Pickard-Cambridge provides the most strenuous arguments against a raised stage, high or low, for fifth-century tragedy); Arnott *Greek Scenic Conventions* pp 1–42; and Hourmouziades *Production and Imagination in Euripides* chapter 3 (the initial part of his discussion applies to the time of Aeschylus). Both Arnott and Hourmouziades present reasonable arguments for a low raised stage from the beginning of the fifth century based on the plays themselves (most notably, in the case of Hourmouziades, on Aeschylean plays); some of these are indicated in the following paragraph of the text. Arnott's other arguments are less convincing, and he had been criticized by Taplin (*Stagecraft* p 441) leaning heavily on late sources; even if this is so, he makes up for it by bringing to his scholarly discussion of the plays a dramatic imagination clearly informed by practical theatrical experience. Cf also nn 12 and 17 (below) for the somewhat different view of N.G.L. Hammond, now followed by M.L. West, on 'elevated utterances' in Aeschylean tragedy and in *Prometheus Bound*.

gical evidence) accords ill with the concentration of interest in the
Chorus whose 'ritual solemnity' and 'prophetic function' he regards as
'embodying the spirit and soul of the poet's teaching.' Some defenders
of the low raised stage, however, argue reasonably that while such a
platform would help to distinguish actors from Chorus during the acts,
both levels (stage and orchestra) would be accessible to both elements,
and communication between them need not be broken. It is on the
evidence of (or perhaps, rather, by inference from) the plays themselves that these scholars base most of their arguments: both Arnott
and Hourmouziades, for example, point to various indications of elevation, look-out points, high rocks, etc or of ascent or descent (eg, to and
from altars) implied in the texts of tragedy, especially of Aeschylean
tragedy. Agreement with such inferences will, of course, depend on
the reader's willingness to accept for early Greek tragedy even the
limited degree of realistic representation involved in this view.

Acceptance of some kind of low-platform stage becomes perhaps
easier once we can be sure of the presence of a temporary wooden *skênê*
or stage building providing a backdrop to the action. This is certainly
required for the palace and temple buildings of Aeschylus' *Oresteia* in
458 BC, and once such a *skênê* was there it seems reasonable to imagine
two or three low steps leading up to the central entrance. The presence
of this platform stage is still easier to accept as a part of this movable
skênê when we know (from the grooves in the supporting stone wall)
that the *skênê* was a regular feature of the Periclean theatre. Indeed,
once the movable *skênê* capable of representing a palace façade is
accepted for the fifth-century theatre (as it must be from at least 458 BC
onwards) acceptance of *some form* of low stage seems quite admissible.
(It is puzzling that Pickard-Cambridge, who is willing to accept that
such façades may have been approachable from the orchestra by 'one
or two broad steps,' is still unwilling to countenance the possibility of a
low raised stage at the same period.)

What other stage properties and mechanisms, if any, did the trage-
dian of Aeschylus' time have at his disposal? Scene-painting
(*skênographia*), we are told by Aristotle, was introduced by Sophocles;
this could, of course, have been during the latter part of Aeschylus'
career, and indeed we are told by Vitruvius (a less reliable source for
fifth-century practice) that a painter called Aristarchus, 'working
under Aeschylus' instruction,' did scene-painting.[5] However, neither

5 Aristotle *Poetics* 1449 A 18; Vitruvius vii, praef. II (Vitruvius, a Roman architect of the
 Augustan period, may be expected to be more knowledgeable about Hellenistic than
 about classical Greek architecture and decoration).

of these (somewhat uncertain) bits of information has very much relevance to our questions. Recent opinion concerning such early *skênographia* tends to regard it as decoration of the *skênê* rather than as literal or even conventionalized depictions of actual settings; though when the *skênê* came to be used for a palace or temple façade (viz, in the *Oresteia*), such scene-painting may have been used to indicate this. (If Aristarchus was indeed involved, this would have been appropriate, since he was known for his interest in problems of perspective in architectural representations.) Of the stage mechanisms used in the classical Greek theatre, probably only the crane (*mêchanê*) is of relevance to the discussion of the staging of *Prometheus Bound*. We do not know the precise date at which this device was introduced. Pollux, a scholar of the second century AD who describes this instrument, draws his examples of its use from Euripides,[6] and it is Euripides' frequent use of the *deus-ex-machina* which Aristophanes parodies in his comedies. Sophocles, at least as far as we can tell from the extant plays and fragments, may not have used the *mêchanê* at all. Nor (apart from *Prometheus Bound*) does extant Aeschylus provide any situations where we may reasonably expect that the *mêchanê* was used, a point which we should bear in mind when considering the probability or otherwise of its use even in the *Prometheus*. (The date of introduction, as well as the precise use, of the *ekkuklêma*, or revolving platform, by which interior scenes were shown, is a matter of further debate; however, this is of no relevance to the staging of *Prometheus Bound*, where, at least in my opinion, there was no occasion for it.)

From the limited external evidence and more particularly from the texts of the plays themselves (where, as recent scholarship in particular has shown us, there are usually implicit indications as to what was going on on-stage and what was left to the audience's imagination working on the poet's descriptions) one forms the impression that Aeschylean theatre depended little on scenic and mechanical effects.[7] The 'illusionist' theatre of later times was the product of a long and laborious development from its somewhat creaking origins in the use of the revolving platform (*ekkuklêma*) and the increasing use of the

---

6　Pollux iv. 128; cf Arnott pp 72 ff.

7　For the important working rule that the words of the plays, properly interpreted, are the best indications of the stage action, see Taplin *Stagecraft* pp 28 ff and, in application, passim throughout his book. See also his valuable appendix B ('The Stage Resources of Fifth Century Theatre') for warnings concerning the unreliability of much of the 'late' ancient evidence (especially that emanating from Roman and Byzantine times) for the fifth-century Greek theatre. Such evidence, he rightly insists, should be used only in corroboration, never in refutation, of the evidence provided by the plays themselves.

mêchanê in the latter part of the fifth century. Recent scholarship is surely right in its constant reminders that simply because uses *can* be found for scene-painting and elaborate mechanical devices in fifth-century tragedy, that is no reason to suppose that they *were* actually used, especially in earlier tragedy.[8] Similarly, one is grateful to Oliver Taplin for doing much to discount Aeschylus' reputation (in later times) for lavish and spectacular stage effects. While admitting that 'the plays themselves do clearly indicate a fair number of exotic and ceremonial spectacles,' Taplin shows that all such spectacles do dramatic work within their plays and that most of them depend not on stage mechanisms and contrivances but on costume, song, dance, and (as in the case of the Chorus of Erinyes) brilliant dramatic conceptions.[9]

On the basis of this general impression of the usages of Aeschylean theatre, let us approach the several problems and uncertainties which arise concerning the original stage presentation of *Prometheus Bound*. While it is not difficult to present the problems, the reader will soon see that solutions to them must inevitably involve an element of subjective judgment, not to say guesswork, based, to a greater or lesser degree, on a close reading of the text and on our very limited knowledge of theatrical procedures in the mid-fifth century. One initial point may perhaps be made. All the major problems in reconstructing the original stage presentation of *Prometheus Bound* are fundamentally of the same kind. Thus it seems wise to attempt answers which will be consistent with one another or, to put it another way, answers which all reflect the same general view of Aeschylean theatrical technique. From what has already been said, it will be clear that our own expectations will favour a production which depends to a high degree on the vivid descriptions in the text and on the imagination of the readers for the visualization of the outlandish setting and the more macabre elements of the physical action.

When the play opens Prometheus is 'discovered' being bound to a lofty mountain crag. (The anachronistic term itself serves as a preliminary indication of 'the willing suspension of disbelief' required of a

---

8 Cf Arnott pp 91–2 on 'Country Settings''; cf also his chapter 5 passim, on 'Stage Machinery.'
9 See Taplin *Stagecraft* pp 39–49. Particularly interesting are his suggestions as to how possible misconceptions about 'the spectacular' in Aeschylean theatre may have come about: from misinterpretation of Aristophanic satire, in *Frogs*, of Aeschylean language and word-pictures; from misapplication of Aristotle *Poetics* 1453 B 8–10 to Aeschylus; and from too-credulous acceptance of comments in the anonymous *Life of Aeschylus.*

modern audience accustomed to illusory rather than conventional stage technique: Prometheus and his captors, Hephaistos, Kratos, and Bia, would, of course, have to walk on-stage to assume their positions before the play begins.) Pickard-Cambridge posits 'some high central erection on the far side of the orchestra from the audience' to which Prometheus is fastened.[10] This suggestion seems to me to create too many unnecessary contingent problems. Even this degree of realism requires scene-painting of a mountainous background surrounding Prometheus' crag with (as Pickard-Cambridge also adds) 'a slope or steps leading up to Prometheus' rock.' Such elaborate scene-painting is, as we have seen, unlikely in Aeschylus' time; moreover (since Pickard-Cambridge is being 'realistic') we would have to accept the improbability of a convenient plateau for the later choral dances immediately below Prometheus' rock. All is, of course, conjecture, but I would prefer Arnott's view (partially supported by suggestive dramatic and artistic comparisons) that the rock to which Prometheus is bound was symbolized by an upright post at the far side of the *orchêstra* from the audience.[11] If the movable *skênê* was by this time a part of the theatrical setting, then it is also possible (as Taplin acquiescently cites Bethe as suggesting) that this simple wooden structure was used to represent Prometheus' rock.[12]

10 Pickard-Cambridge p 38.
11 Arnott pp 97–8.
12 See Taplin *Stagecraft* p 454 and reference to Bethe, there given. For another, recent view of the representation of the enchainment of Prometheus, see Hammond 'Dramatic Production to the Death of Aeschylus' esp pp 422 ff. Hammond believes that throughout the time of Aeschylean drama a rock-outcrop remained at the east side of the orchestra, projecting slightly into it, a little above the eastern parodos. There is archaeological evidence that 'at some time a considerable area of the rock was cut away roughly to the level of the orchestra' (ibid, p 409). Other authorities, notably Dorpfield and Dinsmoor whom Hammond cites, believe (to my mind most reasonably) that the removal of this rock-outcrop occurred when the theatre of Dionysus was first being established on the south slope of the Acropolis. Hammond's belief rests mainly on the rather dubious ground that he can find uses for the rock in all extant Aeschylean tragedy, the rock to which Prometheus is bound being one of his prize examples. (Hammond believes that the rock-outcrop may not have been removed until the construction of the Periclean theatre, completed 420 BC, when the orchestra was moved some fifteen metres forward and the eastern parodos passed over the levelled remains of the outcrop.) West, in *his* suggestions about the staging of *Prometheus Bound*, has recently come out in favour of 'Hammond's rock' but with considerable modifications of Hammond's views to suit theories of his own. (See below, n 17.) Taplin, too (*Stagecraft* pp 448–9), gives partial assent to Hammond's theory but believes that the rock was removed at the time of the introduction of the *skênê*, shortly before the *Oresteia* (cf also ibid p 457).

Before passing on to the next, and more interesting, problem of
stage presentation, we should mention, if only to dismiss, the curiously persistent theory that Prometheus himself was represented by a
large dummy, a view which has been supported and attacked by
almost equally balanced forces of scholarly opinion – at least until
recently when, for the most part, 'the nays have it.'[13] The only cogent
argument in favour of this view, namely that it would reduce to two the
number of speaking actors on stage at once, has little force if the
Prometheus, as seems probable to most who accept its authenticity, was
one of Aeschylus' last plays. Refutation of a theory with little or
nothing to recommend it is, perhaps, superfluous, but of the various
arguments urged against it, the simplest and best might be mentioned:
how, if Prometheus was represented by a dummy, could he be released and move about in the subsequent plays of the trilogy?[14]

Major problems of stage presentation arise in connection with the
entry of the Chorus and their later activities. Let us enumerate these
briefly before following up a few of the many suggestions for meeting
them. First, the Okeanids themselves tell us that they have rushed to
Prometheus (from the depths of the ocean, according to their immediately preceding sentence) in their winged car (135), and we have
already heard Prometheus' startled outcry of the flutter of wings
approaching, before he perceives who his visitors are. Is this winged
chariot visible to the audience? If so how is it introduced and where
does it land? Secondly, the Chorus clearly remain in the chariot all
through the kommatic parodos and the first part of the first episode, till
just before the entry of Okeanos, for Prometheus bids them (272–3)
descend to the ground and listen to his coming woes, and the Chorus
acquiesce (277 ff), obviously suiting the action to their words:

> ... and now, leaving the seat of this speedy chariot
> [κραιπνόσυτον θᾶκον], leaving *aither*, the sacred highway of birds, I
> approach this craggy land ... (278–81)

Thirdly, why does Okeanos, who appears at this moment, completely
ignore his daughters throughout his whole scene with Prometheus?

Wilamowitz, Murray, and others believed that the crane was used to
swing the Chorus on scene in the winged chariot. Wilamowitz suggested that the Okeanids sang the parodos from their airborne car,

13 For 'the lists,' pro and con, in this debate, see Taplin *Stagecraft* p 243, who rejects 'the
   dummy theory.'
14 See Pickard-Cambridge p 42, and others.

disembarked (following v 283) in a ravine behind Prometheus' rock, and made their way, unseen (during the scene between Okeanos and Prometheus), to the level of the *orchêstra*, which they entered, for the first stasimon, after Okeanos' departure.[15] Murray's view is similar except that he thinks that the Chorus and Okeanos may have been balanced on opposite ends of a double crane (!) and that the Chorus may have alighted on a crag at vv 281 ff.[16] Both views surely require more elaborate scenery and more robust mechanical equipment than seems likely to have existed in Aeschylus' time. However, after due allowance is made for lack of realism and for the poet's dependence on the audience's imagination, we cannot doubt, in view of the specific references in the text (135, 272 ff, 278–81), that the Okeanids are seated in the winged chariot during the parodos and that they leave it when they acquiesce in Prometheus' request that they do so. Here the view of Pickard-Cambridge seems quite tenable: that the winged car is pushed forward without use of a crane, onto the top of the stage-building (which could still be quite a rudimentary one) whence the Chorus descend 'whether by concealed steps or [less probably, in my view] from behind the scenes, into the orchestra, while Prometheus is talking to Okeanos.'[17]

15 Wilamowitz *Interpretationen* pp 115–16.
16 Murray *Aeschylus* pp 40–2.
17 Pickard-Cambridge pp 39–40. In order to keep up to date on these matters, one must, I suppose, at least allude to M.L. West's (to my mind) outlandish view of the staging of the Chorus' entry in his 'The Prometheus Trilogy' pp 137–9. West has accepted Griffith's evidence against the Aeschylean authorship of *Prometheus Bound* and so is free to envisage a theatre of a later date than the Aeschylean period (later, as we shall see, even than Griffith's conjecture). He supposes four to six cranes to have been used to swing on the Chorus of twelve Okeanids over a stage *not yet built over*, but sufficiently widened to accommodate the cranes, which would be partially hidden behind screens. 'The rock [see above n 12] has not yet been removed; the east *eisodos* has to skirt it. It follows that *Prometheus* and its companion plays could only have been conceived and produced at a certain fairly short transitional period in the development of the theatre of Dionysus, say between c. 445 and c. 435' (p 138). (Readers of Hammond's article will remember that the main reason given for the preservation of the rock-outcrop during the Aeschylean period was its function as a natural *bema* or speaking platform before the introduction of any kind of constructed stage or steps: cf Hammond 'Dramatic Production' pp 409–10.) The theatrical non sequitur of the Chorus' apparent alighting at 277 ff (after hovering aloft during their initial exchanges with Prometheus) and the entry of Okeanos at v 284 West explains by regarding the Okeanos scene as a later insertion 'made by the poet because he found his play was turning out too short' (p 138). West has poked considerable fun (p 137) at 'the abandoned transport' and other such devices necessary for the Chorus' entry in winged cars, but appears to accept the clutter of his 'four to six' cranes with equanim-

Each of the foregoing suggestions for the Chorus' entry (or rather
entries) seeks to meet both the explicit indications in the text that the
Chorus do not leave their winged chariot until vv 278 ff, *and* the fact
that Okeanos gives no indication of the presence of the Okeanids
during his scene with Prometheus. In unrealistic drama, it is possible
that dramatic convenience could explain this omission, though, as
Taplin points out,[18] it is without parallel in extant Aeschylus. But so
also (as Taplin also observes)[19] is the somewhat informal appearance,
disappearance, and reappearance of the Chorus in the manner suggested above. Those who find the latter anomaly more upsetting than
the failure of Okeanos and the Chorus to recognize one another's
presence may wish to accept Sikes and Willson's less 'realistic' view that
the Chorus' winged car was simply pushed initially onto the
orchêstra.[20] The other view, however, seems preferable, especially
since it also accounts for the long gap between the Chorus' statement
that they will now descend from the chariot and approach Prometheus
on his rock (represented either by the movable stage-building or by a
post on the same level as the *orchêstra*, as we have envisaged it) and
their next activity, at vv 397 ff, the song and dance (first stasimon)
expressing sympathy for Prometheus' woes. Finally, with regard to the
fact that, for theatrical or other reasons, the poet has here provided the
only known instance of a parodos sung (whether in the *orchêstra* or not)
but not danced, there seems little to be said.[21] (Thomson's insistence
that the Chorus not only *do* dance the parodos but that their dance,
symbolizing the flight of sea-nymphs, replaces the need of any winged
equipment,[22] is unacceptable in view of the Chorus' clear statement
(278 ff, well after the parodos) that they are now about to leave their
seat (θᾶκον), previously described as a winged chariot at v 135.) Either

ity. It should be added also that there is no evidence (archaeological or other) of the
'transitional theatre' (complete with natural rock-outcrop, hundred-foot stage, and
numerous cranes, but inconsiderable stage buildings) which he describes as conveniently existing between c 445 and 435 BC.

18 Taplin *Stagecraft* pp 257–8.
19 Ibid p 255.
20 Sikes and Willson p xlvi.
21 Cf, however, the interesting suggestion of Focke ('Aischylos' *Prometheus*') to which
    reference has already been made (chapter 2, p 24 and n 7) that if the *Prometheus* was
    first produced in Sicily, Aeschylus may have reduced the usual demands on the
    Chorus because of a lack of well-trained *choreutae*.
22 Thomson, introduction, p 143. Thomson does not provide evidence for the Chorus'
    alleged 'dance conventionally associated with the flight of sea-nymphs on their
    winged horses.' He also conveniently understands the winged chariot of v 135 (=140

we accept this exceptional feature of the parodos, so clearly indicated in the text, or else we are reduced to the extreme and in this instance surely unjustified recourse of excision. Bethe would conveniently omit vv 271–84; Taplin, who regards the whole Ocean episode with the exception of the 'Typhon digression' as 'turgid, wordy and bathetic,' would eliminate all of it except vv 351–72.[23] Such solutions will not, however, appeal to readers who agree with our earlier appreciation of that scene – or, indeed, to readers who have any respect for the integrity of the received text of the play, whatever its authorship.

Other problems of the staging of *Prometheus Bound* (including even the much debated final scene) are on the whole less perplexing than that of the entry of the Chorus. The entry of Okeanos (at v 284) may have involved the *mêchanê* (a simple use of it, not involving a great weight like that of a Chorus of twelve Okeanids), or Okeanos may simply have entered, probably on the roof on the *skênê* (the usual place for divine epiphanies, once the *skênê* became part of the theatrical setting), possibly simply on the *orchêstra* level. The aforementioned lack of other clear examples of the use of the *mêchanê* in Aeschylus' time (or of much else in the way of illusionist equipment) discourages Arnott from believing in its use here; moreover, as Jebb has pointed out, advance notice in the text is regularly given before the use of the *mêchanê*,[24] and Okeanos enters without any warning at all. Most authorities, however, do accept the use of the crane for Okeanos' entry;[25] a proper answer to the question really depends entirely on the (unknown) date of the first introduction of this equipment. What does seem certain is that Okeanos is mounted on a winged sea-bird of some kind: there would be no point in his repeated mention of it (286–7; 394–6, at his arrival and departure respectively), and especially in his use of the demonstrative τόνδ᾽ at 286, unless the creature was actually present. Since this is the case, Okeanos, if the crane was not used, would probably have to be pushed onstage riding the dummy sea-bird, and this would be contrived more easily on the roof of the *skênê* than at the rear of the *orchêstra*. However, some readers may feel that this

Thomson) to refer to the (imaginary) winged horse of each sea-nymph and the 'seat' of v 279 (=295 Thomson) to its back. Later, in his note on vv 277–83 (=293–9 Thomson) he rather vaguely explains that when the Chorus leave this seat they are merely leaving the *thymelê* (altar) around which they have been clustered since the end of the parodos.

23 Taplin *Stagecraft* pp 258–60: for the reference to Bethe's argument, ibid p 258.
24 See Jebb's note on Soph. *Philoctetes* 1409, to which Arnott refers p 73 and, for the latter's discussion of Okeanos' entry, see Arnott pp 75–8.
25 See Pickard-Cambridge pp 40–1.

monstrous, supposedly airborne apparition, both winged and four-footed, does in fact call for the crane to do its justice.

The Io scene is certainly the most theatrical, spectacular in the best sense of the word, scene in the play and, indeed, one of the most striking, in visual and vocal effects, of any actor-dominated scene in Aeschylus. Enough has been said already, in other parts of this study, of the power and significance of these effects. Here we need remark only on the unique technical feature, for extant Aeschylean productions, of the scene. After an opening series of anapaests (561–5), Io sings and dances a lyrical passage which lasts, with one interruption, for over forty verses. When the form becomes strophic, Io's lyrical questions are answered, after strophe and antistrophe, respectively, by four iambic verses from Prometheus. The unique feature (for Aeschylus) of this epirrhematic structure is, of course (as Taplin observes) that 'both lyric and spoken elements are supplied by the actors.'[26] *Prometheus Bound* is an unusual play in its theme and in its *dramatis personae*, both of which descend to the human level only to depict moments of frenzied suffering induced by the gods: it is not surprising, then, that it should indulge in such unusual technical effects, which are clearly well within the power of its poet to carry off. And the weird mask of Io as the cow-headed maid helps, perhaps, to support a choreographed singing role not normally expected of human figures in Aeschylean drama.

The manner of Hermes' entry at v 944 raises no great difficulty, though various features of the entry announcement for Hermes (particularly the fact that it is made by Prometheus, not the Chorus) have occasioned scholarly comment.[27] There is no indication in the text and no other reason to believe that the *mêchanê* was involved in this entry. Presumably Hermes simply walked on, either at the *orchêstra*-level or, more impressively, onto the roof of the *skênê* (we simply do not know when this was first used as a *logeion*, or speaking platform, for divine *personae*), and left when he had delivered his last warning to the Chorus (1071–9). Wilamowitz thinks Hermes remains during vv 1080–

26 Taplin *Stagecraft* p 266. The conventional form of the so-called 'epirrhematic *kommos*' in Aeschylus (in which the Chorus sing the lyrical parts and the actor 'interrupts' with iambic, 'dramatic' verses) is to be found, for example, at *Ag.* 1407–47. In the Io scene, this dispensing with the Chorus in a passage of the kind where, in terms of typical Aeschylean production, it might have been expected to function reminds us again of Focke's comments and explanation (above, n 21) concerning the reduced role of the Chorus in this play. However, one should add that, in purely dramatic terms, this adaptation of the epirrhematic structure is entirely appropriate.

27 See Taplin *Stagecraft* pp 268–9.

93, but surely the presence of the Titanic figure alone with the faithful Chorus provides a more impressive tableau for Prometheus' description of the cataclysm and for his final cry of defiance and justification.[28]

Scholarly difficulties raised concerning the staging of the final scene of *Prometheus Bound* have been due, in large part, to too literal-minded a conviction that scenic effects must accompany all descriptions. Prometheus' actual fate is, of course, quite clear from the text, and that of the Chorus only slightly less clear. Hermes declares (1016 ff) that Zeus will blast the crag to which Prometheus is bound with the thunderbolt and that it will bear the Titan off in its rocky embrace. Prometheus' ultimate destination is likewise clear from Hermes' further prophecy that he need expect no end of his woes until some god agrees to replace him in Tartaros (1026–9), a threat which Prometheus accepts at face value in his final taunt to Zeus, 'So let him hurl my body headlong to black Tartaros ... !' (1050–2). (It seems necessary to spell this out again, since recently Taplin, who is so eminently sensible in various explanations of the staging of *Prometheus Bound*, refuses to accept more than the prophecy that Prometheus and the Chorus with him will be buried by the thunder-smitten mountain.)[29] That the Okeanids are to share Prometheus' fate also seems clear: Hermes warns them to stand clear, 'away from this place,' lest their wits be crazed by the thunderbolt; the nymphs indignantly reject this course as cowardly and dishonourable: 'with this one, I wish to suffer what must be suffered!' (1963–7); Hermes adjures them not to claim later 'that Zeus has hurled them to unforeseen disaster,' since he has warned them, 'For with full knowl-

28 See Wilamowitz *Interpretationen* p 118. I agree with Taplin, p 270, in believing that Hermes exits at v 1079.

29 Taplin *Stagecraft* p 272 curiously takes Hermes' reference to Prometheus' coming punishment in Tartaros (1027–9) not as part of Hermes' prophetic statements but 'simply as an ἀδύνατον' ie, as a rhetorical expression for an impossibility. But there is, of course, nothing impossible about Zeus' hurling of Prometheus to Tartaros; *if* there is anything of an *adunaton* here present in the mind of Hermes, it might be the contingency that some god actually would ever be willing to fulfil the condition of Prometheus' future liberation by taking his place. This whole statement of Hermes is, as we have seen (above, chapter 5 p 98), one of the passages which anticipate the trilogy development (though it is true that Prometheus will have returned to the mountain-top before the divine substitution is to occur), and as such is clearly prophetic; Hermes would, in any case, be unlikely to invent such a specific situation, which actually is to occur in the future, simply as an *adunaton* chosen at random. Taplin's curious, not to say perverse, treatment of this passage may, perhaps, be related to his reluctance to regard the present play as part of a connected trilogy of the kind usually reconstructed; cf his note 2 to p 272; cf also Taplin's appendix D ('The Authenticity of Prometheus Bound') and his note 'The Title of *Prometheus Desmotes*.'

edge, not suddenly by means of stealth, will you be enmeshed in the inextricable net of *atê* (ruin), through your bad counsel' (1071–9). Thomson, heeding only the first part of Hermes' warnings, concludes, 'All we have to suppose, therefore, is that, stunned and scattered by the earthquake, the Oceanids disappear from the orchestra.'[30]

The reluctance of Thomson and others to accept the clear indications of the text about the fate of the Okeanids stems partly from a sense of moral outrage,[31] partly from misapprehensions about realistic staging. With regard to the first point, it need merely be said that the Chorus are not a collective 'tragic hero' but rather an instrument (however heartless it may sound) of dramatic effect. Once they have established their undying loyalty, they simply become part of the total final cataclysm (and in so doing enhance the worth of Prometheus). Certainly we are not expected to think of the Okeanids' time in Tartaros as if they were to be figures in the subsequent plays of the trilogy! With regard to the second point, scholars concerned with the stage representation of the disposal of Prometheus will, of course, find increased difficulty in dealing with that of the Chorus. Thus Thomson, though accepting as probable the withdrawal of Prometheus on the *ekkuklêma*, naturally jibs at fitting the Chorus onto this machine as well, and even Sikes and Willson, though allowing that Prometheus' description of the final storm replaces 'any actual representation' of it, still posits 'the literal disappearance of the central figure' through a trapdoor, while the Chorus 'flee to right and left from the view of the audience.'

All these difficulties disappear if we accept (justifiably, in my view) Pickard-Cambridge's common-sense solution. Rejecting the editorial view hitherto prevailing, that Prometheus' descent was shown onstage, he believes that the play ends with Prometheus' description of the growing storm as the Chorus cluster around him 'preparing for the worst.'[32] Arnott and Taplin take substantially the same view, that the cataclysm is left to the audience's imagination working on the description provided in the text, but while Pickard-Cambridge regards the victims as still waiting for the cataclysm (to the sound of off-stage storm-noises) as the play ends, Arnott and Taplin (rightly, in my view) recognize that the audience would accept it as actually *happening* (without physical stage effects) during Prometheus' final description beginning 'and now in fact and no longer in prophetic word (καὶ μὴν ἔργῳ

30 Thomson, edition of *Prometheus Bound* p 174.
31 Cf Sikes and Willson p xlvii: '... we can scarcely believe that Aeschylus could have meant to involve the innocent Ocean nymphs in the punishment of the guilty.'
32 Pickard-Cambridge p 38.

κοὐκέτι μύθῳ, 1080) the earth is shaken ...'[33] Arnott generalizes well on the whole technique of this final scene:

> ... a thing can either be described or shown, and there is no need to do both ... if the effect is announced frequently beforehand, and the audience is left in no doubt as to what is coming, we may conjecture that without such notice it would not be appreciated – that is, the effect is symbolic, not realistic.[34]

One further point of an entirely different kind, though still connected with the *physical* action of the play, remains to be mentioned. This is the important and well-demonstrated observation in Taplin's recent study that '*Prom.* departs more than any other play of Aeschylus, and perhaps more than any other surviving tragedy, from the regular association of exit and entry with act-dividing songs.'[35] Taplin notes particularly the lack of exit and entry before and after the parodos; the lack of entry or exit throughout the second episode (436–525), despite the fact that the odes preceding and following it are clearly 'act-dividing songs' and the lack of an entry after the choral song at 907 (Hermes does not enter until 944). The second of these examples is marked as the most egregious: 'it seems almost as though in this play the dramatist is trying to break away from the normal interconnection of song and act with exit and entry.'[36]

Not all readers will agree either with the explanation which Taplin (at one point at least) suggests for what he calls 'the non-coincidence of structure and action' in this play or with the debilitating effect which he claims that it produces. One explanation hinted at is that the phenomenon may be a feature of an unfinished (Aeschylean) play later filled out and patched together.[37] But surely this structural feature recurs too consistently for such a haphazard explanation to be valid. Taplin can find no compensating gain or even reasonable dramatic explanation for the anomaly he notes. On the contrary, in the case of the second episode in particular (436–525), he remarks on 'the undeniable slowness and monotony which results from the rejection of new incident,'[38] and his impression of the play as episodic and discon-

33 See Arnott pp 123–9; Taplin *Stagecraft* p 273
34 Arnott pp 123–4.
35 Taplin *Stagecraft* p 268; for his whole discussion of this point, see pp 245–69.
36 Ibid p 262.
37 Ibid p 250; cf pp 258–9.
38 Ibid p 264.

nected is imputed in part, at least, to its lack of entries and exits at the expected points. (One would expect the Io episode, which *is* provided with an entry and exit at beginning and end respectively, to fare better ... and so it does, to a degree, but, alas, its 'internal coherence' only helps to make it 'a kind of play within a play [which] lacks any significant connection with what goes before and after it'!)[39]

This is not the place to return to a detailed defence of the structure of *Prometheus Bound*; readers must decide for themselves whether its various parts (including the scenes with Okeanos and with Io), as discussed earlier in their relation to the whole,[40] have seemed episodic, disconnected, or otherwise haphazard. One or two observations may, however, be ventured with regard to Taplin's specific complaint. In the case of two-actor or even three-actor tragedy (particularly when, as in Aeschylus, three actors are seldom actively employed at the same time), the necessary retention of the protagonist on-stage throughout is likely to result in less than the usual number of entries and exits, and a corresponding change in what Taplin describes as the normal structure in relation to 'act-dividing songs' is thus to be expected. Add to this the emphasis on the isolation of Prometheus (which Taplin mentions only to dismiss in this connection), and it is not surprising that an address by Prometheus (either in soliloquy or to the Chorus as the conventionally present sounding-board) should frequently begin a scene where in normal circumstances a new actor might be introduced. Admittedly, then, the poet abandons, in the dramatic circumstances, the usual structural relation between choral songs and exits and entrances. Even so, is the unusual timing of entrances always so malapropos as Taplin suggests? The mid-scene entry of Okeanos (and, indeed, the whole Okeanos scene) Taplin finds particularly irritating. We have seen, however, that when the structure is viewed in relation to the thematic development ('Prometheus in relation to the gods' ... 'Prometheus in relation to man'), 'the Okeanos scene provides the dramatic conclusion (at just the right moment) to the first part of the play, while the longer Io episode provides the dramatic conclusion to the second part *and* the significant connection between the two.

So, too, in the Hermes episode, it is essential that Prometheus voice his fatal defiance of Zeus *after* the departure of Io and after the second part of the choral frame surrounding the Io episode. (Otherwise this fatal defiance would become part of the Io episode when, in fact, it is

39 Ibid p 267.
40 See above, chapter 3; cf also chapter 2.

something altogether different, though causally related to it.) Since it is this defiance which brings Hermes on-stage, it is inevitable also that his entry should be thus postponed. In brief, the critic should be willing to adjust his structural expectations to the dramatic requirements of the play.

Bibliography

1 Editions, commentaries, etc

NOTE For the text of *Prometheus Bound* I have used mainly Gilbert Murray's text (Oxford Classical Texts 1938, second edition, 1955) and for fragments of Greek tragedy, A. Nauck and Bruno Snell *Tragicorum Graecorum Fragmenta* (Hildesheim 1964). Other editions, commentaries, and translations, as noted below, have also been consulted.

Grene, David, and Lattimore, Richmond, edd   *The Complete Greek Tragedies* vol I. *Aeschylus* Chicago 1959

Groeneboom, P., ed   *Aeschylus Prometheus* Groningen 1928 [1966]

Herington, C.J.   *The Older Scholia on the Prometheus Bound* Leiden 1972

Herington, C. John and Scully, James *Aeschylus: Prometheus Bound* (translation and introduction) New York and London 1975

Lloyd-Jones, Hugh See Smythe, H.W.

Long, H.S.   *Notes on Aeschylus' 'Prometheus Bound': Proceedings of the American Philosophical Society* No 102 (1958)

Mazon, Paul, ed   *Eschyle* I. Neuvième tirage. Budé, Paris 1966

– ed   *Hésiode* (Budé series) Paris 1928

Merkelbach, R., and West, M.L., edd   *Fragmenta Hesiodea* Oxford 1967.

Mette, H.J.   *Die Fragmente der Tragoedien des Aischylos* Berlin 1959

Murray, Gilbert, ed   *Aeschyli septem quae supersunt tragoediae* Oxford 1938; second edition, 1955. Oxford Classical Texts

Page, Denys, ed   *Aeschyli septem quae supersunt tragoediae* Oxford 1972

Paley, F.A., ed   *The Tragedies of Aeschylus, re-edited with an English commentary* Fourth edition. Oxford 1924

Prickard, A.O., ed *Aeschylus, Prometheus Bound, with introduction and notes*
Oxford 1878 [1924].

Rackham, H., ed *The Prometheus Bound of Aeschylus* Cambridge 1899 [1957].

Rzach, A., ed *Hesiodi Carmina* Second edition. Leipzig 1908.

Scully, James See Herington, C. John

Sikes, E.E., and Willson, St. J.B.W., edd *The Prometheus Bound of Aeschylus,
with introduction and notes* London 1898

Sinclair, T.A., ed *Hesiod, Works and Days, with introduction and notes* London
1932.

Smyth, H.W., ed *Aeschylus, with an English translation* 2 vols. The Loeb Classical Library. Cambridge and London 1956–7 (appendix to vol II, edited by
Hugh Lloyd-Jones)

Thomson, George, ed *Aeschylus, The Prometheus Bound, edited with introduction,
commentary and translation* Cambridge 1932

Wecklein, N., ed *The Prometheus Bound of Aeschylus, with introduction and notes*
(translated by F.D. Allen) Boston 1893

West, M.L. *Hesiod, Theogony, edited with prolegomena and commentary* Oxford
1966

– *Hesiod, Works and Days, edited with prolegomena and commentary* Oxford 1978
– See Merkelbach and West

Wilamowitz-Moellendorff, Ulrich von., ed *Aeschyli Tragoediae* Berlin 1914

2 Books

Arnott, Peter *Greek Scenic Conventions* Oxford 1962

Beck, R.H. *Aeschylus as Playwright Educator* The Hague 1975

Bolton, J.D.P. *Aristeas of Proconnesus* Oxford 1962

Bremer, J. *Hamartia* Amsterdam 1969

Cole, Thomas *Democritus and the Sources of Greek Anthropology* A.P.A. Mono-
graph No 25. 1967

Coman, Jean *L'Authenticité du Prométhée enchaîné* Bucarest 1943

Dale, A.M. *The Lyric Metres of Greek Drama* Cambridge 1968

Detienne, M. and Vernant, J.-P. *Les Ruses de l'Intelligence: La Mètis des Grecs*
Paris 1974. See also Lloyd, Janet, translator.

Dodds, E.R. *The Ancient Concept of Progress and Other Essays on Greek Literature
and Belief* Oxford 1973

Dorig, J., and Gigon, O. *Der Kampf der Götter und Titanen* Lausanne 1961

Duchemin, Jacqueline *Prométhée, Histoire du Mythe, des ses Origines orientales à
ses Incarnations modernes* Paris 1974

Dumortier, J. *Les Images dans la Poésie d'Eschyle* Paris 1935

Earp, F.R. *The Style of Aeschylus* Cambridge 1948
Edelstein, Ludwig *The Idea of Progress in Classical Antiquity* Baltimore 1967
Freeman, Kathleen *The Pre-Socratic Philosophers* Cambridge, Mass. and Oxford
   1946
Gagarin, Michael *Aeschylean Drama* Berkeley 1976
Garvie, A.F. *Aeschylus' Supplices: Play and Trilogy* Cambridge 1969
Golden, Leon *In Praise of Prometheus* Chapel Hill 1962
Griffith, Mark *The Authenticity of Prometheus Bound* Cambridge 1977
Grossmann, G. *Promethie und Orestie* Heidelberg 1970
Guthrie, W.K.C. *In the Beginning* London 1957
– *A History of Greek Philosophy* Cambridge 1969
Havelock, E.A. *Prometheus* Seattle and London 1968
– *The Liberal Temper in Greek Politics* London 1957
Herington, C.J. *The Author of the 'Prometheus Bound'* Austin and London 1970
Hourmouziades, N.C. *Production and Imagination in Euripides* Athens 1965
Jaeger, Werner *Paideia*, vol I. Second edition (translated by Gilbert Highet)
   New York 1945
Kitto, H.D.F. *Greek Tragedy* Second edition. London 1950
Kranz, W. *Stasimon* Berlin 1933
Lattimore, Richmond *The Poetry of Greek Tragedy* New York 1958
Lebeck, Anne *The Oresteia* Cambridge, Mass. 1971
Lesky, Albin *Greek Tragedy*² (translated by H.A. Frankfort) London 1967
Lloyd, Janet, tr *Cunning Intelligence in Greek Culture and Society* Sussex and New
   Jersey 1978. See Detienne and Vernant
Lloyd-Jones, Hugh. *The Justice of Zeus* Berkeley 1971
Méautis, G. *L'Authenticité et la Date du Prométhée enchaîné* Génève 1960
Murray, Gilbert *Aeschylus* Oxford 1940
Owen, E.T. *The Harmony of Aeschylus* Toronto 1952
Pickard-Cambridge, A.W. *The Theatre of Dionysus in Athens* Oxford 1946
Podlecki, A.J. *The Political Background of Aeschylean Tragedy* Ann Arbor 1966
Pohlenz, M. *Die Griechische Tragödie*. Second edition. Göttingen 1954
Reinhardt, Karl *Aischylos als Regisseur und Theolog* Berne 1949
Rosenmeyer, Thomas G. *The Masks of Tragedy* Austin 1963
Sansone, David *Aeschylean Metaphors for Intellectual Activity. Hermes Einzel-
   schriften* 35. Wiesbaden 1975
Schmid, Wilhelm *Geschichte der griechischen Literatur* I. 3. Munich 1940
– *Untersuchungen zum Gefesselten Prometheus* Stuttgart 1929
Séchan, L. *Le Mythe de Prométhée* Paris 1951
– *Etudes sur la Tragédie grecque dans ses Rapports avec la Céramique* Paris 1926
Smyth, H.W. *Aeschylean Tragedy* Berkeley 1924

Snell, Bruno *Aischylos und das Handeln im Drama* Leipzig 1928
Solmsen, Friedrich *Hesiod and Aeschylus* Ithaca 1949
Stanford, W.B. *Aeschylus in his Style* Dublin 1942
Stoessl, Franz *Die Trilogie des Aischylos* Baden bei Wien 1937
Taplin, Oliver *Greek Tragedy in Action* Berkeley and Los Angeles 1978
– *The Stagecraft of Aeschylus* Oxford 1977
Trendall, A.D. and Webster, T.B.L. *Illustrations of Greek Drama* London 1971
Thomson, George *Aeschylus and Athens* Third edition. London 1966 [1941]
Unterberger, Rose *Der Gefesselte Prometheus des Aischylos* (Tübingen Beiträge zur Altertumswissenschaft, Heft 45) Stuttgart 1967
Vandvik, E. *The Prometheus of Hesiod and Aeschylus* Oslo 1943
Vernant, J.-P. See Detienne
Webster, T.B.L. See Trendall
Welcker, G. *Die Aischylos Trilogie Prometheus* Darmstadt 1824
West, M.L. *Textual Criticism and Editorial Technique* Stuttgart 1973
Westphal, R. *Prolegomena zu Aischylos' Tragoedien* Leipzig 1869
Wilamowitz-Moellendorff, Ulrich von *Aischylos Interpretationen* Berlin 1914
– *Griechische Tragödien* I Berlin 1910

3 Articles and reviews

Adams, S.M. 'The Four Elements in the *Prometheus Vinctus*' *CP* 28 (1933) 97–103
Burns, Alfred 'The Meaning of the *Prometheus Vinctus*' *Class. et Med.* 27 (1966) 65–71
Case, Janet 'On *Prometheus Desmotes*, Lines 980–81' *CR* 18 (1904) 99–100
Ceadel, E.B. 'Resolved Feet in the Trimeters of Euripides' *CQ* 35 (1941) 66–89
Davidson, J.A. 'The Date of the *Prometheia*' *TAPA* 80 (1949) 66–93
Dawson, Christopher 'Notes on the Final Scene of the *P.V.*' *CP* 46 (1951) 237–8
Dodds, E.R. 'Morals and Politics in the *Oresteia*' *PCPS* ns 6 (1960)
Farnell, L.R. 'The Paradox of the *PV*' *JHS* 53 (1933), 40–50
Fitton-Brown, A.D. '*Prometheia*' *JHS* 79 (1959) 52–60
Focke, F. 'Aischylos' *Prometheus*' *Hermes* 65 (1930) 259–304
Fowler, Barbara Hughes 'The Imagery of the *Prometheus Bound*' *AJP* 78 (1957) 173–84
Fraenkel, Eduard 'De novo Acii fragmenta' *Gnomon* 6 (1930) 663
Garzya, A. 'Le Tragique du *Prométhée enchaîné*' *Mnem.* 18 (1965) 113–25
Grene, David '*Prometheus Bound*' *CP* 35 (1940) 22–38
Griffith, Mark 'Aeschylus, Sicily and Prometheus' *Dionysiaca. Nine Studies in Greek Poetry, Presented to Sir Denys Page.* Cambridge 1978
Hammond, N.G.L. 'Personal Freedom and its Limitations in the *Oresteia*' *JHS* 85 (1965) 42–55

- 'Dramatic Production to the Death of Aeschylus' *GRBS* 13 (1972) 387–450
Herington, C.J. 'A Study in the *Prometheia*. Part I: The Elements in the Trilogy'
    Phoenix 17 (1963) 180–97; 'Part II: *Birds* and *Prometheia*' *Phoenix* 17 (1963)
    236–43
- 'A Unique Technical Feature in the *Prometheus Bound*' *CR* 13 (1963) 5–7
- 'Some Evidence for a Late Dating of the *Prometheus Bound*' *CR* 14 (1964)
    239–40
- 'Aeschylus: The Last Phase' *Arion* 4 (1965) 387–403
- 'Aeschylus in Sicily' *JHS* 87 (1967) 74–85
Hermann, Gottfried 'De Compositione Tetralogiarum Tragicarum' *Opuscula*
    II. Lipsiae 1827
Hoppin, J.H. 'Argus, Io and the *Prometheia* of Aeschylus' *JHS* 86 (1966) 78–85
Jocelyn, H.D. 'Greek Poetry in Cicero's Prose Writing' *Yale Classical Studies* 23
    (1973) 61–111
Kitto, H.D.F. 'The *Prometheus*' *JHS* 54 (1934) 14–20
Lesky, Albin 'Decision and Responsibility in the Tragedy of Aeschylus' *JHS* 86
    (1966) 78–85
Lloyd-Jones, Hugh 'The Guilt of Agamemnon' *CQ* ns 12 (1962) 187–97
- 'Zeus in Aeschylus' *JHS* 76 (1956) 55–67
- Review of Rose Unterberger *Der Gefesselte Prometheus des Aischylos*, *CR* 20
    (1970) 241–2
Morrison, J.S. 'The Place of Protagoras in Athenian Public Life' *CQ* 35 (1941)
    1–16
Podlecki, A.J. 'Reciprocity in the *Prometheus Bound*' *GRBS* 10 (1969) 287–92
Robertson, D.S. 'Prometheus and Chiron' *JHS* 71 (1951) 150–5
Stevens, P.T. 'Colloquial Expressions in Aeschylus and Sophocles' *CQ* 31
    (1937) 182–91
Stinton, T.C.W. Review of C.J. Herington *The Author of the Prometheus Bound*,
    Phoenix 28 (1974) 258–64
- '*Hamartia* in Aristotle and Greek Tragedy' *CQ* ns 25 (1975) 221–54
- 'Interlinear Hiatus in Trimeters' *CQ* ns 27 (1977) 67–72
Taplin, Oliver 'Aeschylean Silences and Silences in Aeschylus' *HSCP* 76 (1972)
    57–97
- 'The Title of *Prometheus Desmotes*' *JHS* 95 (1975) 184–6
Thomson, J.A.K. 'The Religious Background of the *Prometheus Vinctus*' *HSCP*
    31 (1920) 1–37
Todd, O.J. 'The Character of Zeus in Aeschylus' *Prometheus Bound*' *CQ* 19
    (1925) 61–7
Tracy, S.V. '*Prometheus Bound* 114–117' *HSCP* 75 (1971) 59–62
Vernant, J.-P. 'Mètis et les mythes de souveraineté' *Revue de l'histoire des
    religions* 180 (1971) 29–76

Vlastos, Gregory 'On the Pre-History in Diodorus' *AJP* 67 (1946) 51–9
Wartelle, André 'La Pensée théologique d'Eschyle' *Bulletin de l'association Guil-
laume Budé* 1971, 535–80
West, M.L. 'The Prometheus Trilogy' *JHS* 99 (1979) 130–48
Yorke, E.C. 'Trisyllabic Feet in the Dialogue of Aeschylus' *CQ* 30 (1936) 116–19
– 'The Date of the *Prometheus Vinctus*' *CQ* 30 (1936) 153–4
Young, Douglas 'Miltonic Light on Professor Denys Page's Homeric Theory' *G
and R* (1959) 96–108
Yu, Anthony C. 'New Gods and the Older Order' *Journal of the American
Academy of Religion* 39 (1971) 19–42

This book

was designed by

ANTJE LINGNER

and was printed by

University of

Toronto

Press